DATE DUE

REFORMING FEDERAL
LAND MANAGEMENT

REFORMING FEDERAL LAND MANAGEMENT
Cutting the Gordian Knot

Allan K. Fitzsimmons

ROWMAN & LITTLEFIELD PUBLISHERS, INC.
Lanham • Boulder • New York • Toronto • Plymouth, UK

Published by Rowman & Littlefield Publishers, Inc.
A wholly owned subsidiary of The Rowman & Littlefield Publishing Group, Inc.
4501 Forbes Boulevard, Suite 200, Lanham, Maryland 20706
www.rowman.com

Estover Road, Plymouth PL6 7PY, United Kingdom

British Library Cataloguing in Publication Information Available

Library of Congress Cataloging-in-Publication Data
Fitzsimmons, Allan K.
  Reforming federal land management : cutting the Gordian knot / Allan K. Fitzsimmons.
    p. cm.
  Includes bibliographical references and index.
  ISBN 978-1-4422-1596-2 (cloth : alk. paper) — ISBN 978-1-4422-1595-5 (electronic)
  1. Public lands—United States—Management. 2. Public lands—United States. I. Title.
  HD216.F58 2012
  352.5'70973—dc23

                                                                    2011051198

♾™ The paper used in this publication meets the minimum requirements of American National Standard for Information Sciences—Permanence of Paper for Printed Library Materials, ANSI/NISO Z39.48-1992.

Printed in the United States of America

Contents

List of Tables

Preface

We shall succeed only so far as we continue that most distasteful of all activity, the intolerable labour of thought.

—Learned Hand

"MR. SECRETARY, THE WHITE HOUSE CALLED; they need a briefing paper in two hours."

"Senator, here is the proposed new legislation, all 100 pages of it. The vote is tomorrow at noon."

The clock and calendar often apply pressure to members of the executive and legislative branches of government. In November 2009, for example, members of the Senate were given seventy-two hours to read a two-thousand-page health care bill prior to voting on bringing it to the Senate floor for debate. That pressure leaves too little opportunity for comprehensive thinking. Over time, the cumulative impacts of legislative and administrative efforts aimed at addressing the problem of the moment can produce widespread, unintended, adverse consequences of great significance. So it is with management of America's federal lands.

For over a century we Americans have thrown laws, processes, objectives, priorities, and rules into the stew of federal land management with little thought to how each new ingredient may affect its overall flavor. We now find ourselves with conflicting laws, unclear priorities, procedural mazes, and an antiquated bureaucratic structure. We have created an atmosphere where processes and procedures often impede rather than aid the accomplishment of management actions intended to advance good stewardship. The overall result is a loss of public benefits and undesirable impacts on natural resources. The time for thoughtful review and far-reaching reform has come.

With this book I seek to help stimulate a vigorous debate on how we manage our federal lands by arguing for major changes and offering ideas for how they may be accomplished. I contend that collaboration, cooperation, and political courage can result in a comprehensive federal land management regime adapted to the twenty-first century—a regime that advances human well-being as well as good stewardship of the land.

I propose that Congress clearly define and order land management priorities for each agency, redistribute the public lands among the agencies to reflect the clarified priorities, evaluate existing judicial interpretations of laws influencing federal land management for consistency with current congressional intent, evaluate the scientific basis of existing statutes impacting federal land management in light of new understanding gained since the laws were enacted four decades ago, institute change to enhance the power of those members of the public most directly impacted by management decisions, and reduce the management role of the courts. I further propose Congress establish a new public land law review commission to help it address these proposals, a commission whose recommendations must receive an up or down vote in Congress.

Assumptions

The federal lands attract authors with considerable variation in academic training, experience, outlook, and purpose. Economists, political scientists, ecologists, lawyers, geographers, foresters, and other disciplinary specialists write about federal lands. Land managers, academics, environmentalists, ranchers, wildlife aficionados, outdoor recreationists, concessioners, and commodity producers write about federal lands. Philosophers, poets, and politicians also make their contributions.

All of us bring a set of assumptions to our thinking and writing based on our storehouse of knowledge and understanding gained through education and practice. Counting years in graduate school that yielded a master's thesis and doctoral dissertation on national parks, I have spent some four decades inside and outside the federal government working on natural resource and public land questions. During this time I have developed basic points of view. In the interest of full disclosure, I bring the following overarching assumptions to this book.

1. Americans rightly view the federal lands as a vital national asset and they should be retained in public ownership.

2. The classic congressional twofold division of federal lands into multiple-use areas (typically managed by the Bureau of Land Management or the Forest Service) and those whose potential uses are more limited owing to their unique characteristics (like wilderness areas, national parks, and national wildlife refuges) continues to make sense.

3. People, not nature, determine landscape preferences because nature does not have a preferred state.

4. Policy-neutral science—science that reports true and false and an honest estimate of uncertainty about the natural world without reflecting the researcher's policy biases—is an important component of good federal land management.

5. Collaboration among federal land management agencies and between federal, state, tribal, and local governments—coupled with public review and comment—is essential to good management.

6. Benevolent anthropocentrism (the forwarding of human well-being with a good steward's concern for nonhuman biota) offers the most rational basis for good management.

7. The proper location of federal land management policy and management decision-making is the Congress and the executive branch, not the federal courts.

8. Under our form of government, only Congress can wield the sword that cuts the Gordian Knot.

Plan of the Book

The introduction illustrates the scope and magnitude of the problem using three contemporary management issues: the restoration of Yosemite Valley after the flood of 1997, the cumulative impact on the availability of oil and natural gas resources generated by uncoordinated land management decisions, and the self-identified "process predicament" facing the Forest Service. I then present examples of several recent suggestions for overhauling federal land management followed by a look at the roles of values and science. I conclude the introduction with a summary of my recommendations regarding the steps needed to reform federal land management.

In chapters 1, 2, and 3 I set the stage for the analyses and recommendations found in chapter 4.

Chapter 1 provides the reader with a contemporary snapshot of federal lands. I present their geographic distribution (which makes it clear why this book is fundamentally about the West) and characteristics, describe the wide variety of resources they contain, and show how these multiple resources contribute to the nation. The chapter gives the reader an understanding of the patterns of federal lands managed by each of the four major federal land managing agencies: the Bureau of Land Management (BLM), the Fish and Wildlife Service (FWS), the Forest Service (FS), and the National Park Service (NPS), which collectively manage 99 percent of our federal lands. It discusses agency missions. I use the effort to create a Tallgrass Prairie National Preserve to demonstrate why missions matter. Snapshots, no matter how useful, remain incomplete because landscapes reflect both natural and societal forces acting through time, so chapter 2 adds temporal context.

Chapter 2 explores major aspects of human interaction with the landscape and federal lands through time. Using changing views of fire as a management tool and wilderness as a landscape type, I show how people alter their perceptions of the landscape and how it should be managed as time passes. The chapter considers how changing settlement patterns and economic activity based on federal lands influence our relationship with the land. The chapter investigates differences in views among longtime residents and relative newcomers to areas with abundant federal land. While federal lands persist in space and time, we manage them through legislative, administrative, and judicial actions. Chapter 3 addresses these aspects of federal land management.

Federal land management falls under the sway of each of our three branches of government. Congress makes laws, shapes the budget, and requires specific actions. The executive oversees planning, rulemaking, and day-to-day management while issuing broad policy directives. The judiciary reviews executive branch action for consistency with the law. In chapter 3, I discuss these sources of influence, with particular attention to the role of the courts. I go on to examine the difficulty of moving the law to the landscape using three issues as examples: the Clinton Roadless Rule, northern spotted owls, and wetlands. With the preparatory work done, chapter 4 contains my recommendations for cutting the Gordian Knot.

In chapter 4, I argue that Congress bears the greatest responsibility for ending the current federal land management turmoil. I begin the chapter with a brief analysis of the suggestions for reform presented to the reader in the introduction. I then offer eight specific recommendations needed to cut the Knot. Detailed discussions, including examples of the problems to be overcome and how that might be accomplished, accompany each recommendation.

The conclusion restates the necessity for a far-reaching overhaul of federal land management to secure for this and future generations the full range of benefits society can obtain from its public lands.

"You are out of your mind" nicely paraphrases the reaction of a longtime friend when we discussed the scope of the changes I suggest in this book. Perhaps. I admit to proposing daunting tasks, but the value of the federal lands to our country is too great to continue along the present chaotic, band-aid-laden course.

I am concerned here with federal lands only; thus, the remaining 70 percent of the nation's land that falls under private, state, and tribal ownership lies outside my purview. As a result, I do not address major issues influencing natural-resource management such as private property rights and takings, federal–private sector efforts in cooperative conservation, or free-market environmentalism.

Many people and situations have contributed to the storehouse of knowledge and understanding (no matter how large or small it may be) leading up to my writing this book. My parents took their young son to national parks in and around California, experiences that fostered an everlasting appreciation for such special places and for broad landscapes that I later learned were federal lands. Bob Durrenberger at California State University Northridge as well as Joe Spencer and Tom McKnight at UCLA were instrumental in my becoming a geographer. My students asked a lot of questions requiring a review of my assumptions and a restatement of arguments. My government bosses— Mary Lou Grier, Bill Horn, Lynn Scarlett, and Gale Norton at the Department of the Interior and Linda Stuntz at the Department of Energy—provided me with opportunities to evaluate and participate in the development of federal land management policies. Extensive interaction with career land management and program officials contributed heavily to my understanding of federal lands and their management.

As for the book itself, I am indebted to Bill Horn and Bob Lackey for their comments as well as to an anonymous reviewer. My daughter, Shannon Doolan, provided a critical review that helped me clarify arguments, eliminate extraneous verbiage, and generally sharpen my writing.

Finally, thanks to my wife, Ruth Ann, for her continuous support.

Introduction

The Nature and Scope of the Problem

A "Gordian Knot" of contradictory law, policy and precedent holds the
public lands captive. . . . It is time for a sea-change in public land policy.

—Jack Ward Thomas and Alex Sienkiewicz

FOR OVER 2,000 YEARS, THE GORDIAN KNOT has represented perplexing problems unsolvable by traditional means. The ancient kingdom of Phrygia
occupied what is now central Turkey. It sat astride the land route from Greece
to Asia. Legend has it that Gordius, the Phrygian king, devised a Knot so
intricate that the individual who untied it would become king of Asia. Many
tried, but none succeeded. Then the Macedonian king, Alexander the Great,
encountered the Knot. When he, too, failed to unravel the Knot by conven-
tionally tugging here and pulling there, he drew his sword and cut it half. By
326 BC Alexander's empire reached eastward to the Indus River in today's
Pakistan, some 3,000 miles from his homeland. The complexities enveloping
federal land management today call to mind both King Gordius's puzzle and
Alexander's solution.

The federal government has acquired and disposed of millions of acres
since our nation's founding (see box intro.1). Today, federal lands, which
comprise some 28 percent of the United States, make vital and varied contributions to the nation. They provide natural resources essential for modern
life, recreation and renewal for hundreds of millions of annual visitors, and
habitat for countless other living things. Yet good management of these lands
is thwarted by more than a century of now-conflicting laws haphazardly pil-
ing priority upon priority and objective upon objective with little thought to

---

Box Intro.1.   Federal Land Acquisition and Disposal

Through acquisition and disposal, Congress has significantly altered the federal estate over time. At inception, the nation reached from the Atlantic Seaboard to the Mississippi River with the federal lands chiefly composed of territory ceded by the original thirteen colonies between the Allegheny Mountains and the river. To these original 237 million acres, the Louisiana Purchase added 530 million acres in 1803 and a variety of other actions throughout the first half of the nineteenth century contributed an additional 696 million acres. The purchase of Alaska in 1867 increased the federal estate by 378 million acres. It essentially ended large-scale federal land acquisition. Overall the federal government held title to over 1.8 billion acres of land at one time or another.

For much of our history Congress generally saw the public lands as a currency to spend in service to developing the nation. Transferring public lands was a way to finance the new government, pay Revolutionary War soldiers, and aid states. Until the 1930s, a principal goal of federal land law was the disposition of these lands via statutes such as the Homestead Act of 1862 and the Desert Lands Entry Act of 1877. Under one law or another, Congress transferred some 815 million acres to private entities while title to over 450 million acres shifted to the states. Thus, Congress passed ownership of approximately two-thirds of the lands once owned by the federal government into nonfederal hands.

Source: Kristina Alexander and Ross W. Gorte, *Federal Land Ownership: Constitutional Authority and the History of Acquisition, Disposal, and Retention* (Washington, D.C.: Congressional Research Service, 2007), available at http://opencrs.com/document/RL34267/ (accessed August 29, 2011).

---

their cumulative impact, the continued use of land-managing agencies better suited to conditions of 1910 than 2010, and the emergence of logic-defying procedural mazes. The public interest suffers.[1]

Congress and the executive branch cannot satisfactorily address the Gordian Knot constricting federal land management by tinkering with existing laws, rules, plans, or procedures. They need to muster the wisdom and will to, like Alexander, cut the Knot via major changes in all facets of federal land management.

A post–Gordian Knot landscape would be expected to yield multiple benefits to society. Reformed management would clearly state the public purpose of federal lands and prioritize objectives within distinct land-management categories. It would eliminate duplicative agencies, clarify missions, and rectify boundaries. It would elevate the importance of collaborative land-use planning involving state and local officials and shield the results from those interests that did not get their way through open and public processes.

The Gordian Knot thwarts good management at all levels—from on-the-ground project implementation to rational bureau-wide allocation and use of resources. The three widely divergent examples I describe below illustrate the breadth and depth of the current problem and the need for comprehensive reform. The first example deals with the National Park Service's efforts to repair damage caused by flooding in Yosemite Valley. This is a place- and project-specific example of a kind faced by managers throughout the country. The second example looks through a different lens, one that focuses on a type of resource—oil and natural gas—rather than on a specific place or bureau. This example shows the Gordian Knot's cumulative impact on the availability of domestic resources critical to modern life. The final example adopts a bureau-level perspective by looking at the impacts of the current land-management situation on the Forest Service.

Yosemite Valley Post-Flood Restoration

Management of the valley has been controversial since at least 1913, when Secretary of the Interior Franklin K. Lane permitted automobiles to enter it. That year some 25,000 people reached the approximately seven-square-mile valley that is the heart of Yosemite National Park. Today visitation exceeds 3 million annually. It is easy to see that over time, management pressures mounted as more and more people came to the valley and the National Park Service (NPS) sought to balance its dual mandate of providing for visitor enjoyment while conserving park resources. Management had grown increasingly difficult as various interests hardened their positions regarding appropriate uses of the valley and levels of visitation.

In the early 1990s, the NPS started new planning efforts intended to address four management issues in the valley: housing, restoration of natural resources, transportation, and visitor services. These efforts were overcome by events when the Merced River flooded the valley in 1997. The river raged through the valley, destroying roads, bridges, and campgrounds. It poured into buildings and played havoc with water and sewer systems. Precisely because it was so destructive, the flood provided an opportunity for multiple interests to step back and take a comprehensive look at management of the valley. The NPS provided the vehicle for doing so by combining its four pre-existing planning efforts into a single comprehensive Yosemite Valley Plan, which it prepared after extensive public involvement.

The NPS issued the Yosemite Valley Plan in December 2000.[2] The plan enjoyed widespread public support as well as that of environmental organizations like the National Parks and Conservation Association, the Wilderness

Society, and the Natural Resources Defense Council. As a *San Francisco Chronicle* staff writer noted in January 2007: "Years of acrimonious debate over how to manage a crown jewel of America's national park system gave way to consensus that the Park Service had finally gotten it right."[3]

In our present Gordian Knot world, consensus does not necessarily translate into actual management in the public interest. While the NPS was preparing the Yosemite Valley Plan, it also had to prepare a Merced Wild and Scenic Comprehensive Management Plan because Congress had declared the Merced to be a national wild and scenic river, a designation requiring a separate plan. Two small, largely unknown environmental groups have been in the federal courthouse since 2000 seeking to advance their own vision for the valley. Friends of Yosemite Valley and Mariposans for Environmentally Responsible Growth have successfully used a series of court actions to prevent implementation of the Merced River Plan (and, collaterally, major aspects of the Yosemite Valley Plan).[4] Among other things, these groups tried to prevent relocation of sewer lines whose continued presence in wet meadows threatened these natural resources and repairs to existing flood-damaged roads.

Seeking to move forward with the sewer and road repair projects, Mike Tollefson, the apparently very frustrated park superintendent, told the court on March 5, 2007:

> In my Eighth Declaration . . . I provided extensive information about why these two vital repair projects enjoined by the U.S. District Court [at the request of Friends of Yosemite Valley and Mariposans for Environmentally Responsible Growth] must be allowed to proceed. . . . I have also provided information about how these specific projects will restore and protect natural and cultural resources, while enhancing visitor experience and making Yosemite a safer place to visit. . . . I am compelled to reiterate and underscore the serious ramifications of the District Court's injunction of the Utilities Project and Loop Road Project. . . . Not only does this injunction *prevent* [emphasis in the original] NPS from protecting the visitor experience, natural and cultural resources, and the values of the Merced River, but it also puts the health and safety of park visitors and residents at significant and unnecessary risk. . . . As the manager responsible for Yosemite National Park, I have presented this assessment . . . [based] on volumes of supporting documentation.[5]

On March 22, 2007, the district court permitted the park to proceed with the two projects in question but left the overall halt to implementation of the comprehensive restoration plan in place. Ultimately, however, the district court ordered the NPS to start over, a decision upheld by the Ninth Circuit Court of Appeals in July 2009—over a decade of work thrown out (more on this in chapter 4).[6]

Our federal estate not only houses highly valued landscapes like Yosemite Valley and other national park lands but also contains critical natural resources, none of which are more valuable to human well-being than the energy resources needed to power today's society.

Oil and Gas Availability

The idea of oil and natural gas development on public lands often prompts spirited debate. Advocates point to economic and societal benefits while opponents see harm to the environment and limitations on other land uses. Over the years Congress and the executive branch placed a patchwork of multiple restrictions—withdrawals, moratoria, rules, lease stipulations, and so forth—on energy development in the name of environmental protection.[7] They did so without regard to their cumulative effect on domestic energy production. That changed in the first decade of this century when Congress and two administrations decided to take stock of that impact. In November 2000, President Clinton signed the Energy Policy and Conservation Act (EPCA), which called for an inventory of oil and gas resources beneath *onshore* federal lands in western states and an evaluation of the "the extent and nature of any restrictions or impediments to the development of the resources."[8] With support from the Bush administration, Congress amended the EPCA in 2005 to include Alaska and federal lands in the east.[9] The resulting analysis is revealing.

The departments of the Interior, Energy, and Agriculture issued their EPCA report in May 2008 describing the cumulative effects of various restrictions on the production of oil and gas from beneath onshore federal lands.[10] They estimate the amount of land overlaying oil and gas resources, the amount of oil and gas beneath those lands, and the amount of both land and resources impacted by restrictions. They offer these estimates.

- Two hundred seventy-nine million federal acres lie astride technically recoverable oil or gas resources.[11] These acres represent 44 percent of the total 627 million acres overseen by the four federal land-managing agencies.[12]
- Sixty percent of the 279 million acres are inaccessible for oil and natural gas exploration and development for one legislative or administrative reason or another.[13]
- Twenty-three percent of the 279 million acres can be reached only under various conditions that exceed the requirements of standard lease terms.[14]
- The remaining 17 percent of the 279 million acres are available using standard leasing provisions (this comprises 8 percent of the 627 million

acres supervised by the land-managing agencies or less than 0.5 percent of the country as a whole).[15]

- Federal lands overlay an estimated 30.5 billion barrels of oil and 231 trillion cubic feet of natural gas.[16]
- The restrictions put 62 percent of the country's potentially exploitable oil resources and 41 percent of the natural gas resources completely out of bounds.[17]
- Thirty percent of the oil and 49 percent of the natural gas resources are available only under conditions that exceed those contained within standard leases.[18]
- Eight percent of the oil resources and 10 percent of the gas resources might be tapped under standard lease conditions.[19]

By any reasonable standard, the cumulative impact of the present disjointed management situation places nationally significant amounts of energy beyond reach. If one adds the effects of various moratoria on the production of oil and natural gas from offshore areas, then the impact on the availability of resources critical to the functioning of our society becomes even more pronounced.

The Forest Service Predicament

In the mid-1990s senior Forest Service leadership recognized that the accumulated weight of a century of laws, policies, rules, and processes was harming the agency's ability to effectively manage the land under its care. They began a review of the situation. Although the initial investigation did not go beyond the draft stage, subsequent efforts resulted in the June 2002 publication of the *Process Predicament.* The study reveals the Byzantine nature of the current situation.[20] For example, preliminary analysis shows that project planning for a timber sale on the Pike and San Isabel National Forests involved over 800 planning activities to comply with applicable federal laws and internal Forest Service processes and procedures.[21] Overall, the authors point out multiple impacts flowing from the current state of affairs of which I offer three examples: (1) conflicting mandates given to land managers on the one hand and federal regulators on the other;[22] (2) waste of agency resources in excessive data gathering and analysis spurred by litigation threats; and (3) an emphasis on process over actual management actions. I look at each in turn.

First, difficulties arise from the difference between congressional mandates given federal regulators as opposed to those Congress assigns to federal land managers. The land manager may see a project positively, as one of many needed actions over time and space to accomplish multiple agreed-upon objectives. The same project may be seen negatively by a regulator, such as the Environmental Protection Agency (EPA), which is narrowly concerned with short-term impacts to a single component of the landscape. Current law allows the regulator's view to prevail over that of the land manager. Consequently, projects must be abandoned or revised to meet the regulator's requirements even though doing so inhibits achievement of overall long-term management goals. The *Processes Predicament* notes the following concern raised by a fisheries biologist on the Gifford Pinchot National Forest.

> Roads decommissioning and in-stream restoration (such as culvert removal) can adversely affect water quality in the short term, although the long-term benefits for waters and lands are obvious. Often, such activities are folded into large projects with multiple objectives to achieve greater efficiencies. If consultation delays or prevents such projects from going forward, managers have a perverse incentive *not* [emphasis in the original] to decommission roads or restore streams, but rather to eliminate those components from the project just to get the rest of the work done.[23]

Good stewardship foregone.

Second, the authors of the *Process Predicament* observe that information gathering and analysis routinely far exceed what is needed to support reasoned, well-informed management decisions. Sensitive to the threat of litigation and uncertain about what a reviewing court might demand regarding what constitutes sufficient data gathering and evaluation, Forest Service field managers now often seek to "bullet proof" their decisions through excessive analysis. The money and staff expended on such excessive activities all represent agency resources not devoted to actually accomplishing the agency's land-management mission. While precise estimates of the amounts of money involved are difficult to determine, Forest Service officials estimate some 100 million dollars could become available each year to fund on-the-ground projects if unnecessary planning were eliminated.[24]

Finally, process is not product. Operational delays (whether administrative or judicial in origin) on a dynamic landscape can easily result in harm to the very resources managers intend a project to protect. For example, should a wildland fire burn though an area where hazardous fuels reduction treatments have been forestalled, the fire is far more likely to cause unwanted environmental impacts than if the treatments had been accomplished. Such was the case with the Megram fire that burned 59,000 acres in the Six Rivers National Forest in northern California in 1999. When a winter storm caused a timber blowdown on 35,000 acres of forest in 1995, managers were quick to recognize the creation of a significant fire hazard, which they immediately sought to address. Nonetheless, at the time of the Megram fire the hazard had not been dealt with (only 1,600 acres had received hazardous fuels treatment) owing to the time spent in fulfilling the requirements of multiple applicable laws and administrative procedures as well as the time spent in litigation brought by opponents of the hazardous fuels treatments. While "process" may have been served, the forest was not and neither was the public.

It will be hard for society to develop and implement needed solutions for the quagmire we have created. Cutting the Gordian Knot will bring charges of trying to "gut environmental protections" or similar claims from those advocacy groups who see the current situation as working to their benefit and thus often reject compromise.[25] For example, during the period 1989–2002 federal district court suits against the Forest Service seeking to reduce resource use outnumbered those calling for more resource use by three to one.[26] Recently nineteen environmental groups, joined by the state of California, successfully sued to stop implementation of a sweeping new (2005) Forest Service planning rule that would have addressed some of the concerns raised in the *Process Predicament.*[27] The Forest Service issued a new planning rule in 2008 to comply with the district court's decision on the 2005 rule. They were sued again. The court ruled against them in July 2009 and the Obama administration did not appeal, directing the Forest Service to start over.[28] For some interest groups, overcoming the "process predicament" with a new planning rule constituted an attempt "to roll back protections of the forests."[29] At the end of the first decade of the twenty-first century the "process predicament" remains unresolved and good stewardship suffers as a result. The difficulties we Americans face in extracting ourselves from our current federal land-management dilemma do not arise from a lack of suggestions, a sample of which I briefly outline in the next section.

A Myriad of Reform Proposals

For more than a decade, many learned observers acknowledged the need for the substantial reform of federal land management. During that time they put forward numerous proposals to achieve that end. I summarize several of these efforts to illustrate the breadth of the ideas offered. I comment on these proposals in chapter 4 prior to presenting my own reform ideas.

If there were no federal lands, the nation would not face federal land-management problems. In 1999, notable economists Terry Anderson and Vernon Smith (2002 Nobel Prize winner in economics) advanced an exploratory proposal for the privatization of federal lands managed by the Bureau of Land Management, Forest Service, and National Park Service as well as the continental shelf.[30] In their view federal lands have been mismanaged both economically and ecologically. The solution lies in shifting management responsibility to the private sector and using market forces to identify and capture the highest value land use. Their plan centers on divestiture via the issuance of public land certificates to all American citizens that then become transferable property to be used at auctions concerned with the uses of former public lands.

Daniel Kemmis offers a different method to remove federal control over public lands. Kemmis heads the Center for the Rocky Mountain West at the University of Montana and previously was speaker of the Montana House of Representatives as well as mayor of Missoula. For Kemmis, sovereignty lies at the center of the problem. Focusing on the West, he characterizes present federal land management as "paternalistic and increasingly dysfunctional" and observes that public ownership and federal ownership are not synonymous.[31] He would shift sovereignty over now-federal lands in the West to yet-to-be-constituted regional bodies. Arguing that the West is both sufficiently mature and moving in a bipartisan fashion on environmental and natural resource matters, Kemmis posits that regional collaborative structures would far better represent the interests of the people and communities most directly impacted by actions on the landscape. Devolving power for land management to those most effected by such management is, for Kemmis, a democratic imperative. Hence, "westerners must be in charge of the West."[32]

The University of Maryland's Robert Nelson, a professor of environmental policy in the School of Public Affairs, would also remove federal control from most public lands in the West. Nelson envisions dismantling both the Bureau of Land Management and the Forest Service. Roughly 20 percent of the land managed by these agencies in the West would remain in federal ownership because they possess clearly recognizable national attributes, but all management responsibilities would shift to either the Fish and Wildlife Service or the National Park Service.[33] The states would take control of the divested 80 percent with the ability to pass land on to local governments or the private sector, including nonprofit groups like the Nature Conservancy. Like Kemmis, Nelson argues that land use decisions in the West should be made by those living there and he sees the need for "nothing less than the equivalent of a new constitutional convention for the rural West."[34]

Sally Fairfax would also reorganize federal land-management agencies but would retain the current estate in federal ownership. She is a distinguished professor of forest policy in the College of Natural Resources at the University of California, Berkeley. After analyzing agency missions she sees those of the Bureau of Land Management (BLM), Forest Service, and National Park Service coalescing around the provision of outdoor recreation, thus ending the need for three separate bureaus. Consequently, she calls for Congress to fold these agencies into a new federal entity. In her judgment the key to the future lies in the ability to work with local and regional interests. Since the BLM has a history of working well with local and regional interests she sees it as providing the management model for the new combined agency.[35]

University of Illinois law professor Eric Freyfogle casts the problems of federal land management in completely different terms. He views the issue as being defined by our legal framework, which establishes separate categories of private and public property. Freyfogle, a longtime observer of environmental law and natural resource issues, would revise property law by ending the present legal dichotomy between public and private property. Instead, we should adopt a view wherein land is "owned ultimately by the sovereign people collectively . . . and managed for the common good. But private parties have use rights in this land."[36] He sees in the future "a marked reduction in public lands as we now know them . . . [but only] if we have an even greater reduction in private lands as we now know them" as the land base is shifted to collective ownership.[37] In his judgment, the challenge for land management in this new order will be determining how to sculpt private use rights while determining the structure of collective management regimes to achieve public purposes.

Law professor Robert Keiter approaches the problem from yet another perspective. Keiter heads the Wallace Stegner Center for Land, Resources, and the Environment at the University of Utah's law school. He argues that public land management should "emulate nature" by focusing on ecosystems. To accomplish this goal Congress should enact overarching legislation—a National Ecosystem Management and Protection Act—directing existing agencies to "conserve and restore ecosystem health and biodiversity levels, while preventing any further ecological impairment."[38] According to Keiter, such legislation would establish both a nonimpairment standard for ecosystems and an affirmative requirement that agencies "protect and restore species diversity" on an ecosystem basis.[39] It would supplement, not supplant, existing legislation. Agencies would implement the act using the normal processes of rulemaking and planning, each of which would be subject to administrative appeal and citizen suits. Successful implementation would require an expansion of protected lands and establishment of nonfederal buffer zones coupled with "selective site-specific modifications to our current hands-off wilderness management policies."[40]

Resource economist Randal O'Toole asks, "If privatization is politically infeasible and public management inept, is there a third alternative?"[41] For O'Toole, the answer is yes and takes the form of fiduciary trusts. He proposes the retention of public lands in public ownership but elimination of the four land-managing agencies and existing administrative boundaries. Federal lands would be reorganized into 60 to 120 ecoregions with each being co-managed by a market trust and a nonmarket trust. Market trusts would "maximize the revenue for public land management while preserving the productive capacity of the land," while nonmarket trusts would "maximize the preservation and, as appropriate, restoration of natural ecosystems, historic structures, and prehistoric artifacts important to the history of America."[42] He would retain current restrictions on land use and have the trusts resolve differences regarding land use through "negotiation or monetary exchange." Interested citizens would form a "friends" organization for each trust that would ultimately elect trustees and be able to sue if they did not like trustee decisions.

Some observers find laws insufficient and seek remedies in a constitutional amendment. Several such proposals have emerged over the last three decades and are generally categorized as environmental quality amendments. While not specifically targeting federal lands, their impacts thereon would be dramatic. Writing in the *Ecology Law Quarterly*, published by the University of California at Berkeley School of Law, attorney Dan Gildor proposes to add "Congress shall have the power to preserve, protect, and promote the environment" to the Constitution.[43] Fellow attorney Pamela Schmaltz offers:

> The right of citizens of the United States to the continuing integrity, diversity and viability of the environment and existing ecosystems shall not be abridged by the United States or any State through action or inaction. The Congress shall have power to enforce this article by appropriate legislation.[44]

Defenders of Wildlife president and CEO Rodger Schlickeisen's idea of an amendment is:

> The living natural resources in the United States are the common property of all people, including generations yet to come. All persons and their progeny have an inalienable, enforceable right to the benefits of those resources for themselves and their posterity. The United States and every State shall assure that use of those resources is sustainable and that they are conserved and maintained for the benefit of all the people.[45]

Gildor notes that such proposals have not garnered much support in the past, but now may be the time for reconsideration. Authority for federal environmental legislation flows from the Constitution's Commerce Clause. In 1995 the Supreme Court found that Congress had overreached its power under the Commerce Clause when the court struck down the Gun Free School Zone Act of 1990 in *United States v. Lopez*.[46] Limitations on the reach of the Commerce Clause threaten the body of environmental legislation, in Gildor's opinion, hence, the need for a constitutional amendment.

Gildor bases his case not only on jurisprudence but also on what he sees as a public shift in values not captured in the Constitution. He writes that "a moral revolution has taken place within this country regarding the environment all while the form of national government has remained static."[47] The constitution should be brought into line with new environmental ethics.

Holly Fretwell, a fellow at the Property and Environmental Research Center, offers yet another approach in her book *Who Is Minding the Federal Estate: Political Management of America's Public Lands.*[48] "Entrusting care of federal lands to politicians," she writes, "has resulted in damages that are both widespread and well documented." That is because "Congressional incentives are not in line with resources priorities," rather "they are instead to provide visible benefits for constituents."[49] Since bureaus depend on Congress for their funding, she argues that management decisions are driven by politics, not science, so management incentives are wrong. Fretwell proposes lessening dependence on congressional appropriations by expanding experiments involving land trusts, federal–private sector partnerships, and land use bidding arrangements that generate income that would remain within the land-management unit. Doing so would partially free land managers from congressional pressures that Fretwell argues are not usually consistent with good land management.

Having looked at the variety of proposed solutions to our present federal land-management conundrum, the next section examines the values that underlie many of today's battles.

Values and Federal Land Management

Differences regarding values lie behind most federal land-management conflicts. Should we open a portion of the Arctic National Wildlife Refuge to oil and gas exploration and development? Should we retain or remove major dams on western rivers? Should we increase, decrease, or stop logging on public land? How one answers these questions depends in large measure on how one would answer more basic questions. Is nature a deity, a god apart from the God of Christianity, Judaism, or Islam? Are nature and the God of the western monotheistic religions the same? Does an undisturbed (by humans) nature illustrate the ideal landscape? Do other species have the same rights and value as humans? Should improvement in human well-being be the principal guide in resource use? Americans answer these questions differently. Scholars generally agree that today's values-based differences stand rooted in the countervailing philosophies advanced more than a century ago by John Muir and Gifford Pinchot.[50]

John Muir, founder of the Sierra Club and leader in the effort to establish Yosemite National Park, saw land management as a religious crusade. By the 1870s he had adopted a nature-worshipping philosophy that rejected the monotheistic God of western faiths in favor of "pantheistic spiritualism," according to Muir biographer Stephen Fox.[51] Claiming the moral high ground for himself and his followers, he wrote in the *Sierra Club Bulletin* that "the battle we have fought and are still fighting for the forests is part of the eternal conflict between right and wrong, and we cannot expect to see an end to it."[52] Writing of Muir, environmental historian Roderick Nash observed, "Nature was his church . . . [and] protection of Nature became a Holy War."[53] Nature was worthy of veneration for its own sake rather than as an example of God's work. Nature first.

Gifford Pinchot, appointed the first chief of the Forest Service in 1905, took a utilitarian tack. He saw the transformation of natural resources to human use essential for prosperity. "Conservation," he wrote, "means the wise use of the earth and its resources for the lasting good of men. Conservation is the foresighted utilization, preservation, and /or renewal of forests, waters, lands, and minerals for the greatest good for the greatest number for the longest time."[54] He was unapologetically anthropocentric. People first.

The practical application of Pinchot's and Muir's respective positions first played out on the national scene in the battle to dam the Tuolumne River in Yosemite National Park to provide a water supply for San Francisco. The dam would flood Hetch Hetchy Valley. Muir railed against it. He likened the valley to a holy shrine, calling dam supporters "temple destroyers" with a "perfect contempt for Nature" who instead of "lifting their eyes to the God of the mountain, lift them to the Almighty Dollar."[55] Pinchot favored construction. The city finished building the dam in 1923 after receiving congressional authorization for construction in 1913. It still supplies San Francisco with water.[56]

Today's nature-first federal land-management camp contains multiple tents. One finds Muir's nature-as-deity descendants. One may find those who see God and nature as one as did David Brower, environmentalism's doyen during the final decades of the twentieth century.[57] Brower wrote: "To me, God and Nature are synonymous."[58] One can find secularism among biocentrists and deep ecologists who vest in other species the same rights and relevance as those generally associated with humans. Nature-firsters make appeals to the Christian and Jewish religious communities to join their policy efforts on the basis of a claimed need to protect nature-as-God's-creation.[59] In spite of this variety, the nature-first camp retains a good deal of cohesion because its occupants claim for themselves the moral high ground embodied in adoption of an undefiled nature as the landscape ideal.

The utilitarian camp is likewise an admixture—hikers, skiers, sightseers, ranchers, miners, foresters, energy producers, hunters, fishermen, campers, and others—but it lacks the same intensity of purpose as the nature-firsters because economic concerns do not have the same power to unify as do shared moral convictions. At the same time, the people-first camp is more flexible because people-first means accommodating diverse public desires with their attendant different land-management objectives. People-firsters do not claim for themselves a cape of moral authority; thus, compromise comes more easily to them than to some nature-firsters who tend to think of tradeoffs that balance competing lawful uses of public lands as making deals with the devil.

All this talk of camps should not obscure the fact that many Americans do no associate themselves with any camp and those who do may move their tents closer together or farther apart depending on the issue at hand; context is important (see box intro.2). Indeed, they may even temporarily change camps. Consider two recent examples: nature-firsters' proposal to remove Glen Canyon Dam on the Colorado River and Forest Service plans for development of natural gas leases in Wyoming's Bridger-Teton National Forest.

David Brower, the undeniable head of the nature-first camp in the last decades of the twentieth century, carried Muir's banner until the time of his death in 2000 at age eighty-seven.[60] In the spring of 2000 he helped launch the effort to tear down Glen Canyon Dam on the Colorado River in order to return the Colorado to nature. At the kickoff ceremony launching the initiative, Brower said removing the dam and draining Lake Powell behind it would "bring a lot of joy to the 1,600 miles of Glen Canyon and its side canyons. . . . They are waiting eagerly to be born again. I know, I asked them all."[61]

Removing Glen Canyon Dam may bring joy to the canyon, but it would bring a lot of grief to millions of people in the region, including resident nature-firsters. Lake Powell is the second largest reservoir in the United States.

Box Intro.2.   Attributes of Federal Lands

Americans value federal lands for many reasons. They offer places of active and passive outdoor recreation, and of respite and renewal. They are sources of natural resources needed for daily living. They furnish habitat for many of the biota that share the land with us. They contain landscapes of enormous scenic grandeur. They shelter evidence of our history. Activities based upon them provide jobs that support families and communities. The interplay among these many attributes is complex and subject to multiple pressures that shift in space and time.

It provides water to millions of people in Arizona and Southern California. It receives some 2.5 million recreation visits a year as the central feature of the Glen Canyon National Recreation Area, a unit of the national park system. In 2006, nonlocal visitors boosted the regional economy by spending $123 million in the area.[62] On annual average, the hydroelectric power produced at the dam is sufficient for over 450,000 households, or some 1.1 million people.[63] One can easily imagine the great majority of nature-firsters in the impacted areas of Arizona, Nevada, and Southern California moving into the utilitarian camp on this issue.

Energy plays a major role in Wyoming's economy and enjoys favor in many quarters. Wyoming is an energy-rich state where one can find petroleum, natural gas, coal, coal-bed methane, oil shale, and wind-farm sites. In early 2007, it became evident that the Forest Service was moving forward with allowing lessees to begin new natural gas exploration work in the Bridger-Teton National Forest's Wyoming Range. The Forest Service action sparked opposition from interests normally found in the people-first camp as well as from nature-first quarters. Groups of sportsmen, county commissioners, and chambers of commerce all went on record as opposing lease development.[64]

The landscape proposed for possible development contains a variety of assets. In addition to energy resources, it possesses major scenic attributes and offers habitat for species that draw hunters and fishermen from around the country. The Jackson Hole, Wyoming, Chamber of Commerce opposed development. It wrote the Forest Service that "such extractive activities are in direct conflict with the values and conditions we support and are necessary to sustain commerce and quality of life for our communities."[65] In this case, some utilitarian opponents of energy development see it as harming their particular portion of the multiple-use spectrum. As can be seen from these two examples, context matters.

In a democratic society open debate resulting in tradeoffs and balancing is the means to reconcile differing values-based positions. Cutting the Gordian Knot requires adherence to this basic principle. No matter one's values, all sides routinely claim the mantle of science to increase the appeal of their policy preference or management prescription. The next section looks at the role of science in federal land management.

Science and Federal Land Management

In this section I argue that science is an important but not the determinative factor in establishing land-management objectives and priorities or in crafting management actions. I further argue that the rise and use of so-called normative science risks undercutting the enormous value science has for society and that it has no place in federal land management.

The role of science in federal land management continues to evolve. It began with Pinchot's commitment to scientific forestry following a European model wherein foresters—as scientists—would make land-management decisions grounded in disciplinary understanding.[66] Over the years additional scientific disciplines and increasing specializations within them were added to the mix so that, for example, today we find not only ecologists but also restoration ecologists, aquatic ecologists, and fire ecologists; we find not only biologists, but also those who specialize in specific species. Scientists contribute to a widening circle of issues that now encompasses such topics as finding critical habitat for endangered species, determining how to most effectively manage fire on the landscape, or identifying locations for wind farms to produce renewable energy.

Americans no longer subscribe to Pinchot's idea that management should solely reside in the hands of a scientific cadre because many of the questions faced by land managers fall outside the realm of science.[67] The key questions surrounding removal of dams, development of oil and gas resources, or harvesting timber are simply not resolvable through scientific inquiry, method, or findings. How, for example, can science address the concerns raised by the Jackson Hole, Wyoming, Chamber of Commerce, noted above? Nonetheless, society generally holds knowledge and understanding flowing from science, as well as science itself, in high regard and few would align themselves with land-management policies or actions lacking scientific substance.

What is science? When I use the term *science,* I do so in the context of the following definitions. In pertinent part, the Merriam-Webster online dictionary offers that science is "knowledge or a system of knowledge covering general truths or the operation of general laws especially as obtained and tested through scientific method [and] such knowledge or such a system of knowledge concerned with the physical world and its phenomena."[68] Nobel Prize–winning physicist Richard Feynman thought of science as "the separation of the true from the false [in nature]."[69] Francis Collins, the head of the human genome project, writes: "Science's domain is to explore nature" and to "understand the natural world."[70] Science, as I consider it in this book, is about the systematic determination of true and false in the natural world. It does not include what may be broadly termed social science.

I adopt Robert Lackey's definition of normative science as "information that is developed, presented, or interpreted based on an assumed, usually unstated, preference for a particular policy or class of policy choices."[71] Implicit policy preferences embedded in normative science applicable to federal land management generally champion nature/natural while holding human-induced changes in ecological conditions to be undesirable. As environmental historian William Cronon notes:

> American ecology has long been attracted to a vision of the natural world in which pristine wild systems are regarded as the only legitimate examples of ecological "health." Any human alteration of such systems therefore appears as "disturbance" or worse, a violation of their natural integrity. Seductive as this either/or, bad/good, disturbed/undisturbed dualism may be, it gets us into all sorts of trouble as we confront the challenge of responsible land management.[72]

According to Lackey, common policy preferences found in normative science assume that

> human caused extinctions are inherently bad and should be avoided; unaltered [by humans] ecosystems are preferable to altered; reducing complexity in ecosystems is undesirable; natural evolution is good, human intervention is not; more biological diversity is preferable to less biodiversity; and native or indigenous species are preferable to nonnative species.[73]

One can reasonably argue that these are legitimate policy positions, but as Lackey notes, the converse of these views are equally valid public policy viewpoints. Science compels none of these positions.

Normative science is an inappropriate component of federal land use decision-making whether it incorporates assumptions favoring preservationist or utilitarian management prescriptions.

Finally, scholars, policymakers, land managers, and all concerned with federal land management, or any field employing conclusions reached by science, would do well to remember another definition offered by Feynman: "Science is the belief in the ignorance of experts."[74] Any review of advances in science quickly reveals a landscape littered with the bones of previously well-accepted ideas fallen prey to subsequent understanding.[75] Science is a restless enterprise. While normative science falls short, non-normative science is essential for good federal land management.

Science Is Necessary but Not Sufficient

Scientific analysis in fields such as biology, ecology, forestry, geology, and geography can provide knowledge about the natural world important to the management of federal lands. Scientists can tell policymakers the most likely environmental outcomes of alternative management actions. For example, they can tell the superintendent of Yosemite National Park that locating a campground adjacent to the Merced River in Yosemite Valley is likely to impact species A, B, and C in a particular way, whereas placing it away from the river will affect species D, E, and F. Essentially, science can aid in answering managers' questions of the form "If I do x, what will happen in some portion of the natural world?" The response will be incomplete and speculative in many cases. One cannot ask or expect more of science, but such information is critical to well-informed decision-making.

Science does not offer a calculus on which to base tradeoffs involving ecological considerations, economic factors, societal expectations, and other factors a manager must fold into rational decision-making. In Yosemite Valley, the ecological implications of moving campgrounds away from the Merced River are but one factor; impact on the experience of campers is another. The superintendent, in balancing multiple responsibilities, must weigh these and other considerations when making an overall management decision regarding campground placement. Likewise, the superintendent of Sequoia National Park had to consider multiple factors when deciding to relocate visitor facilities away from Giant Forest after park scientists determined their presence was causing problems with regeneration of the giant sequoias within that grove, even though their historic location provided an unparalleled visitor experience (one I enjoyed often). The following discussion of the removal of dams to protect salmon illustrates this point in more detail.

The Columbia River and its tributaries such as the Snake River have many uses. They are not all fully compatible. Salmon have long used these rivers. Declines in salmon populations returning to the Snake River resulted in the National Marine Fisheries Service listing sockeye salmon as endangered in 1991, spring/summer Chinook salmon as threatened in 1992, and fall Chinook as threatened in 1997. It also added steelhead in 1997. Officials have taken numerous actions to improve conditions for the salmon. An additional action called for by some interests is the removal of four dams on the Snake River because the dams increase mortality among juvenile salmon heading for the ocean and among adults returning to spawn.[76] Yet, while adversely affecting salmon, the dams offer important benefits. Collectively, they create a 140-mile stretch of pooled water from the point where the lower Snake River flows into the Columbia River upstream to Lewiston, Idaho. The dams provide hydroelectricity while the pools permit barge navigation, water for irrigation and human consumption, wildlife habitat, and recreational opportunities.

In general, Native Americans and national environmental organizations favor dam removal, but not necessarily for the same reasons. Five tribes in the region—the Nez Perce, Confederated Tribes of the Umatilla Indian Reservation, Yakama Nation, Confederated Tribes of Warm Springs, and the Shoshone-Bannock Tribes—historically had close cultural and economic ties to salmon in the lower Snake River. The salmon catch offers commercial, subsistence, and ceremonial benefits and dam removal would result in the reappearance of an estimated 14,000 acres of land previously used for cultural purposes.[77]

Nature-first environmentalists often favor removing dams because doing so moves the landscape toward a more natural state. Dams on the lower Snake River provide good targets of opportunity. In his article in the *Atlantic* on the salmon issue, James Fellows writes that "the debate's underlying—and usually unspoken—agenda . . . is the desire to limit development of pristine territory, and return rivers where possible to their unspoiled, pre-dammed condition— not necessarily for the sake of the salmon."[78]

Many regional residents and their congressional representatives oppose dam removal. No dams means no barges, which means area farmers would need to use more costly truck and rail transportation to move crops to ports while transportation costs for goods now moving upstream would also increase. The absence of dam-created pools means communities depending on the river for potable water would have to retrofit all their pool-dependent withdrawal systems. Removal means changes in recreational opportunities and wildlife habitat. If irrigation water became unavailable, the value of farmland is estimated to fall by some $130 million.[79] No dams means no low-cost hydroelectric power and electricity users would see their bills increase by an estimated $400–550 million annually.[80] The majority of concerns raised by tribes, environmentalists, and dam beneficiaries alike lie outside a quest for truth about the natural world, so the decision to breach or not breach dams is not within the realm of science.

Scientific information is a necessary but not sufficient condition for wellinformed decision-making. Every day, federal land managers incorporate science into decision-making: in planning, in preparing NEPA documents, in selecting which issues to tackle with limited budget and personnel resources, and in determining the preferred way to accomplish a specific task. Congress and the executive branch look to science to inform law and policy. But neither manager nor member nor secretary can ask science to make the decision for them, for to do so would be to ignore relevant nonscientific management and policy information.

The Importance of Policy-Neutral Science

Policymakers, land managers, and the public alike rely on the findings of science to help enlighten decisions regarding our public lands. These science consumers expect researchers to provide unbiased, objective information regarding land-management matters. They expect scientific information to be policy neutral and based on firm concepts rooted in the pursuit of truth about the natural world rather than on the preferences of a study's author.

Scientists bring their personal values and beliefs to the office, but that is not an excuse for blurring the line between facts and values in conducting or reporting scientific work. If normative science and vague ideas dominate the scientific enterprise, then the public will rightly lose its faith in the objectivity of scientific findings and the recommendations championed by scientists. People will see scientists as just another agenda-driven special interest at a great cost to us all because science is a cornerstone of societal advancement. Some fear that day may already be upon us.

"They distrust science," writes Douglas Futuyma when speaking of the public and scientists in his editorial in *BioScience*, the flagship publication of the American Institute of Biological Sciences (AIBS).[81] As AIBS president, he sees the problem as one of scientific illiteracy among the public, noting:

> The biggest challenge to biology and to science is not to achieve deeper understandings of genomes or ecosystems or black holes—that understanding is coming along just fine. . . . Scientists need to convince people that they have developed honest procedures for understanding how the world works.

We can clearly increase the understanding of science within the general population but the distrust will not go away just by educating people about science. One reason the public now rejects scientific forestry as the only guide to managing national forests is that many people feel that foresters advocated a particular management action, cutting timber, and that they employed normative science in doing so. Former Forest Service chief Jack Ward Thomas writes: "In the early 1970s . . . FS timber management activities were met with public backlash in two very different parts of the country [Montana and West Virginia]."[82] The Forest Service was emphasizing timber harvest but "values relating to fish and wildlife, recreation, watershed, and minerals were moved to the FS' 'back burners.'"[83] What is now equally clear is that many scientists within ecology and conservation biology likewise have management agendas driving their work.

The question of the proper place of policy advocacy within science and by scientists has been with us for some time.[84] What has changed in recent years is the growing acceptance by some scholars that they are on a mission and that their research should forward that mission. Reed Noss, a major figure in conservation biology, writes: "The entire field rests on the value assumption that biodiversity is good and ought to be conserved. Human actions that protect and restore biodiversity are good; those that destroy or degrade biodiversity are bad."[85]

The Society for Conservation Biology addressed the matter of normative science and advocacy during its 2006 annual meeting. The society published a series of papers on the topic in the February 2007 issue of its journal, *Conservation Biology*. In one article, J. Michael Scott and his coauthors report on their analysis of forty-five research articles in each of six peer-reviewed journals focused on

applying science to "conservation and management."[86] Normative language—
phrases like "profound ecosystem consequences," "natural resources can be
negatively affected," "suffered from lower nesting success," "favorable conditions," and "massive degradation"—appeared in 254 of the 270 (94 percent)
articles reviewed, while particular policy preferences appeared in 149 papers. For
those who have been involved with developing and implementing federal land-
management policies and who look to the scientific community for information
and advice, these findings are disheartening (although not surprising for those
of us who read scientific literature).

The normative phrases identified by Scott et al. presume a desired state. They
reflect what the researcher believes to be good or bad or what ought to be or
to happen. Such language lacks scientific justification because science properly
concerns itself with "is" or "was" or "may/will be" in the natural world. Science
has no means or measures to determine if having ten acres in wilderness is better
or worse than if those same acres were converted to a cornfield or a parking lot.
It has no way to determine if the vegetative community on a patch of ground
today is better/worse or more or less desirable than the vegetative community
occupying the same land 100 or 1,000 or 10,000 years ago. Ought is the concern
of society at large, as in we ought to protect nature's bald eagles but destroy nature's poliovirus since we judge eagles to be good and the poliovirus to be bad
largely for reasons having little to do with true and false in nature. Scott and his
coauthors conclude their article with this admonition:

> We believe that scientists and professional societies should strive to conduct
> policy-relevant science, to report it in value-neutral language, to state clearly
> policy implications of the findings, and to be vigorous in their efforts to bring
> that information to the attention of decision makers and all interested parties.

On the assumption that the "policy-relevant science" they refer to is not normative, then their call is precisely how science should help inform decision-
making.

The next section—"Summary of Recommendations"—arises from my experience in government. When a senior policymaker asks you for advice and
recommendations, they expect it to be clear and concise, a bottom line based
on in-depth understanding. When they want detailed information they ask.
You, the reader, are entitled to no less.

Summary of Recommendations

The recommendations touch on many aspects of federal land management
but not all. Nonetheless, the ideas cover enough ground to paint a reasonably

full picture of needed actions. Here, then, is a summary of my basic recommendations, which I flesh out significantly in chapter 4. The action falls largely on Congress because it is the land-management equivalent of Phrygian king Gordius; it crafted today's Gordian Knot.

Congress should reaffirm the basic twofold division of federal lands of multiple use and protected areas and in doing so clarify management priorities.

Congress should review judicial interpretations of existing law to determine if they represent contemporary congressional intent and make changes in the laws as needed.

In the light of new scientific understanding, Congress should reexamine the scientific basis for decades-old laws on the one hand and determine if old laws can satisfactorily address new scientific concerns on the other.

Congress should significantly reduce the role of the courts in federal land management by reducing ambiguity in legislative language, clarifying priorities, and reducing the opportunities to appeal publicly vetted and widely supported management decisions.

Congress should abolish the Forest Service and reassign its lands to the Bureau of Land Management, Fish and Wildlife Service, and National Park Service.

Congress should establish new management mechanisms giving greater weight to the voices of those living close to federal lands compared with residents of more distant places.

Congress should convene and empower a new Public Land Review Commission to conduct a sweeping review of federal land management and make comprehensive recommendations for reform.

The president should remove policy and land-management authority from the Office of Management and Budget.

As I outlined in the preface, the next three chapters set the stage for the detailed arguments leading to these conclusions. Chapter 1 begins this effort by looking at a contemporary snapshot of our federal lands.

Notes

1. This should not be construed as a critique of federal land managers; by and large they do a good job within the constraints in which they find themselves.

2. See the Yosemite Valley Plan, available at www.nps.gov/archive/yose/planning/yvp/seis/vol_Ia/chapter_1.html#0010 (accessed January 8, 2010).

3. Chuck Squatriglia, "Blueprint to Beautify, Restore Yosemite Tangled Up in Court," *San Francisco Chronicle*, January 21, 2007, A-1.

4. Court filings of Friends of Yosemite Valley and Mariposans for Environmentally Responsible Growth as well as the government's responses are available at www.nps.gov/archive/yose/planning/litigation (accessed August 31, 2010).

5. Michael Tollefson, "Ninth Declaration of Michael J. Tollefson in Support of Defendants' Reply Brief for Motion for Stay of Pending Appeal," March 5, 2007, in the U.S. District Court for the Eastern District of California Fresno Division, case no. CV-F-00-6191 DLB, *Friends of Yosemite Valley v. Dirk Kempthorne.*

6. Mark Grossi, "Yosemite Seeks Ideas about Crowd Control," *Fresno Bee*, July 8, 2009.

7. National wilderness areas and units of the national park system have always been off-limits to oil and gas production except where provisions for oil or gas development were included in the legislation establishing a specific unit, as with Big Cypress National Preserve in Florida. There are no serious proposals for national parks or wilderness areas to be opened to energy development. All energy-development projects on federal lands must comply with the full range of environmental legislation.

8. *Energy Policy and Conservation Act*, Public Law 106-469 §604, 42 U.S.C. §6217.

9. *Energy Policy Act of 2005*, Public Law 109-58 § 364, 42 U.S.C. 16801 note.

10. U.S. Departments of the Interior, Agriculture, and Energy, *Inventory of Onshore Federal Lands' Oil and Gas Resources and the Extent and Nature of Restrictions or Impediments to Their Development*, Washington, D.C., 2008. BLM/WO/GI-03/002+3100/REV08. www.blm.gov/epca.

11. U.S. Departments of the Interior, Agriculture, and Energy, *Inventory of Onshore Federal Lands' Oil and Gas Resources*, xxviii.

12. Federal acreage by bureau: Bureau of Land Management (255.8 million acres), Forest Service (192.8 million acres), Fish and Wildlife Service (94.5 million acres), and National Park Service (84.2 million acres).

13. U.S. Departments of the Interior, Agriculture, and Energy, *Inventory of Onshore Federal Lands' Oil and Gas Resources*, xxviii.

14. U.S. Departments of the Interior, Agriculture, and Energy, *Inventory of Onshore Federal Lands' Oil and Gas Resources*, xxix.

15. Standard leasing conditions require compliance with the full range of federal environmental statutes as well as those protecting cultural resources, like the National Historic Preservation Act.

16. U.S. Departments of the Interior, Agriculture, and Energy, *Inventory of Onshore Federal Lands' Oil and Gas Resources*, xxviii.

17. U.S. Departments of the Interior, Agriculture, and Energy, *Inventory of Onshore Federal Lands' Oil and Gas Resources*, xxix.

18. U.S. Departments of the Interior, Agriculture, and Energy, *Inventory of Onshore Federal Lands' Oil and Gas Resources*, xxix.

19. U.S. Departments of the Interior, Agriculture, and Energy, *Inventory of Onshore Federal Lands' Oil and Gas Resources*, xxix.

20. Forest Service, *The Process Predicament: How Statutory, Regulatory, and Administrative Factors Affect National Forest Management* (Washington, D.C.: USDA Forest Service, 2002).

21. Forest Service, *The Process Predicament*, appendix D, 16.

22. Federal regulators are charged with devising and overseeing compliance with regulations implementing specific statutes—for example, the Endangered Species Act (ESA). Their focus is generally narrow. Land managers have a much broader

perspective normally centered on a specific piece of ground. Some agencies have both regulators and land managers; for example, the Fish and Wildlife Service oversees compliance with the ESA and manages wildlife refuges.

23. Forest Service, *The Process Predicament*, 18.

24. Forest Service, *The Process Predicament*, 5.

25. For discussions of the reluctance of some organizations to untie the Gordian Knot, see, for example, Mark Sagoff, *Price, Principle, and the Environment* (Cambridge: Cambridge University Press, 2004), 212–22, and Michael Hibbard and Jeremy Madsen, "Environmental Resistance to Place-Based Collaboration in the U.S. West," *Society and Natural Resources* 16 (2003): 703–18.

26. Denise M. Keele, Robert W. Malmsheimer, Donald W. Floyd, and Jerome E. Perez, "Forest Service Land Management Litigation 1989–2002," *Journal of Forestry* (June 2006): 196–202.

27. U.S. Government Printing Office, *Federal Register* 70, no. 3 (January 5, 2005): 1023–61. *Citizens for Better Forestry et al. v. U.S. Dept. of Agriculture et al.*, U.S. District Court Northern District of California, No. C 05-1144 PJH, filed March 30, 2007.

28. *Citizens for Better Forestry et al. v. U.S. Department of Agriculture*, U.S. District Court for the Northern District of California, No. C 08-1927 CW, filed June 30, 2009, available at www.fs.fed.us/emc/nfma/includes/2009_06_30_SJ_Order.pdf (accessed September 8, 2010).

29. Wilderness Society, "Welcoming a New Era for the Forest Service," August 20, 2009, available at http://wilderness.org/content/welcoming-new-era-forest-service (accessed September 8, 2010).

30. Terry L. Anderson, Vernon L. Smith, and Emily Simmons, "How and Why to Privatize Federal Lands," *Policy Analysis* 363 (December 9, 1999).

31. Daniel Kemmis, *This Sovereign Land* (Washington, D.C.: Island Press, 2001), 175–76.

32. Kemmis, *This Sovereign Land*, 232.

33. Robert Nelson, *A Burning Issue* (Lanham, MD: Rowman & Littlefield, 2000), 178.

34. Nelson, *A Burning Issue*, 182.

35. Sally K. Fairfax, "When an Agency Outlasts Its Time," *Journal of Forestry* (July/August 2005): 264–67.

36. Eric T. Freyfogle, "Goodbye to the Public-Private Divide," *Environmental Law* 36 (2006): 24.

37. Freyfogle, "Goodbye," 23.

38. Robert B. Keiter, *Keeping Faith with Nature* (New Haven: Yale University Press, 2003), 308–9.

39. Keiter, *Keeping Faith with Nature*, 309.

40. Keiter, *Keeping Faith with Nature*, 308.

41. Randal O'Toole, "A Matter of Trust: Why Congress Should Turn Federal Lands into Fiduciary Trusts," *Cato Institute Policy Analysis* 630 (January 15, 2009): 11.

42. O'Toole, "A Matter of Trust," 10.

43. Dan L. Gildor, "Preserving the Priceless: A Constitutional Amendment to Empower Congress to Preserve, Protect, and Promote the Environment," *Ecology Law Quarterly* 32 (2005): 823.

44. As cited in Gildor, "Preserving the Priceless," 823.

45. Rodger Schlickeisen, "The Argument for a Constitutional Amendment to Protect Living Nature," pp. 221–42 in *Biodiversity and the Law*, ed. William J. Snape III (Washington, D.C.: Island Press, 1996), 234.

46. Gildor, "Preserving the Priceless," 830–33.

47. Gildor, "Preserving the Priceless," 861.

48. Holly Fretwell, *Who Is Minding the Federal Estate: Political Management of America's Public Land* (Lanham, MD: Lexington Books, 2009).

49. Fretwell, *Who Is Minding the Federal Estate*, 95–96.

50. Bryan G. Norton, *Sustainability: A Philosophy of Adaptive Ecosystem Management* (Chicago: University of Chicago Press, 2005), ix.

51. Stephen Fox, *John Muir and His Legacy: The American Conservation Movement* (Boston: Little, Brown, 1981), 50. Also see: Donald Worster, *A Passion for Nature: The Life of John Muir* (New York: Oxford University Press, 2008), and Thurman Wilkins, *John Muir: An Apostle for Nature* (Norman: University of Oklahoma Press, 1995).

52. As quoted in Norton, *Sustainability,* ix.

53. Roderick Nash, *Rights of Nature* (Madison: University of Wisconsin Press, 1989), 41.

54. Gifford Pinchot, *Breaking New Ground*, reprinted in Roderick Nash, *The American Environment: Readings in the History of Conservation* (Reading, MA: Addison-Wesley, 1976 [1947]), 62.

55. John Muir, *The Yosemite*, reprinted in *John Muir: Nature Writings* (New York: Library of America, 1997 [1912]), 817.

56. Two recent books chronicle the Hetch Hetchy controversy; see: John Warfield Simpson, *Dam: Water, Power, Politics, and Preservation in Hetch Hetchy and Yosemite National Park* (New York: Pantheon, 2005), and Robert Righter, *The Battle over Hetch Hetchy* (Oxford: Oxford University Press, 2005). Don Hodel, then secretary of the interior, kindled efforts to restore Hetch Hetchy in 1987 by having the Bureau of Reclamation conduct a preliminary study on the availability of water from other sources. In July 2006 the State of California released the *Hetch Hetchy Restoration Study* concluding that much more analysis was required before decisions on dam removal could be made. Available at www.hetchhetchy.water.ca.gov (accessed September 8, 2010).

57. Brower headed the Sierra Club for seventeen years and started Friends of the Earth, the League of Conservation Voters, and the Earth Island Institute.

58. David Brower, *Let the Mountains Talk, Let the Rivers Run* (New York: Harper Collins West, 1995), 176.

59. For example, see E. O. Wilson, *The Creation: An Appeal to Save Life on Earth* (New York: W.W. Norton, 2006). Wilson, a self-described secular humanist who rejects the idea of creation as the manifestation of God, begins the book with a "Letter to a Southern Baptist Minister."

60. Newspapers covered his passing under headlines like "nature's crusader" and "dean of the greens." See the *Mercury News*, November 6, 2000, and *Seattle Post-Intelligencer*, November 7, 2000.

61. Jeffrey St. Clair, "David Brower's Last Chance: Taking Out Glen Canyon Dam," *In These Times*, April 17, 2000.

62. Daniel Styles, *National Park Visitor Spending and Payroll Impacts* (Washington, D.C.: National Park Service, 2007), table A-1.

63. Glen Canyon Dam Adaptive Management Program, "Frequently Asked Questions," 2007, available at www.gcdamp.gov/faq.html (accessed September 8, 2010).

64. Noelle Straub, "Sportsmen in D.C. Lobby for Wyoming Range," *Casper Star-Tribune*, February 16, 2007; Associated Press, "Thomas Supports Range Lease Ban," *Billings Gazette*, May 30, 2007; Star-Tribune Editorial Board, "Gov Makes Good Case to Protect Wyoming Range," *Casper Star-Tribune*, May 7, 2007, Jennifer Frazer, "Oil and Gas Buyback Proposed," *Wyoming Tribune-Eagle*, May 30, 2007.

65. Star-Tribune Editorial Board, "Gov Makes Good Case to Protect Wyoming Range."

66. Pinchot was part of the Progressive Era, which emphasized scientific management—cadres of professionals—playing a major role in societal decision-making.

67. See Nelson, *A Burning Issue*; Keiter, *Keeping Faith with Nature*; Fairfax, "When an Agency Outlasts Its Time"; and Joseph DiMento and Helen Ingram, "Science and Environmental Decision Making: The Potential Role of Environmental Impact Assessment in the Pursuit of Appropriate Information," *Natural Resources Journal* 45 (2005): 283–309.

68. Merriam-Webster Online, available at www.m-w.com/dictionary/science (accessed September 8, 2010).

69. Richard P. Feynman, *The Pleasure of Finding Things Out* (New York: Basic Books, 1999), 240.

70. Francis Collins, *The Language of God* (New York: Free Press, 2006), 6.

71. Robert Lackey, "Science, Scientists, and Policy Advocacy," *Conservation Biology* 21 (2007): 13.

72. William Cronon, "Resisting Monoliths and Tabulae Rasae," *Ecological Applications* 10 (2000): 675.

73. Lackey, "Science, Scientists, and Policy Advocacy," 14.

74. Feynman, *The Pleasure of Finding Things Out*, 187.

75. See Bill Bryson, *A Short History of Nearly Everything* (New York: Broadway Books, 2003).

76. U.S. Army Corps of Engineers, *Summary: Improving Salmon Passage, Final Lower Snake River Juvenile Salmon Migration Feasibility Report/Environmental Impact Statement* (Walla Walla, WA: U.S. Army Corps of Engineers, 2002), 3.

77. U.S. Army Corps of Engineers, *Summary*, 36.

78. James Fallows, "Saving Salmon or Seattle?" *The Atlantic* 286 (2000): 20–26.

79. U.S. Army Corps of Engineers, *Summary*, 33.

80. Bonneville Power Administration, *Fact Sheet: The Costs of Breaching the Four Lower Snake River Dams*, March 2007, available at www.bpa.gov/corporate/pubs/fact_sheets/07fs/fs030207.pdf (accessed September 8, 2010).

81. Douglas J. Futuyma, "Science's Greatest Challenge," *BioScience* 57 (2007): 3.

82. Jack Ward Thomas and Alex Sienkiewicz, "The Relationship between Science and Democracy: Public Land Policies, Regulation and Management," *Public Land and Resources Law Review* 26 (2005): 51.

83. Thomas and Sienkiewicz, "The Relationship between Science and Democracy," 51.

84. See generally *Conservation Biology* 21 (2007) for a recent collection of articles on the subject. See also: Mark A. Davis and Lawrence B. Slobodkin, "The Science and Values of Restoration Ecology," *Restoration Ecology* 12 (2004): 1–3, and Keith Winterhalder, Andre Clewell, and James Aronson, "The Science and Values of Restoration Ecology—A Response to Davis and Slobodkin," *Restoration Ecology* 12 (2004): 4–7.

85. Reed Noss, "Values Are a Good Thing in Conservation Biology," *Conservation Biology* 21 (2007): 18.

86. J. Michael Scott et al., "Policy Advocacy in Science: Prevalence, Perspectives, and Implications for Conservation Biology," *Conservation Biology* 21 (2007): 29–35. The journals examined were *Conservation Biology, Ecological Applications, Forest Science, Journal of Range Management, Journal of Wildlife Management,* and the *North American Journal of Fisheries Management.*

1

Federal Lands in the First
Decade of the Twenty-first Century

The conservation of natural resources is the fundamental problem.

—Theodore Roosevelt

EVERY STATE IN THE UNION CONTAINS SOME FEDERAL LAND, but the federal lands in Massachusetts differ dramatically from those in Montana. Regional differences in their physical geography, resource characteristics, and share of the landscape are among the factors coloring how people think of federal lands and their management. Westerners, for example, find that federal lands dominate their landscapes. So it is not by accident that for the past fifty years, representatives from western states have routinely held majorities on congressional committees overseeing federal lands.[1] In this chapter, I present a snapshot of federal lands, including their distribution by region and land-management agency, physical characteristics and resources, and economic and noneconomic societal benefits.[2] I also discuss land-management agency missions and why they matter.

Geographic Distribution

Federal lands are distributed quite unevenly across the country (see table 1.1). In broad regional terms, thirteen western states comprise some 49 percent of our total land area while containing 93 percent of our federal land.[3] Even without Alaska, the western concentration of federal lands remains evident. The eleven contiguous western states account for 40 percent of total acreage in the lower forty-eight states but have 88 percent of the federal land therein. Comparatively, the Northeast is nearly devoid of federal lands; indeed neighboring Yellowstone and Grand Teton National Parks in Wyoming alone contain more federal land than all nine northeastern states combined. Comparing the Midwest and South, one finds similar amounts of federal land and overall acreage.[4] Even though the Midwest and South contain significantly more federal land than does the Northeast, every western state (except Hawaii and Washington) has nearly as much or more federal land than is found in either of these two regions (see appendix). Little wonder that westerners pay attention to federal land management.

Any time a few land managers control large portions of the countryside their actions attract a good deal of local, regional, or statewide attention. Such is the case in western states where, on average, federal lands occupy more than 50 percent of a state's territory (compared with less than 5 percent in other regions).[5] Management actions on federal lands impact many facets of local and regional life, including economic activity, employment opportunity, public revenue, and the land costs of activities ranging from housing to schools. If, as in the case of federal lands, interests far removed from the land in question play major roles in determining the actions of those managers, then local and regional concerns increase all the more, a situation that helps inspire reform proposals like those of Kemmis and Nelson that I summarized in the introduction.[6]

Any discussion of federal lands must include a separate look at Alaska, owing to the sheer number of federal acres it houses. Alaska contains 38 percent of our federal lands; by comparison, the second ranking state—Nevada—is home to 9 percent. Alaska contains:

- Eighty-one percent of the land in the wildlife refuge system;[7]
- Sixty-five percent of the land in the national park system;[8]
- More national forest land than any other state;[9]

TABLE 1.1
Federal Acreage (in Thousands) by Region and Bureau, 2008

	BLM	FWS	FS	NPS	Total
Northeast	0	262.7	1,715.6	502.5	2,480.8
Midwest	343.3	4,874.0	13,062.2	1,710.2	19,989.8
South	50.9	4,448.8	14,341.8	5,639.9	24,481.4
West	255,378.8	84,918.8	163,646.6	76,391.3	580,344.5
Total	255,782.1	94,504.3	192,766.2	84,243.9	627,296.5

Source: Appendix. These four agencies manage nearly 99 percent of total federal lands.

- Fifty-three percent of federally designated wilderness;
- The largest wildlife refuge (Arctic at 19.3 million acres) and all of the nation's twelve refuges exceeding 1 million acres in size; and
- The largest national park (Wrangell–St. Elias Park and Preserve at 13.2 million acres) and nine of the nation's ten national park system units exceeding 2 million acres in size.

By any federal land measure, Alaska stands apart and when considering national-level data, one must always consider Alaska's share.

One only has to look at the National Wildlife Refuge System to see the value in understanding Alaska's contribution to our federal lands. The Fish and Wildlife Service manages some 550 refuges nationwide covering 94.5 million acres, for an average size of 171,000 acres. Without Alaska's 47 refuges covering 76.8 million acres, the average size of refuges becomes 35,000 acres. Instead of picturing landscapes with relatively large refuges, leaving out Alaska allows us to envision the wildlife refuge system as it really is in the contiguous states: a series of relatively small parcels dotting various portions of the country.[10]

Just as we do not find our 627 million federal acres distributed evenly by region, we do not find them equally apportioned among the four land-managing agencies (see table 1.1). The BLM (41 percent) and the FS (26 percent) manage most federal land. All bureaus have a strong western focus, but it is greatest for the BLM and least for the FS.

Having placed the federal lands in their geographic and agency context, I discuss differing agency management missions in the next section because uses of a given parcel of federal land depend heavily upon which agency Congress entrusted with its management. Each bureau has its own set of legislative and administrative directions.

Agency Management Missions

The Bureau of Land Management and the Forest Service are presumptive multiple-use agencies and may permit a wide range of human uses on their lands (see box 1.1). Multiple-use does not mean that all uses may be permitted everywhere because some are mutually incompatible. Managers evaluate development proposals against their impacts on other legitimate uses of the land when deciding on whether or not to allow the activity. In some cases, Congress or the executive branch has made its will known regarding management of specific tracts of BLM and FS managed lands. On lands managed by the BLM, either Congress or the executive branch has placed some kind of

---

Box 1.1.   Bureau Mission Statements

It is the mission of the Bureau of Land Management to sustain the health, diversity, and productivity of the public lands for the use and enjoyment of present and future generations.

The mission of the USDA Forest Service is to sustain the health, diversity, and productivity of the Nation's forests and grasslands to meet the needs of present and future generations.

The mission of the U.S. Fish and Wildlife Service is working with others to conserve, protect, and enhance fish, wildlife, plants, and their habitats for the continuing benefit of the American people.

The National Park Service preserves unimpaired the natural and cultural resources and values of the national park system for the enjoyment, education, and inspiration of this and future generations. The Park Service cooperates with partners to extend the benefits of natural and cultural resource conservation and outdoor recreation throughout this country and the world.

Sources: BLM—www.ntc.blm.gov/leadership/leader_blm_mission_html. FS—www .fs.fed.us/aboutus/mission.shtml. FWS—www. fws.gov/infopocketguide/fundamentals .htm. NPS – www.nps.gov/legacy/mission.html.

---

conservation-first special management designation on approximately 73 million of the agency's 255.8 million acres (29 percent). One finds the 73 million acres scattered among categories such as: wilderness areas, wilderness study areas, areas of critical concern, national conservation areas, herd management areas, and national monuments.[11] The situation repeats itself on lands managed by the Forest Service, where some 44 million acres carry special designations such as wilderness, botanical areas, and scenic and research areas (also see the "Oil and Gas Availability" section in the introduction).[12] In addition, over 50 million acres of the national forests are managed as roadless areas.[13]

The Fish and Wildlife Service emphasizes resource conservation chiefly in the form of providing wildlife habitat in national wildlife refuges (NWRs). In its founding documents Congress declared recreation based on wildlife (e.g., observation, photography, hunting, and fishing) to be the primary public uses on refuge lands.[14] Congress also provided for a wider range of uses *if* the refuge manager determined they would be compatible with the purpose of the refuge and refuge system as a whole. An example is a commercial timber harvest at the Great Dismal Swamp NWR on the Virginia–North Carolina border.

Hurricane Isabel swept through the refuge in September 2003, severely damaging the refuge's now-rare stands of Atlantic white cedar (AWC). The blowdown created an extreme fire threat by loading the erstwhile forest floor with excessive amounts of fuel. In 2004 refuge managers began implementing the commercial harvesting of up to 3,000 acres of standing and damaged AWC and mixed hardwoods.[15] Offering downed and damaged trees for commercial harvesting removed the fire danger while creating an opportunity to restore AWC stands and doing so at a profit rather than at a cost. In general, then, refuge managers operate with less management flexibility regarding land use than do BLM and FS managers, but greater flexibility than their NPS counterparts.

National Park Service lands contain the greatest restrictions on land use. Law and policy limit activities to those related to visitor use and enjoyment of park resources. NPS lands are presumptively off-limits to uses and activities not associated with public appreciation of the features giving rise to the unit's establishment. The nearly 400 units of the national park system provide opportunities for the public to view spectacular scenery and wildlife, enjoy a variety of resource-based outdoor recreational activities, and visit places central to the nation's history and culture.[16] Consumptive uses of nonrenewable natural resources rarely occur on NPS lands. Congress may have permitted them only if they existed prior to an area being designated a part of the national park system as part of the political horse-trading needed to obtain majority support for the new unit. Over time, Congress has reinforced land-use restrictions (even those that would aid park visitors) by declaring 52 percent of the national park system's 84 million acres to be wilderness wherein access is limited to nonmechanized means, no facilities may be built, and land managers must carefully control all acceptable activities like hiking, backpacking, and canoeing (see table 1.2). Periodically, someone claims parks are being, or will shortly be, opened to resource exploitation and development. As a practical matter, such alarms lack a basis in reality in the twenty-first century and are best viewed as fund-raising efforts.

TABLE 1.2
National Wilderness Acreage, 2009

Bureau	Wilderness Acreage (millions)	Percent of National Wilderness Acreage	Percent of Total Managed Acres
BLM	8.7	7.9	3.4
FWS	20.7	19.0	22.0
FS	36.2	33.0	18.8
NPS	43.9	40.1	52.1
National Total	109.5	100.0	17.4

Source: Department of the Interior, "Secretary Salazar Joins President Obama in Commemorating 40th Anniversary of Wilderness Act," news release, August 3, 2009.

Public understanding and experience with agency management direction significantly impact their views regarding who is to manage what, where. As an example, I turn to the effort to establish a tallgrass prairie unit of the National Park System.

Why Perceptions of Management Missions Matter

The NPS long sought to add a unit centered on preserving remnants of the tallgrass prairie plant community. The tallgrass once extended over tens of millions of acres in the center of the country. An attractive opportunity presented itself in 1983 within Osage County, Oklahoma, when the trustees of the Barnard Ranch announced that its 29,000 acres of high-quality tallgrass prairie were for sale.[17] Complexity accompanied the opportunity, however, for while tallgrass prairie covers the surface, oil and natural gas lie beneath it. Moreover, those who own the land do not own the mineral rights. The county had once been the Osage Reservation, but tribal members sold the land decades ago while retaining subsurface rights. Oil and natural gas production provides a major source of income for the tribe and its members. The tribe did not trust the NPS, fearing that NPS control of the surface would eventually result in termination of energy production and related income. The NPS mission mattered. Cattlemen and farmers were also concerned about NPS management. Conversely, many residents of nearby Pawhuska, Oklahoma, were supportive. They saw potential tourist income generated by the presence of a unit of the national park system as a welcome boost for a community in economic doldrums. Likewise, environmental organizations strongly favored creation of a new park system unit. In this atmosphere, efforts began to craft a compromise that would gain the bipartisan support of Oklahoma's congressional delegation.[18]

Work to reach agreement on creating a new unit of the national park system based on preservation of the tallgrass plant community paid off in 1987. All members of the Oklahoma congressional delegation cosponsored legislation to establish a 100,000-acre Tallgrass Prairie National Preserve that also had the support of the Reagan administration, the governor, and the state legislature.[19] The bill called for a 50,000-acre core area consisting of lands purchased from willing sellers and a surrounding 50,000 acres whose tallgrass resources were protected through easements. Oil and gas production could continue under pre-preserve regulations administered by the Bureau of Indian Affairs. It was a preserve, not a park, but it achieved the public purpose of protecting tallgrass prairie for the use and enjoyment of present and future generations.[20] The legislation pleased neither the Osage nor many environmentalists. The tribe was not convinced the legislative language would protect their interests and some members of the environmental community wanted a bigger unit and were unhappy with the continuance of oil and gas production.

On May 26, 1988, the Senate Energy and Natural Resources Committee held a hearing on the legislation.[21] In his opening statement, Oklahoma's senior senator, David Boren, made it clear the bill represented a compromise that the delegation was convinced struck the right balance between competing viewpoints. Changes, especially by expanding acreage, would unravel the agreement.[22] Nonetheless, after the hearing the Sierra Club immediately called upon its members to push Congress for a larger preserve.[23] Mickey Edwards, the congressman in whose district the preserve was to have been located, had also publicly warned against lobbying for a larger preserve. Moreover, he thought he had an agreement with interested parties not to do so.[24] The Sierra Club's action caused Edwards to cry foul and he pulled his support of the bill. The remainder of the Oklahoma delegation followed and the legislation died; yet today the NPS has a Tallgrass Prairie National Preserve.

On November 12, 1996, President Clinton signed the Omnibus Parks and Public Lands Management Act (P.L. 104-333) into law. Buried in the bill, which touched 113 sites and 41 states, was the creation of the Tallgrass Prairie National Preserve. It was not, however, the 100,000-acre area proposed in Oklahoma. After the collapse of the Osage County effort, attention had turned to Kansas. Following years of tumultuous debate—again centered on the implications of NPS land ownership—the Kansas congressional delegation ultimately supported an 11,000-acre preserve in Flint Hills of which the NPS could not own more than 180 acres.[25] The act President Clinton signed names these 11,000 acres the Tallgrass Prairie National Preserve. They are but a shadow of what was within reach in Oklahoma if only all parties had respected a carefully crafted compromise that recognized how affected parties perceive the importance of agency missions.

Having looked at the extent and distribution of federal lands and touched upon the missions of federal land-managing agencies, I now outline what is on and beneath these lands and illustrate some management issues.

Resources of Federal Land

The wide range of geologic, geomorphologic, geographic, and climatic conditions one finds on federal lands means that surface and subsurface resources abound. They may be living or inanimate; they may be tangible or intangible; and they may be renewable or nonrenewable. Such variety makes federal land management all the more challenging. I begin with living resources.

Home for Other Species[26]

Many other living things share the land and waters of the United States with us humans. Researchers have identified over 200,000 species of fungi, plants, and animals as U.S. residents but generally recognized that perhaps hundreds of thousands of species have yet to be described.[27] Federal lands offer habitat to many of these biota because of their extensive environmental diversity, a situation that helps account for estimates that they provide habitat for nearly 60 percent of the species listed as threatened or endangered under the Endangered Species Act.[28] Of course, many of these same species also reside on nonfederal land as well; indeed private lands provide homes to over 60 percent of listed species, and state lands harbor about the same number of species as do the federal lands.[29] Biota do not care who owns the land they call home, but it is clear federal lands attract an extensive array of living things and that they comprise a major resource thereon.

Federal lands will continue to provide habitat for other species in the United States and many believe their importance will grow as development and habitat fragmentation occur, especially on nonfederal lands.[30] As I point out in the section that follows and in chapter 2, rural land use is changing. Species favoring large territories, those that migrate long distances, or those that are adverse to humans at some stage of their lives may find some of the changes harmful. One must resist the temptation, however, to assume federal lands are becoming the last refuge of living things in the United States, especially in the contiguous states. Here nonfederal rural lands (forests, cropland, rangeland, and pasture) account for 71 percent of total land use compared to 21 percent in federal lands and 6 percent in cities, towns, and roads combined.[31] We need to consider more than amounts of, and changes in, human land use when thinking about species and federal lands; invasive species and shifting spatial distributions of biota are but two such considerations.

Invasive species thrive on federal lands throughout the country.[32] Their presence makes it harder for forest supervisors, refuge managers, park superintendents, and BLM district managers to achieve the agreed-upon land-management objective of maintaining native species populations. Each agency considers invasives a major management issue. In his 2003 Earth Day speech then-Chief of the Forest Service Dale Bosworth highlighted invasives as one of four great issues facing management of our national forests (the others were wildland fire, habitat fragmentation, and unmanaged recreation).[33] All bureaus maintain active programs to address invasives. The NPS, for example, has established seventeen Exotic Plant Management Teams that specialize in a particular region of the country so as to maximize scientific expertise and take best advantage of local and regional knowledge.

Even without invasives, management tied to biota and habitat is difficult because living things move through space over time while management boundaries remain static. Change occurs at many spatial and temporal scales as biota respond to shifting physical conditions without regard to management plans or congressional directives. As a consequence, we need to think of the biotic components of a given place as a *temporary assemblage* of plants and animals at a particular time.[34] We cannot fossilize landscapes.[35] In addition, each species has its own living requirements so that one cannot speak of good or bad habitat outside a reference to a particular species. There are no easy answers regarding management issues tied to biota.

Timber

We humans have long used wood in multiple ways to improve our lives. We make homes, tools, and furnishings from wood. We make paper on which we impart knowledge, ideas, and information from wood. We warm ourselves and cook our food with wood. Time and technology have added to the means of accomplishing these tasks but wood remains a major material in the twenty-first century. I write this in a wood-framed house with wooden rafters, a wooden roof, and a wooden deck. My computer sits on a wooden desk. If you are reading this in hard copy, at some point the paper on which these words are printed was part of a tree. The overall trend in U.S. consumption of wood is upward; for example, it was 86 percent greater during 2001–2005 than it was during 1965–1969.[36] Demand for wood persists.

Unlike petroleum or some mineral resources, the United States has ample forest resources; its 750 million forested acres make it the fourth most forest-rich country on the earth (trailing Russia, Brazil, and Canada).[37] The public—chiefly through federal agencies—owns some 44 percent of the nation's forests (see table 1.3). Forestland, however, is not synonymous with timberland. The

TABLE 1.3
Forest and Timber Acreage by Owner, 2007

Ownership	Forestland		Timberland	
	Acres	*% U.S. Total*	*Acres*	*% U.S. Total*
Public				
Federal	250	33	113	22
State/local	80	11	45	9
Public Total	329	44	158	31
Private	421	56	354	69
U.S. Total	750		513	

Source: Forest Service, *Forest Resources of the United States, 2007*, 2009, tables 1 and 10.

latter refers to forestland that "is producing or is capable of producing crops of industrial wood and not withdrawn from timber utilization by statute or administrative regulation."[38] The nation contains some 513 million acres of timberland, of which 113 million are managed by federal agencies. Less than one-half of all federally managed forests are deemed timberlands.

Timber production from the national forests fluctuates over time. Like all commodities, it reacts to domestic and international market forces as well as to policy and management decisions, and (increasingly in recent years) to extensive use of administrative and judicial processes by those opposed to cutting trees on multiple-use federal lands.[39] Current harvests have declined to levels not seen since the early 1940s (see table 1.4) and come at a time when annual net wood growth is several times greater than the amount of timber cut.[40] Although an important potential source of renewable timber resources, the multiple-use timberlands in the national forests supply only some 2 percent of total national production.[41] As a result, wood imports reached 17 percent of consumption during the period 2000–2005, the highest such dependence in history.[42] In addition to imports, increased harvesting from private lands has helped satisfy Americans' appetite for wood. However, the future of such production is in doubt because between 2000 and 2005 the timber industry sold approximately 60 percent of its best timberland to real estate and long-term investment companies that are likely to turn the land away from sustainable forest product production and toward housing and

TABLE 1.4
Average Annual National Forest Timber
Harvest by Ten-Year Intervals, 1908–2007

Interval	Average Annual Harvest (million board fee)
1908–1917	494,993
1918–1927	947,708
1928–1937	1,046,827
1938–1947	2,399,250
1948–1957	5,218,326
1958–1967	9,666,264
1968–1977	11,353,617
1978–1987	9,965,076
1988–1997	7,050,411
1998–2007	2,264,699

Source: U.S. Forest Service, "Number of Sales, Value and Price per MBF of Convertible Timber Cut & Sold Forest Service Wide," 2009. Available at www.fs.fed.us/forest-management/reports/sold-harvest/documents/1905-2008-_Natl_Sold_Harvest_Summary.pdf.

other nonforest land uses as market conditions and opportunities dictate.[43] One can expect, therefore, that pressure for expanded timber production on federal multiple-use lands will increase. Forests, of course, provide far more than timber; they and other federal lands also serve as locations for a variety of recreational activities, which I sketch in the next section.

Recreation

Is there a reader who has not visited our federal lands at some time? I suspect there are very few. These lands registered some 645 million visits in 2010 (see table 1.5). Continued population growth as well as the broad public interest in the outdoors and connecting with our history assures that our national parks, forests, and other areas will continue to draw large numbers of visitors in the future. This is certainly the expectation of bureau managers and planners. Yet recreation has become controversial.[44] In 1999, Mike Dombeck, then chief of the Forest Service, noted: "Now we see law suits, not only against oil, gas and mining, but also to stop recreational use."[45]

Visitors arrive with highly divergent expectations and desires, each of which changes over time. Wilderness aficionados, skiers, hunters, climbers, day-hikers, fishermen, auto-borne scenery devotees, wildlife observers, off-highway-vehicle (OHV) enthusiasts, power boaters, and others all seek out federal lands. Some need roads, restaurants, grocery stores, lodgings, and other facilities to enjoy their experience. Others prefer trails and solitude. Some want motors; others prefer muscle. Some want chair lifts while others strap on snowshoes. Expectations conflict. The principal divide lies between

TABLE 1.5
Visitation to Federal Lands by Bureau, 2010

Bureau	Visitation (millions)	Percent National Total
BLM	58.6	9.1
FS	170.8	26.5
FWS	44.5	6.9
NPS	281.3	43.6
Reclamation	90.0	13.9
Total	645.2	

Sources: Bureau of Land Management, *Public Land Statistics 2010,* available at www.blm.gov/public_land_statistics/index.htm (accessed September 12, 2011). Bureau of Reclamation, "Bureau of Reclamation Facts and Information," available at www.usbr.gov/main/about/fact.html (accessed September 13, 2011). FWS data from personal communication with Chris Tollefson, FWS public affairs office, Washington, D.C., September 14, 2011. NPS data from National Park Service Public Use Statistics Office, *Annual Summary Report for 2010,* available at www.nature.nps.gov/stats/viewReport.cfm (accessed September 12, 2011). FS data from *National Visitor Use Monitoring Report,* available at: http://apps.fs.usda.gov/nrm/nvum/results (accessed October 13, 2011).

those whose use of public lands requires a discernible human presence and those whose use does not. The question of Grand Canyon National Park over-flights illustrates this point.

The effort to resolve the question of overflights at Grand Canyon National Park has continued for some twenty years. Aircraft noise offends some visitors for whom "natural quiet" is a highly desirable park resource, while hundreds of thousands of other visitors wish to see the canyon's grandeur from the air. While at the Department of the Interior (DOI) in the 1980s, I was part of the group addressing these conflicting concerns. Our pursuit of a solution was made more complicated by the differing operational needs of fixed-wing and helicopter tour operators and assuring whatever plan emerged met the safety requirements of the Federal Aviation Administration. The work resulted in publication of new flight rules establishing limited flight corridors in 1988. They were apparently inadequate, however, as a series of subsequent efforts to further reduce aircraft noise while providing for overflights continues to the present day.[46] Overflights are but one recreational public-use conflict facing land managers. The Forest Service and the BLM, for example, face significant OHV-management issues, and controversies surrounding downhill skiing in our national forests continue. Reconciling competing recreational desires will continue to be a major aspect of public-land management.

Water

Federal lands, agencies, and officials play a major role in securing the ben-efits of water for humans and other species. This is especially true in the West, where an estimated 65 percent of the water supply for the contiguous eleven states comes from BLM, FS, and NPS land.[47] The geographic characteristics of federal land in combination with congressionally mandated responsibilities heighten the importance of the federal presence to the availability of water.

Elevation, topography, and vegetation combine to explain the physical linkage between federal land and water supply. Federal agencies, in particular the Forest Service and the National Park Service, manage a significant por-tion of the higher elevation and mountainous land in the Cascade and Sierra Nevada Mountains, as well as similar lands throughout the individual moun-tain ranges comprising the Rocky Mountains. These mountains trend north–south and intercept eastward-moving and moisture-laden air masses arriving from over the Pacific Ocean. Rising over the mountains, the air masses cool so that water vapor condenses and falls in some form of precipitation to ulti-mately supply the West's major rivers with water. In turn, the rivers provide much of the water for cities, towns, and irrigated agriculture throughout the West, as well as habitat for a wide variety of wildlife.

Policymakers long ago understood the link between forests, water, and development. Congress passed the Forest Reserve Act in 1891, creating public forests. Six years later it enacted what came to be known as the Organic Administration Act (or the Forest Management Act) regarding reserve management, which stipulated three goals for the forest reserves, one of which was to "secure favorable water flows." This mission passed to the Forest Service, which Congress created in 1905 to manage the 56 million acres within the forest reserves.[48]

In 1902 Congress formally recognized the importance of water to western development by establishing the Bureau of Reclamation (BOR) within the DOI.[49] The BOR occupies the central position in western water management (see box 1.2). Therefore, it deserves our attention even though students of federal lands do not count it as one of the federal land-managing agencies because it oversees only about one-tenth of the acreage managed by the NPS.

Water development historically dominated the agency.[50] Over time, Congress authorized and funded the building of the 472 dams and 348 reservoirs presently operated by the BOR, thus making it the dominant entity in the management and provision of water in the West. Together these facilities yield widely felt and diversified benefits. For example, BOR dams and reservoirs:

- Provide water to 31 million people (five times Arizona's population);
- Produce 17 percent of the nation's hydroelectric power (second largest provider);
- Supply water for 60 percent of the nation's vegetable crop;
- Furnish water for 25 percent of the nation's fruit and nut crop; and
- Receive some 90 million water-oriented recreation visits annually.[51]

The BOR's infrastructure helps assure that the West's water continues to flow, but the agency also plays an important role as a broker between competing interests, especially regarding the waters of the West's single most significant river, the Colorado.

Box 1.2.   Bureau of Reclamation Mission

The Bureau of Reclamation's mission is to manage, develop, and protect water and related resources in an environmentally and economically sound manner in the interest of the American public.

Source: www.usbr.gov/main/about/mission.html.

The Colorado River basin encompasses seven states wherein disputes over water allocation have continued for the better part of a century. Colorado, New Mexico, Utah, and Wyoming comprise the so-called upper basin, while the lower basin consists of Arizona, California, and Nevada. The upper basin provides most of the river's water. Western water law operates on a first-in-time-first-in-right basis, meaning that the first users of water have a prior or superior right to water compared with later users. In the early part of the last century the upper basin states feared that western water law would preclude their future use of Colorado River water because preexisting uses in lower basin states would prevent diversion to newer uses in the upper basin states. The 1922 Colorado River Compact, a negotiated agreement between the seven states and the federal government, called for a 50-50 split between upper and lower basin states. Congress ratified the compact in the Boulder Canyon Project Act of 1928 but that hardly ended disputes whose resolution increasingly utilizes consensus-building, which finds the BOR at the center.[52]

Two recent pacts illustrate this point. Under an agreement fostered by the BOR by federal and state authorities on December 13, 2007, the signatories agreed to turn first to consultation and negotiation before running to the courthouse. On signing, Interior Secretary Dirk Kempthorne said, "This is the most important agreement among the seven basin states since the original Colorado River Compact of 1922."[53] Four years earlier in October 2003, Kempthorne's predecessor at Interior, Gale Norton, signed another agreement brokered by the BOR in which the state of California agreed to limit its withdrawals to levels consistent with commitments made in the 1920s in conjunction with the compact.[54] Part of the BOR's success as a broker stems from doing policy-neutral science (see "The Importance of Policy-Neutral Science," in the introduction).

Recognizing the need to address long-standing and worsening water conflicts in the West, Secretary Norton directed the BOR to lead a collaborative effort to find better ways to manage and distribute water in the West. The result was *Water 2025: Preventing Crises and Conflict in the West.*[55] The project gathered federal, state, local, and tribal government representatives from throughout the West in addition to people representing the panoply of groups with an interest in federal lands and their management. From the beginning participants used what became known as the "Hot Spot" illustration as a basis for their work. The illustration is a map showing areas having various potentials for a supply crisis by 2025. The BOR produced the map after an analysis of "hydrologic conditions, weather patterns, endangered species locations, and population growth trends."[56] Because participants generally judged the "Hot Spot" illustration to be policy-neutral, it provided a level playing field on which they could gather.[57] Thus, the overall project avoided the heated acrimony over facts that so often characterize resource-management debates.

Nonenergy Mineral Resources

Today's society relies on the availability of nonfuel mineral resources for the successful functioning of such widely diverse fields of endeavor as medicine, communication, manufacturing, construction, and national defense. Further advances in these and other fields depend on a continued supply of these resources. For example, automobiles using traditional gasoline-fueled engines contain about sixty pounds of copper, but new gasoline-electric hybrid cars require nearly three times that amount, which manufacturers generally require to be new rather than recycled.[58] Federal lands began providing desired minerals in the early 1800s.[59] Today, they supply major portions of the domestic production of such minerals as copper, lead, zinc, gold, silver, uranium, potash, common sand, gravel, and stone.[60] These and other resources come from active mining operations that occupy significantly less than 1 percent of the 627 million federal acres; indeed, the National Research Council (NRC) estimated that in the late 1990s, active mining sites accounted for only .06 percent of land managed by the BLM whereon most mining occurs.[61] Mining operations take place on such a limited land base owing to the cumulative impact of multiple forces affecting mineral development.

Candidacy for mineral production requires that a given piece of federal land meet three fundamental conditions: a valuable mineral must be present, the site must be available for mineral entry, and development must be economically viable. The first criterion needs no elaboration. The second reflects societal preferences regarding use of public lands. Of the 627 million federal acres, approximately 166 million acres are unavailable for mineral entry, including national parks and monuments, wildlife refuges, and congressionally designated wilderness and wilderness study areas.[62] Society places a higher value on nonmineral attributes of these lands and regards mining activity as posing an unwanted risk to them. While domestic considerations drive the land's availability for mining activity, international factors play a large role in mineral economics.

The minerals industry operates worldwide in a market-driven environment influenced by such factors as technological change, political stability-instability in producing nations, and the emergence of large international corporations as dominant worldwide producers.[63] International demand and supply increasingly determines the price of minerals, which in turn stimulates or dampens industry interest in producing minerals from federal lands. Change in price can occur quickly. Rapid increases in the world price of copper, gold, and uranium in the first decade of this century stimulated significant new mining interest in federal lands. Changes in worldwide conditions impacting the price, production, and movement of energy resources likewise help stimulate interest in the energy resources associated with federal lands.

Energy Resources—Fossil Fuels

Our way of life depends on the availability of inanimate energy at reasonable prices. Such energy comes from multiple sources: for example, petroleum, natural gas, coal, nuclear fission, wind, hydropower, solar, and biomass. New sources, such as hydrogen fuel cells, are under development. Since the 1880s, when coal replaced wood as the nation's chief inanimate energy source, fossil fuels have dominated our energy supply.[64] In 2008, they accounted for 84 percent of the energy consumption and 79 percent of energy production in the United States.[65] The Energy Information Administration concludes: "The outlook for the next couple of decades (assuming current laws, regulations, and policies) is for continued growth and reliance on the major fossil fuels."[66] These resources can only be produced from where nature put them millions of years ago and that is often beneath what are now federal lands.

Federal lands have grown in importance as sources of domestic fossil-fuel production over the last half century. Prior to 1950 they accounted for only a few percent of total domestic fossil-fuel production, a figure that rose to 13 percent by 1970 and 32 percent in 2008.[67] In 2008 they provided 43 percent of the coal, 24 percent of the natural gas, and 26 percent of the petroleum produced domestically (the bulk of oil and gas production from federal lands comes from offshore).[68] As for coal, energy analysts estimate over 950 billion short tons of it lie beneath federal lands in the contiguous western states, compared to total national coal production of 1.2 billion short tons in 2008, so it is clear that enough federal coal exists to supply domestic demand for the foreseeable future under any possible set of policy and technologic scenarios.[69] Geology dictates that our domestic fossil-fuel future depends heavily on production from federal lands.

Many people look to federal lands for other than fossil fuels, and well they may, since these lands already make major contributions to the domestic production of energy unrelated to fossil fuels.

Renewable Energy

The allure of renewable-energy resources attracts increasing interest from many quarters and has for many years.

- President George H. Bush's National Energy Strategy of 1991 helped launch a series of federal reports, recommendations, and action items aimed at increasing renewable-energy production on western federal lands.[70]

- The Western Governors' Association stresses expanded development of renewable energy as part of its Clean and Diversified Energy Initiative begun in 2004.[71]

- In the Energy Policy Act of 2005 Congress declares:

> It is the sense of the Congress that the Secretary of the Interior should, before the end of the 10-year period beginning on the date of enactment of this Act, seek to have approved non-hydropower renewable energy projects located on the public lands with a generation capacity of at least 10,000 megawatts of electricity.[72]

- In May 2008, the Department of Energy issued a report that proposed a very aggressive target of producing 20 percent of the nation's electricity from wind by 2030, which would require 300,000 megawatts of wind-generated electricity, compared to the 12,000 megawatts produced in 2006.[73]

There is much room for growth in the renewable energy sector and federal lands in the West can play a significant role in that future (see table 1.6).

Western federal lands hold much promise for the future production of renewable fuels (except for hydropower).[74] Climate and topography endow them with large areas suitable for harnessing wind and solar energy while geology placed geothermal resources beneath them. Natural growing assures the presence of a sustainable supply of woody biomass for use in electric power generation, space and process heating, and production of biofuels.

TABLE 1.6
U.S. Energy Consumption by Fuel Type, 2008

Fuel Type	Consumption (quadrillion BTUs)	Percent National Consumption
Petroleum	37.1	37
Natural Gas	23.8	24
Coal	22.4	23
Nuclear	8.5	9
Biomass*	3.9	4
Hydro*	2.5	3
Wind*	.5	< 1
Geothermal*	.4	< 1
Solar*	.1	< 1
U.S. Total	99.3	

Source: Energy Information Administration, *Annual Review, 2008*, 2009, table 1.3.
* Renewable sources

Compared to fossil fuels, however, development of renewables (except hydro and geothermal power) is a recent addition to the portfolio of federal land-management issues, and development remains limited. The BLM, for example, manages some 23 million acres with solar energy potential, of which only 1.5 million acres had been included in permitting applications by mid-2009.[75] It manages some 20.6 million acres with wind energy potential. By mid-2009 those acres had attracted 28 development projects, with 437 megawatts of installed power (compared with, for example, the 1,300 megawatts for Glen Canyon Dam).[76] Development of solar and wind energy resources is subject to many of the same challenges facing oil and gas in that they can be deemed of lesser priority than conservation-oriented land uses.

Federal lands offer a large and sustainable source of woody biomass for energy production. It comes as a byproduct of other land-management activities such as timber harvesting to habitat restoration, but chiefly it originates from management efforts to reduce the threats posed by wildland fire. Devastating scenes of wildland fire leapt from our TV screens in the summer of 2000 and have remained a fixture of the evening news ever since. Removal of hazardous fuels from federal (and tribal) lands enjoys widespread public and bipartisan political support (no governor asks for fewer acres to be treated within their state). In 2007, the hazardous fuels program provided some 2.7 million tons of woody biomass that could have been used as a fuel.[77] The potential is far greater but transportation costs presently limit use of woody biomass in boilers, and its use in the production of liquid fuels is not yet economically competitive with other biofuels.[78]

Having described the resources federal lands contain, I end the chapter with a brief look at two examples of the economic benefits they provide.

Economic Contributions

People gain economic benefits from federal lands in multiple ways. The federal treasury obtains income from numerous activities. Use of federal lands and resources creates jobs. Spending by tourists stimulates local and regional economies, and so it goes. This section only touches upon two of these benefits—revenue collection and disbursement tied to mineral production, and the economic contributions of the national parks—by way of suggesting both their variety and dollar value.[79]

The land-managing agencies collect revenues of many kinds. Tourists pay entrance fees. Resource developers pay rents, bonuses, and royalties. There are grazing fees and fees for harvesting timber. The BOR sells power. All told, the revenue streams from onshore activities amounted to over $6 billion in 2007, with receipts tied to oil, natural gas, and coal accounting for over 70 percent of the total.[80] Portions of these monies variously go into the general treasury, are returned to the collecting land-management unit such as a national park, or are passed back to states and counties wherein a revenue-producing activity occurred.

The minerals program (broadly considered) not only generates the largest federal income stream but also provides the greatest source of money passed back to the states via revenue-sharing provisions of federal law. In 2009, thirty-three states received money deriving from federal mineral activities within their borders. Some 87 percent of the payments went to four western states: Wyoming, New Mexico, Utah, and Colorado (see table 1.7).

The public recreational use of federal lands offers another aspect of their economic benefits. Visitors spend money for food, lodging, transportation, souvenirs, and amusements. The National Park Service, in cooperation with Michigan State University, developed a methodology to assess the economic impact of park system units on areas within fifty miles of park boundaries.[81] In 2006, 273 million park visitors spent some $10.7 billion nationwide in addition to park payrolls totaling $790 million.[82] Tourist expenditures and park payrolls support an estimated 226,000 jobs (84 percent of which are in the private sector) while producing some $5.8 billion in personal income and $8.3 billion in value added.[83] As expected, national totals mask regional variations.

TABLE 1.7
Federal Mineral Revenue
Sharing with States, 2009

State	Payment (millions)
AK	32.7
CA	51.3
CO	187.3
MT	46.6
NV	20.8
NM	388.5
ND	61.1
UT	128.6
WY	957.2
Total U.S.*	1,902.5

Source: Department of the Interior, *The United States Department of the Interior Budget Justifications and Performance Information Fiscal Year 2011, Minerals Management Service,* 2010, table 40, available at www.doi.gov/budget/2011/data/greenbook/FY2011_MMS_Greenbook.pdf.
* Only states receiving at least $10 million are listed here. A total of 33 states received a payment of some kind.

The data in table 1.8 may surprise some readers. They reveal the economic importance of the cultural and historic units within the national park system. For example, the District of Columbia, Pennsylvania, Massachusetts, and New York each depend on such sites for most of their NPS visitor-generated dollars. The Mall in Washington, D.C., with its monuments, the Liberty Bell and battlefields like Gettysburg in Pennsylvania, and the Statue of Liberty in New York Harbor all attract large numbers of tourists seeking to see and know more about the nation's vital historic places. Nonetheless, those units where visitors come to observe spectacular scenery and wildlife or to participate in resource-based outdoor recreation make the most significant contributions to local economies.[84]

The relative significance of federal activity within the local or regional scheme of things merits our consideration. In 2009, Colorado and Utah received a similar amount of income from mineral activities on federal lands within their respective states (see table 1.7). Yet total economic activity in Colorado is significantly larger than that in Utah so the money has less im-

TABLE 1.8
Impacts of Visitor Spending and NPS Payroll on Local Economies by State, 2006

State	Recreation Visits (millions)	Non-Local Visitor Spending ($ millions)	Total Jobs (thousands)	Total Income ($ millions)
AZ	10.5	662.6	16.8	329.4
CA	32.7	924.5	22.4	642.8
CO	5.3	306.1	8.4	220.1
DC	32.4	15.4	22.2	765.8
FL	8.0	461.8	9.9	256.8
GA	6.5	201.0	4.6	130.7
HI	5.3	290.9	6.3	144.0
MA	203.5	378.8	8.1	203.5
MT	138.0	236.8	5.7	138.0
NY	197.2	313.6	7.1	197.2
NC	20.1	644.4	13.3	304.9
PA	8.8	309.3	8.2	216.2
TN	7.8	448.2	9.0	225.7
TX	5.5	214.3	4.9	120.1
UT	7.8	409.4	9.5	198.0
VA	23.4	419.8	9.7	240.7
WA	6.5	207.7	5.3	133.0
WY	5.3	385.7	7.4	196.0

Source: Daniel Stynes, *National Park Visitor Spending and Payroll Impacts 2006* (Washington, D.C.: National Park Service Social Science Program, 2007), A-24, table A-4.
Note: Only states with total income exceeding $100 million are included. Total jobs include both private sector and NPS jobs. Total income includes both private sector and NPS payrolls plus income of sole proprietors.

pact at the state level in Colorado than in the Beehive State. Of even greater significance are the impacts at local or regional levels. Many communities throughout the West depend heavily on the activity associated with federal lands for their economic well-being, which may significantly impact local views of federal land management on local lands compared to those of people living some distance away.

With a broad picture of our 627 million federal acres now in hand, I can move on to look at how we as a society interacted with those lands over time, for neither the landscape nor our desires regarding its management have remained static.

Notes

1. Robert S. Wood, "The Dynamics of Incrementalism: Subsystems, Politics, and Public Lands," *Policy Studies Journal* 34 (2006): 8.

2. In this book I am concerned with the lands managed by the four principal federal land-management agencies and the data in these tables only reflect acres under their control. They account for approximately 96 percent of all federal land. Lands managed by the Department of Defense (e.g., bases and weapons-testing ranges, the Bureau of Reclamation, and other agencies) are not considered herein.

3. I adopt the regions used by the Census Bureau. The Northeast region comprises Connecticut, Maine, Massachusetts, New Hampshire, New Jersey, New York, Pennsylvania, Rhode Island, and Vermont. The Midwest contains Illinois, Indiana, Iowa, Kansas, Minnesota, Missouri, Nebraska, North Dakota, Ohio, South Dakota, and Wisconsin. The South includes Alabama, Arkansas, Delaware, Florida, Georgia, Kentucky, Louisiana, Maryland, Mississippi, North Carolina, Oklahoma, South Carolina, Tennessee, Texas, Virginia, and West Virginia. The West comprises Alaska, Arizona, California, Colorado, Hawaii, Idaho, Montana, Nevada, New Mexico, Oregon, Washington, and Wyoming.

4. The South and Midwest cover 561 million and 483 million acres, respectively.

5. See appendix.

6. Officials outside the West also pay attention to management actions on federal lands within their jurisdiction. Management of the Everglades National Park, for example, has long drawn widespread interest in Florida.

7. U.S. Fish & Wildlife Service, *Annual Report of Lands under Control of the U.S. Fish & Wildlife Service as of September 30, 2006* (Washington, D.C.: U.S. Fish & Wildlife Service, 2007), available at http://digitalcommons.unl.edu/usfwspubs/23/ (accessed August 30, 2010).

8. National Park Service, "National Park Service, Listing of Acreage as of 12/31/2006," Land Resources Division, Washington, D.C., 2007, available at www.nature.nps.gov/stats/Acreage/acrebypark06cy.pdf?CFID=12673239&CFTOKEN=77591089 (accessed August 30, 2010).

9. Forest Service, *Lands Area Report as of September 30, 2006* (Washington, D.C.: Forest Service, 2007), available at www.fs.fed.us/land/staff/lar/LAR06/table6.htm (accessed August 30, 2010).

10. One reason this book does not contain national maps of public lands is precisely that many units of the national refuge system and the national park system (chiefly the historic and cultural units) simply are too small to appear at a scale allowing the United States to be shown on these pages.

11. Bureau of Land Management, *Public Land Statistics—2009* (Washington, D.C.: Bureau of Land Management, 2010), tables 5-1, 5-15, and 5-16, available at www.blm .gov/public_land_statistics/pls09/pls5-16_09.pdf (accessed August 30, 2010).

12. Personal communication with Holly Martin, FS lands staff, August 29, 2007.

13. Management of these lands is controversial. For a detailed discussion of this controversy, see chapter 3.

14. *National Wildlife Refuge System Administration Act of 1997*, Public Law 105-57, 16 U.S.C. § 742f.

15. *National Wildlife Refuge System Administration Act of 1997*.

16. There are fourteen categories of park system units: national park, national monument, national preserve, national historic site, national historical park, national memorial, national battlefield, national cemetery, national recreation area, national seashore, national lakeshore, national river, national parkway, and national trail. See "Designation of National Park System Units," available at www.nps.gov/legacy/ nomenclature.html (accessed August 30, 2010), for a brief description of each category.

17. Tallgrass Historians, L. C., *Tallgrass Prairie National Preserve Legislative History, 1920–1996* (Omaha, NE: National Park Service, 1998), available at www.nps.gov/ history/history/online_books/tapr/index.htm (accessed November 27, 2011). See the section titled "The Osage Prairie National Preserve Proposal: 1980s Interlude," available at www.nps.gov/history/history/online_books/tapr/tapr_6.htm (accessed August 30, 2010). Also see Rebecca Conard, *Tallgrass Prairie National Preserve Legislative History 1920–1996* (Iowa City, IA: Tallgrass Prairie Historians, 1999), and Cass Peterson, "'Sea of Grass' Future Rests on a Reed-Thin Compromise: Public vs. Private Interests at Issue," *Washington Post*, December 25, 1987, section A.

18. As a special assistant to the assistant secretary for fish and wildlife and parks (who oversees the NPS and the FWS) at the DOI, I was the principal DOI staffer working on the project and met with Osage tribal officials and cattlemen in Washington and Oklahoma as legislation was developed to create the unit while meeting the needs of diverse interests.

19. Mickey Edwards (the House member representing the district wherein the unit would be located) along with Congressmen Inhofe, English, McCurdy, Synar, and Watkins as cosponsors, introduced H.R. 3803 to establish the Tallgrass Prairie National Preserve in the state of Oklahoma on December 18, 1987. Senators Boren and Nickles introduced S. 1967, the like-titled Senate companion bill, on the same date.

20. The NPS defines *national preserve* as "areas having characteristics associated with national parks, but in which Congress has permitted continued public hunting, trapping, oil/gas exploration and extraction. Many existing national preserves, with-

out sport hunting, would qualify for national park designation." See "Designation of National Park System Units" for a brief description of each category.

21. I was present at the hearing.

22. David Boren, "Statement of Hon. David L. Boren, U.S. Senator from Oklahoma," before the Subcommittee on Public Lands, National Parks, and Forests of the Committee on Energy and Natural Resources, U.S. Senate. Hearing on S. 1967, To Provide for the Establishment of the Tallgrass Prairie National Preserve in the State of Oklahoma, and for Other Purposes, 100th Cong., 2nd sess., Committee Print, S. Hrg. 100-871, 29–30.

23. "The Osage Prairie National Preserve Proposal."

24. Mickey Edwards, "Statement of Congressman Mickey Edwards on the Introduction of Legislation to Create a National Tallgrass Prairie Preserve," press release, December 18, 1987. On file with the author.

25. Tallgrass Historians, L.C., "Convergence: 1994–1996," in *Tallgrass Prairie National Preserve Legislative History, 1920–1996*, available at www.nps.gov/history/history/online_books/tapr/tapr_10.htm (accessed August 30, 2010).

26. This section addresses species rather than the broader issue of biodiversity, of which species are only a part. *Biodiversity* has come to mean diversity within and among four levels of organization: genes, species, ecosystems, and landscapes. For explanations of biodiversity, see: Juha Siikamaki, "Biodiversity: What It Means, How It Works, and What the Current Issues Are," *Resources* 168 (2008): 13–17, available at www.rff.org/biodiversity (accessed August 30, 2010). Also see: Jonathan Adams, Bruce Stein, and Lynn Kutner, "Biodiversity: Our Precious Heritage," pp. 3–18 in *Precious Heritage: The Status of Biodiversity in the United States*, eds. Bruce Stein, Lynn Kutner, and Jonathan Adams (Oxford: Oxford University Press, 2000).

27. David Wilcove and Lawrence Master, "How Many Endangered Species Are There in the United States?" *Frontiers in Ecology and the Environment* 3 (2005): 414–20.

28. Craig Groves et al., "Owning Up to Our Responsibilities: Who Owns Lands Important for Biodiversity?" pp. 275–300 in *Precious Heritage: The Status of Biodiversity in the United States*.

29. Researchers tally a species each time it occurs regardless of land ownership; hence, a given species may be tallied under multiple landowner categories.

30. It is important to note that lands managed by the Department of Defense are particularly important with regard to the provision of threatened and endangered species habitat. See: Bruce Stein, Cameron Scott, and Nancy Benton, "Federal Lands and Endangered Species: The Role of Military and Other Federal Lands in Sustaining Biodiversity," *BioScience* 58 (2008): 339–47.

31. U.S. Department of Agriculture, *Summary Report: 2007 National Resources Inventory* (Washington, D.C.: Resources Conservation Service; Ames: Center for Survey Statistics and Methodology, Iowa State University, 2009), available at www.nrcs.usda.gov/Internet/FSE_DOCUMENTS//stelprdb1041379.pdf (accessed November 27, 2011).

32. An invasive species is one that is not native to an area and whose presence is likely to cause unwanted environmental or economic consequences or harm human

health. See: U.S. Fish & Wildlife Service, "Invasive Species," available at www.fws.gov/
invasives (accessed August 30, 2010). Also see the National Invasive Species Information Center at www.invasivespeciesinfo.gov (accessed August 30, 2010). On August
1, 2008, the federal government adopted the 2008–2012 National Invasive Species
Management Plan under the auspices of the National Invasive Species Council, created by Executive Order 13112 and signed on February 3, 1999. The plan and current
information are available at www.invasivespecies.gov/ (accessed August 30, 2010).

33. Dale Bosworth, "Managing the National Forest System: Great Issues and Great
Diversions," speech before the Commonwealth Club of San Francisco, April 22, 2003.

34. Simon Levin, "The Problem of Pattern and Scale in Ecology," *Ecology* 73
(1992): 1943–67.

35. Norman Christensen et al., "The Report of the Ecological Society of America
Committee on the Scientific Basis for Ecosystem Management," *Ecological Applications* 6 (1996): 665–91.

36. Calculated from data in table 5a in James. C. Howard, *U.S. Timber Production,
Trade, Consumption, and Price Statistics 1965–2007*, U.S. Forest Service, Forest Products Lab, Research Paper FLP-RP-637, 2007.

37. Society of American Foresters, *State of America's Forests* (Bethesda, MD: Society of American Foresters, 2007), 31, available at www.safnet.org/aboutforestry/
StateofAmericasForests.pdf (accessed January 28, 2008).

38. W. Brad Smith et al., *Forest Resources of the United States*, Forest Service, North
Central Research Station, General Technical Report NC-241, 2004, 17.

39. The Sierra Club, for example, has opposed all logging activities on all lands that
"are environmentally unsustainable, or that jeopardize fully functioning ecosystems"
since 1992. Both of these presumed standards are completely idiosyncratic, having
no agreed-upon scientific definitions, measures, or baselines; hence the club is free to
oppose logging whenever and wherever it chooses in keeping with Muir's nature-first
philosophy. See: Sierra Club, "Sierra Club Conservation Policies—Forest Management in the United States," available at www.sierraclub.org/policy/conservation/
forest.aspx (accessed August 30, 2010).

40. See generally W. Brad Smith et al., *Forest Resources of the United States—2007*,
U.S. Forest Service, Washington, D.C., General Technical Report WO-78, 2009.

41. The BLM also manages timberlands but their harvests are small in comparison
to those from the national forests. James C. Howard, *U.S. Timber Production, Trade,
Consumption, and Price Statistics 1965–2007*, U.S. Forest Service, Forest Products Lab,
Research Paper FLP-RP-637, 2007, iv, and Smith et al., *Forest Resources of the United
States*, 9.

42. Calculated from data in table 5a in Howard, *U.S. Timber Production, Trade,
Consumption, and Price Statistics 1965–2007*.

43. Dale Bosworth, "In the Spirit of Earth Day: Connecting People to the Land,"
speech at the University of California, April 22, 2006, available at www.fs.fed.us/
news/2006/speeches/04/earth-day.shtml (accessed August 30, 2010).

44. For discussions of recreation on public lands, see: Sally Collins and Hutch
Brown, "The Growing Challenge of Managing Outdoor Recreation," *Journal of
Forestry* 105 (2007): 371–75, available at www.fs.fed.us/news/2007/briefings/12/

recreation.shtml (accessed November 27, 2011), and Kori Calvert and Carol Hardy Vincent, *CRS Issue Brief for Congress—Recreation on Federal Lands* (Washington, D.C.: Congressional Research Service, 2008), available at www.ncseonline.org/nle/crsreports/08Oct/RL33525.pdf (accessed August 30, 2010).

45. As quoted in James Brook, "Environmentalists Battle Growth of Ski Resorts," *New York Times*, January 19, 1999, available at www.nytimes.com/1999/01/19/us/environmentalists-battle-growth-of-ski-resorts.html?pagewanted=1 (accessed August 30, 2010).

46. The NPS and the Federal Aviation Administration are jointly preparing an Environmental Impact Statement on restoring "natural quiet" to the park. They released a draft in February 2011 with a public comment period ending in June 2011.

47. Thomas Brown, Michael T. Robins, and Jorge A. Ramirez, "The Source of Water Supply in the United States," U.S. Forest Service, Discussion Paper, Rocky Mountain Research Station, September 16, 2005, RMRS-WU-4851, table 7. The 65 percent estimate includes lands managed by the BLM, the FS, and the NPS only. FWS lands are found within an "Other federal category," whose total of 5.2 x 109 cubic meters per year is less than 0.5 percent of the total for the BLM, the FS, and the NPS. They also did not include Alaska.

48. Dale Bosworth, Testimony before the Committee on Agriculture, U.S. House of Representatives on the Centennial of the Forest Service, 109th Cong., 1st sess, June 22, 2005, available at www.fs.fed.us/congress/109/house/oversight/bosworth/062205.html (accessed August 30, 2010).

49. *Reclamation Act of 1902*, Public Law 57-161, 43 U.S.C. § 371.

50. I do not include the U.S. Army Corps of Engineers (USACE) in the discussion, as their water-related actions are generally centered on navigation and flood control not tied to federal lands. For an overview of USACE history and activities, see: www.hq.usace.army.mil/history.

51. Bureau of Reclamation, "Bureau of Reclamation Quickfacts," available at www.usbr.gov/facts.html (accessed August 27, 2010).

52. Public Law 70-642, 43 U.S.C 617.

53. Department of the Interior press release, "Secretary Kempthorne Signs Historic Decision for New Colorado River Management Strategies," December 13, 2007.

54. Department of the Interior, "Secretary Norton to Sign Historic Colorado River Pact," press release, October 13, 2003.

55. U.S. Bureau of Reclamation, *Water 2025: Preventing Crises and Conflict in the West* (Washington, D.C.: Bureau of Reclamation, 2005), available online at http://biodiversity.ca.gov/Meetings/archive/water03/water2025.pdf (accessed November 27, 2011).

56. U.S. Bureau of Reclamation, *Water 2025*, 3.

57. The reader should not take this to mean that everyone agreed with every depiction found on the map; some observers felt their area should be included as place of potential conflict, and the location of specific regional boundaries is always open to question. Such qualifiers, however, do not diminish the map's contribution to the project's success or the importance of doing policy-neutral science and analysis.

58. Statement of Henry Bisson, deputy director of the BLM, before the Subcommittee on Energy and Mineral Resources, Committee on Natural Resources, U.S.

House of Representatives, on H.R. 2262, the Hardrock Mining and Reclamation Act of 2007, 110th Cong., 1st sess., July 26, 2007.

59. Most land between the Appalachian and Rocky Mountains that was once part of the federal estate has passed from federal control.

60. See generally: National Research Council, *Hardrock Mining on Federal Lands* (Washington, D.C.: National Academy Press, 1999), and U.S. Geological Survey, *Mineral Commodity Summaries 2007* (Washington, D.C.: U.S. Geological Survey, 2007).

61. National Research Council, *Hardrock Mining on Federal Lands*, 19. The states involved are: Alaska, Arizona, California, Colorado, Idaho, Montana, Nevada, New Mexico, Oregon, Utah, Washington, and Wyoming.

62. Bureau of Land Management, *Public Land Statistics—2006* (Washington, D.C.: Bureau of Land Management, 2007), 11.

63. This does not including sand, gravel, rock, and so forth used in construction, railroad ballast, and similar activities.

64. Energy Information Administration, *Annual Energy Review 2006* (Washington, D.C.: Energy Information Administration, 2007), xx. The Green River formation in Colorado, Utah, and Wyoming contains an estimated 800 billion barrels of recoverable oil in oil shales. Federal agencies manage some 72 percent of the 16,000 square miles of land atop the formation. The BLM published a proposed rule regarding oil shale management in the *Federal Register* 73, no. 142 (July 23, 2008): 42926–75. Nonetheless, I have not included oil shale in the discussion of fossil fuels because commercial production is years away at best. Congress established the EIA in 1977, as a statistical agency of the U.S. Department of Energy. Its "mission is to provide policy-neutral data, forecasts, and analyses to promote sound policy making, efficient markets, and public understanding regarding energy and its interaction with the economy and the environment." See http://tonto.eia.doe.gov/abouteia (accessed August 30, 2010).

65. Calculated from tables 1.2 and 1.3 in Energy Information Administration, *Annual Energy Review 2008* (Washington, D.C.: Energy Information Administration, 2009).

66. Energy Information Administration, *Annual Energy Review 2008*, xx.

67. Energy Information Administration, *Annual Energy Review 2008*, figure 1.14.

68. Energy Information Administration, *Annual Energy Review 2008*, table 1.14.

69. U.S. Departments of Energy, Interior, and Agriculture, *Inventory of Assessed Federal Coal Resources and Restrictions to Their Development* (Washington, D.C.: U.S. Departments of Energy, Interior, and Agriculture, 2007), 1, prepared in compliance with the *Energy Policy Act of 2005*, Public Law 109-58.

70. Department of Energy, *National Energy Strategy* (Washington, D.C.: Department of Energy, 1991).

71. Western Governors' Association, "Clean Energy, a Strong Economy and a Healthy Environment" (Denver: Western Governors' Association, 2006), available at www.westgov.org/wga/publicat/CDEAC06.pdf (accessed November 27, 2011), and Western Governors' Association, "Clean Energy, a Strong Economy and a Healthy Environment: 2007 Update" (Denver: Western Governors' Association, 2007), available at www.westgov.org/wga/publicat/CDEACReport07.pdf (accessed November 27, 2011).

72. *Energy Policy Act of 2005*, Public Law 109-58, § 211.

73. U.S. Department of Energy, *20% Wind Energy by 2030: Increasing Wind Energy's Contribution to U.S. Electricity Supply*, Washington, D.C., DOE/GO-102008-2578, May 2008.

74. No new dams are likely to be built on federal lands, meaning that any increase in hydropower would come from the installation of more efficient equipment or additional generating capacity at existing facilities.

75. Bureau of Land Management, "Renewable Energy and the BLM: Solar," Fact Sheet, Washington, D.C., 2009, on file with author.

76. Bureau of Land Management, "Renewable Energy and the BLM: Wind," Fact Sheet, Washington, D.C., 2009, on file with author.

77. U.S. Department of Agriculture, Forest Service, *Fiscal Year 2009 President's Budget: Budget Justification* (Washington, D.C.: U.S. Department of Agriculture, 2008), 3–12.

78. Woody biomass is heavy and must be hauled to points of consumption. In contrast, wind arrives at the turbine and solar radiation at the photovoltaic cell without any human help.

79. For a number of years some ecologists and economists have sought to determine the value of so-called ecosystem services. I do not include them for the simple reason that I do not think they exist. Providing services implies a provider, but as I have argued in detail elsewhere, ecosystems are mental constructs, models, for better understanding the natural world. Advocates for ecosystem services fall prey to what British mathematician and philosopher Alfred North Whitehead termed "the fallacy of misplaced concreteness": scholars mistaking their models for reality. What advocates call *ecosystem services* are nothing more than the results of biota going about the business of living coupled with the operation of physical laws and processes on biotic and abiotic components of the environment, the transitory results of which humans may deem positive or negative at a particular time and place. For representative discussions of ecosystem services, see: Timothy Fitzgerald and Myrick Freeman III, "Counting the Wealth of Nature: An Overview of Ecosystem Evaluation," pp. 211–34 in *Accounting for Mother Nature: Changing Demands for Her Bounty*, eds. Terry Anderson, Laura Huggins, and Thomas Powers (Palo Alto: Stanford University Press, 2008); James Sanchirico and Juha Siikamaki, eds., "Putting a Value on Nature's Services," *Resources*, no. 165 (spring 2007); and Gretchen Daily, "What Are Ecosystem Services?" pp. 1–10 in *Nature's Services: Societal Dependence on Natural Ecosystems*, ed. Gretchen Daily (Washington, D.C.: Island Press, 1997). I make a case for the view that ecosystems are but mental constructs in "Ecosystem Health: A Flawed Basis for Federal Regulation and Land Use Management," pp. 187–98 in *Managing for Healthy Ecosystems*, eds. David Rapport et al. (Boca Raton, FL: Lewis Publishers, 2002), and *Defending Illusions: Federal Management of Ecosystems* (Lanham, MD: Rowman & Littlefield, 1999).

80. Department of the Interior, *Fiscal Year 2009 the Interior Budget in Brief* (Washington, D.C.: Department of the Interior, 2008), appendix N, and U.S. Department of Agriculture, Forest Service, *Fiscal Year 2009 President's Budget*, appendix F. These totals do not include revenue from outer continental shelf oil and natural gas activities.

81. Daniel Stynes, *National Park Visitor Spending and Payroll Impacts 2006* (Washington, D.C.: National Park Service, 2007). The analysis does not include NPS construction activity or NPS purchases from local firms.

82. Stynes, *National Park Visitor Spending and Payroll Impacts 2006*, 3 and table 5.

83. Stynes, *National Park Visitor Spending and Payroll Impacts 2006*, table 6. Stynes defines *value added* as "the sum of personal income, profits and rents, and indirect business taxes. It can also be defined as total sales net of the costs of all non-labor inputs." He argues, "Value added is the preferred economic measure of the contribution of an industry or activity to the economy."

84. In 2006, eight units had a value added exceeding $100 million: Great Smoky Mountains National Park, Grand Canyon National Park, Blue Ridge Parkway, Yosemite National Park, Yellowstone National Park, Grand Teton National Park, Lake Mead National Recreation Area, and Rocky Mountain National Park. See Stynes, *National Park Visitor Spending and Payroll Impacts 2006*, A-2 and table A-1.

2

Americans and the Land

Change through Time

In wildness is the preservation of the world.

—Henry David Thoreau

The first principle of conservation is development. . . . In the second place conservation stands for the prevention of waste. . . . [The] third principle . . . is . . . natural resources must be developed and preserved for the benefit of the many, and not merely the profit of a few.

—Gifford Pinchot

H UMANS MANAGE THE LAND TO IMPROVE THEIR LIVES. How they do it changes over time under the influence of shifts in technology, settlement patterns, scientific understanding, economic factors, and other forces that shape societal perceptions and values regarding the land. Because they are publicly owned, societal judgments play a particularly important role in the management of federal lands. Perceptions of fire (as a land-management tool) and wilderness (as a landscape condition) offer good examples of how change over time plays out in federal land management. Alterations in western settlement patterns and economic conditions as well as diverse attitudes of urban and rural residents are further examples of changes that influence our views of proper federal land management. In this chapter I examine these issues in turn. First, however, I look at the conditions of the land of the United States at the time of European settlement. I do this because those conditions, both real and imagined, helped shape our initial societal relations with landscape and color contemporary perceptions of it.

The Land at European Settlement

People have inhabited what is now the United States for at least 14,000 years.[1] Anthropologists, archeologists, geographers, historians, and others have long worked to sort out their imprint on the land.[2] For most of that time, the various groups made their living via hunting and gathering and saw the world accordingly. Such peoples generally valued what was on the land (e.g., game, edible and medicinal plants), rather than the land itself.[3] They developed land-management practices to yield plant communities more attractive to game and more favorable for gathering food.

At the time of European contact, however, agriculture had displaced hunting and gathering for most Native Americans.[4] They used permanent fields as well as more temporary fields associated with slash-and-burn methods. Gardens were common, as was supplemental gathering of wild plants and the taking of game.[5] Native Americans cleared and managed land to produce crops with different needs than the plants gathered by their forbearers; for example, maize cultivation was widespread. They cleared fields from woodlands, built canals, terraces, and hilled and ridged fields, and they did so in numerous places throughout the eastern half of the country and the Southwest.[6] Under circumstances where people invested much capital in a plot of land, the land itself took on greater value compared to its value to earlier hunting-and-gathering peoples.

Agriculture and vegetation management provided the most significant human elements of the pre–European contact landscape, but not the only ones. Permanent Native American settlements ranged from small villages in the East to the major centers of the Mound Builders in the Mississippi Valley and pueblos in the Southwest. They became the focal points for transportation routes and trade. They altered forests through demands on wood for fuel and building material.[7] Science writer Charles Mann neatly sums up current scholarly understanding regarding pre-Columbian human impacts on the North American environment: "Indians worked on a very large scale, transforming huge swaths of the landscape for their own ends. . . . It is apparent that many though not all Indians were superbly active land managers—they did not live lightly on the land."[8] Geographer Michael Williams, in his extensive study of forest history in the United States, comes to a similar conclusion: "The idea of the forest as being in some pristine state of equilibrium with nature . . . has been all too readily accepted as a comforting generalization and as a benchmark against which to measure all subsequent change. When Europeans came to North America the forest had already been changed radically."[9] Broadcast fire was the tool of choice for landscape management, as it had been for humans since time immemorial.[10]

Fire as a Land-Management Tool

Native Americans used fire to create conditions that favored desired species—plants and animals alike—from coast to coast.[11] They employed fire in hunting and warfare. In Yosemite Valley, for example, the indigenous Ahwanhee learned that the black oaks whose acorns were a major food source were fire tolerant while the confers that also grew in the valley were not. They created conditions favorable to oaks but not conifers while providing better habitat for game species by annually burning the valley floor. When European descendants first arrived in 1851 they found a very open, park-like setting. They soon ended the practice of annual burning and the conifers began to displace the oaks. As a result, today's visitor sees a valley floor whose vegetation differs significantly from that of 150 years ago.[12]

This general storyline repeats itself, with multiple variations in scope and detail, over hundreds of millions of acres throughout the United States. The most dramatic example concerns the creation of grasslands. In his classic study, *Fire in America*, Stephen Pyne writes, "Taken in its broadest sense . . . grasslands were probably the dominant cover type in North America at the time of European discovery. . . . Nearly all these grasslands were created by man, the product of deliberate, routine firing."[13] These grasslands included such widely separated places as the Central Valley in California and Virginia's Shenandoah Valley. They included much of the Great Plains and were evident in the Midwest and the Atlantic coastal plain. Few large areas of the country were untouched by Native American fire.

Changes in vegetative communities brought changes in species habitat. Mann points out that when Europeans arrived, bison could be found from New York to Georgia. These plains-dwelling creatures followed the new vegetation communities created by Native Americans burning many hundreds of miles eastward from their original homes in the Midwest. In New England, Native American burning created favorable habitat for many species—elk, deer, turkey, and others—whose abundance early European colonists remarked upon.[14] So it was that when European settlers began arriving they encountered a continent whose landscape had been altered by Native Americans who depended on fire as their chief land-management tool.

Europeans brought with them multiple views regarding the use of fire for landscape management. New arrivals from Scandinavia often carried with them traditions of slash-and-burn agriculture, and those from Spain bore the torch of pastoralists who routinely burned large tracts to encourage fodder for their herds.[15] Conversely, colonists from Britain, France, and Germany generally brought with them different experiences regarding fire. People had used fire in those places to push back forests in favor of fields and pasture, but widespread application of fire for such purposes chiefly took place long before colonization and settlement of the seventeenth and eighteenth centuries.[16] Hence, while people from these countries understood and used fire, they did not bring with them a recent history of aggressive, unregulated application of fire to create or maintain desired landscape conditions. Coming from places where timber was an increasingly scarce and valuable resource, they sometimes saw Native American burning practices as being wantonly destructive of an important commodity. The new environment with its seemingly endless forest resources, however, helped fuel a change in view.

Early settlers' attitudes toward fire quickly began to more closely resemble those of Native Americans because they were quick to see its benefits. Writing about early English colonists in Massachusetts, William Cronon observes: "The use of fire to aid in clearing land was something English settlers borrowed from their Indian predecessors, but they applied it for different purposes and on a much more extensive scale. Instead of burning the forest to remove the undergrowth, they burned it to remove the forest itself."[17] Of the South, Pyne finds that "perhaps nowhere else in the country were Indian burning practices more thoroughly adopted and maintained than in the piney woods, in the remote hills, and on the sandy soils."[18]

It was a more practical way to clear land than more labor-intensive methods, an especially important factor as settlement pushed into new territory where labor was in short supply. Potash produced from burning woodlands provided a valuable export commodity. It was the only practical way to keep unwanted vegetation at bay once fields or pastures were established. Yet as a land-management tool, fire was not without its problems.

Even as they adopted fire, European settlers recognized its attendant difficulties and sought their mitigation. People took steps to protect towns, cabins, barns, mills, and other investments susceptible to fire. In various places they put restrictions on the time and season of burning and held individuals responsible should their fires damage others. They formed entities to fight fire. They plowed firebreaks and built berms to halt the spread of fire. Such measures helped to maintain fire's acceptability as a viable land-management technique in the minds of many for a long time.

As the decades rolled by, more people began to think of fire as a bane not a boon. The attitude shift had multiple causes, not the least of which was changing perceptions of forests. Many colonists in the seventeenth century arrived with a dual view of forests. The managed European forest presented a cultivated or tamed look. Like a field or pasture it was a place of order, a part of Eden's garden landscape. Juxtaposed with these civilized woodlands were unmanaged forests. Anthropologist Roberta Dods writes that such places were thought of as "waste" or "wilderness" outside the boundaries of Eden.

She goes on to observe, "These places were equated with the economically, socially and spiritually 'unprofitable.' The 'mythic identification of the forest as waste' marked it as the abode of madmen, thieves, elves, witches, the refuge of pagans and heretics."[19] Upon seeing and experiencing the forests of North America, Europeans placed them in the second category. They saw the application of fire as a civilizing activity to expand Eden's boundaries.

By the early decades of the nineteenth century, views of unmanaged forests were changing. Romantic poets and transcendentalists put God, not wickedness, in the wilderness (more on this in the next section). The uncontrolled forest no longer threatened souls; quite to the contrary, many now thought of it as a place where people could reconnect with God through nature.[20] Thoreau offered his oft-repeated quote, cited at the beginning of this chapter, in 1851. He and others extended Eden's boundaries beyond the garden's edge to include landscapes their Puritan ancestors regarded as the devil's playground. So while economic reasons for using fire as a management tool in wooded environments persisted, justifications based on being the morally or spiritually correct thing grew less important.

More than philosophy was at work in the nineteenth century and the early part of the twentieth century. Large and devastating wildland fires of human origin visited several parts of the country.[21] They hit the lake country of Michigan, Minnesota, and Wisconsin particularly hard (see table 2.1).

TABLE 2.1
Selected Large Historic Fires

Year	Fire Name	State	Acres Burned (in thousands)	Fatalities
1825	Miraich/Maine	Maine/ New Brunswick	3,000	160
1845	Great Fire	OR	1,500	Undetermined
1853	Yaquina	OR	450	Undetermined
1868	Coos	OR	300	Undetermined
1871	Pestigo	WI/MI	3,780	1,500
1881	Lower Michigan	MI	2,500	169
1894	Hinkley	MN	160	418
1894	Wisconsin	WI	Several million	Undetermined
1898	Multiple Fires	SC	3,000	Undetermined
1902	Yacoult	OR/WA	1,000	38
1903	Adirondack	NY	637	Undetermined
1910	Great Idaho	ID/MT	3,000	85
1918	Cloquet-Moose Lake	MN	1,200	450

Source: National Interagency Fire Center, *Fire Information—Wildland Fire Statistics, Historically Significant Wildland Fires,* available at: www.nifc.gov/fire_info/historical_stats.htm.

Europeans and their descendants began to settle the lakes region in the second and third decades of the nineteenth century.[22] Logging became a major economic activity because forests were widespread and contained the nation's largest stands of white pine, the most coveted species at the time. By 1870, Michigan produced more lumber than any other state. In 1890, the three states combined for 35 percent of nation's total lumber output but had so depleted their forests by 1910 that they could no longer supply even their own needs.[23] Along with loggers came farmers eager to open up new lands for agriculture. Railroads began to penetrate the region to haul products to markets. Individually, each of these activities impacted fire; together they gave rise to impacts far beyond those of earlier times.

Fire had long been part of the north woods. All fires require three things: fuel, ignition, and oxygen. Prior to the arrival of Europeans, forests provided the fuel that Indians and nature ignited in the presence of nature's oxygen. With European settlement came changes in fuel loads and ignition sources. Highly wasteful logging practices significantly altered fuels by leaving huge slash piles and other debris on the land, which people then often removed via deliberate burning. Like other dense fuels they could and did reburn. Widespread use of land-clearing fires to advance the agricultural frontier added new and extensive ignition sources, while sparks from wood-fired steam engines started their share of fires. Land-clearing by farmers burned trees that loggers wanted to harvest and for a few decades a race ensued that served to worsen the fire situation. As Pyne puts it, "The fire pattern in the north woods, in short, was like a self-reinforcing dynamo: the more the forest was cut, the greater the influx of land clearing farmers and the greater the fire hazard; the greater the fire hazard, the more rapidly and wastefully logging had to proceed."[24] The pattern included conflagrations like the Peshtigo Fire, perhaps the most devastating fire in the nation's history.

In October 1871, Peshtigo, Wisconsin, was a thriving lumber town of about 1,700 people located some ten miles west of Green Bay.[25] For weeks prior to the town's destruction, wild fires had burned in the surrounding countryside abetted by extraordinarily dry conditions. By the night of October 8, Peshtigo's residents had become accustomed to smoke-filled air and fire-fighting and thought the worst was over when in fact it had not yet arrived.

The Wisconsin State Centennial Committee begins its description of the Peshtigo Fire this way:

> "Look! Look! The sun is rising in the West!" The sawmill foremen had been roused from his bed by a roar like a long freight train on a trestle apparently passing overhead. But instead of a sunrise, he and his wife were looking upon fiery death riding on the wings of a tornado bringing . . . horror and destruction.[26]

Fire fell out of the sky. Reports indicate that the entire town was ablaze in the space of ten minutes. Heat was such that logs floating in the Peshtigo River burst into flames. Most people died; only two buildings survived. The estimate of 1,500 deaths is but a rough guess of lives lost to the fire. For comparison, the Great Chicago Fire, which occurred on the same day, took 250 lives.[27] The figure of 3.8 million acres burned may be a low estimate (see table 2.1).[28] Yet numbers alone do not adequately portray the fire.

The local Catholic priest, Father Pernin, wrote a firsthand account of the scene at the edge of the Peshtigo River, where many people fled. It includes observations such as:

- "The air was no longer fit to breathe, full as it was of sand, dust, ashes, cinder sparks, smoke and fire."
- "People seemed stricken dumb with terror . . . people standing there, motionless as statues, some with eyes staring upward toward heaven and tongues protruded."
- "Above my head . . . I saw nothing but immense volumes of flames . . . rolling over one another with stormy violence."
- "Once in the water up to our necks, I thought we would at least be safe from fire but it was not so, the flames darted over the water as they did over land. . . . The air itself was on fire."[29]

Small wonder that the Peshtigo Fire gave rise to the term *firestorm*.[30]

As bad as the Peshtigo Fire was, major changes in attitudes regarding fire as a land-management tool had to await further developments. The attraction of wealth to be gained from logging and agricultural expansion that employed fire persisted in a nation where more than three-quarters of the population lived outside metropolitan areas.[31] Indeed, another two or three decades had to pass before net forest losses to agricultural clearing in eastern forests came to a general halt.[32] As for the town of Peshtigo, the Wisconsin State Centennial Committee reports that "within a few months, Peshtigo was again a thriving sawmill town."[33]

Fires like Peshtigo did, however, aid in creating more ambivalence within a society regarding fire as a land-management tool. It and other fires began to draw attention to the extraordinary resource waste caused by fire-related land-management practices of the day. Further, by the 1870s and 1880s agricultural settlement had pushed westward beyond the eastern forests, exposing the finite nature of our woodlands to the general public and thereby spurring calls for more responsible forest management.[34] The most influential voice was that of President Theodore Roosevelt. In his 1908 State of the Union speech he said:

Thanks to our own recklessness in the use of our splendid forests, we have already crossed the verge of a timber famine in this country, and no measures that we now take can, at least for many years, undo the mischief that has already been done. But we can prevent further mischief being done; and it would be in the highest degree reprehensible to let any consideration of temporary convenience or temporary cost interfere with such action, especially as regards the National Forests which the nation can now, at this very moment, control.[35]

Roosevelt's position reflected that of the conservation movement, whose acknowledged father was Gifford Pinchot, appointed by Roosevelt as the first chief of the Forest Service in 1905. With his appointment, Pinchot brought his ideas on fire as a land-management tool to federal lands.

Pinchot advocated scientific management of forests as practiced in Europe, where he gained his education as a forester. Fire was not part of his French and German forestry professors' toolkits. He opposed using fire to manage vegetation, seeing it as destructive and wasteful. Instead he argued for fire control and for changing attitudes among those who saw fire as a legitimate tool or as an inevitable part of the landscape. In 1910, he argued, "Today we understand that forest fires are wholly within the control of man."[36] He went on to write, "In all these matters of waste of natural resources, the education of the people to understand they can stop the leakage comes before the actual stopping and after the means of stopping it have long been in our hands."[37] Claiming the mantle of science, the Forest Service extended its antifire position beyond the forest to include rangelands.[38] Suppression became the policy of the NPS upon its creation in 1916.[39] A policy and administrative environment heavily oriented toward fire suppression and control did not provide a fertile seedbed for the idea of using fire as a land-management tool.[40]

Not everyone rejected fire. Some landowners, field personnel in the Forest Service and Fish and Wildlife Service, and nonfederal foresters saw multiple benefits deriving from fire.[41] Landowners saw light surface-burning as a vital component of fire protection and as a way to guard valuable timber resources from conflagrations. Some farseeing western stockmen viewed reintroduction of fire as a way of ridding the landscape of invasive woody species (caused chiefly by overgrazing and fire exclusion) for the purpose of the reestablishment of bunch grasses. Finally, of course, some settlers saw burning as efficient land-clearing. Lines were drawn.

The Forest Service insisted its position be applied across the landscape in the name of coordinated fire suppression.[42] Speaking to the Forestry Conferences in 1919, then-Chief Henry Graves said:

Effective fire protection is achieved only through a joint under-taking between public and private agencies in which all lands, regardless of ownership, are brought under an organized system. . . . There should be incorporated in the forest laws of every State requirements to bring all forest owners into the protective system, and to extend it to all cut-over and unimproved lands in the State.[43]

The "protective system" had no place for views contrary to FS orthodoxy.

People who objected to fire-exclusion policies championed its use in a variety of environmental circumstances and places across the country. The most vigorous early debate centered on what came to be known as light or Paiute burning, which is the deliberate ignition of wildland fire to burn light or surface fuels to accomplish land-management goals.[44] This debate predated the Forest Service as it emerged in California in the 1880s and went on for decades.[45]

Writing on Paiute forestry in 1920, Aldo Leopold summed up the Forest Service position:

> A new problem now confronts the administrators of the forests, namely, the propaganda recently started by the Southern Pacific Railroad and certain timber interests in favor of "light burning" or the so-called "Piute [sic] Forestry." . . . Foresters generally are strenuously opposing the light-burning propaganda. . . . The Forest Service policy of absolutely preventing forest fires insofar as humanly possible is directly threatened by the light-burning propaganda.[46]

He went on to argue that light burning adversely impacts forest productivity and escaped burns pose a "constant risk" to both forests and infrastructure. The Forest Service argument carried the day in California as state agencies weighed in against Paiute forestry and maintained that position for decades. That did not end the debate. The light-burning controversy would play out again, this time in the South, but with a different result.

The Forest Service arrived in the South after the passage of the Weeks Act in 1911.[47] They brought with them their fire-suppression policies and loathing of light burning as a legitimate management technique.[48] But the South was not California. Significant differences existed regarding such factors as forest composition, rate of vegetation growth, and climate as well as in land uses and in commonly used land-management tools. Southerners, including timber producers, had long practiced some form of light burning and did not welcome efforts to eliminate its use.

Foresters inside and outside the Forest Service recognized the value of light burning in an environment where rapid growth of nontree species could prevent forest regeneration. Moreover, researchers were becoming increasingly aware of the importance of fire in the life cycle of longleaf pine, a major commercial species of the South. By the mid-1920s researchers, including H. H. Chapman, dean of the Yale School of Forestry, had established the importance of periodic burning to southern forestry.[49] Nonetheless, the FS retained its official opposition to light burning in the South until 1943. It took until 1974, however, for the Forest Service to relax its opposition to light burning elsewhere in the country. In doing so, it joined the NPS, which had acknowledged the importance of fire as a land-management tool in 1968.[50] The FS had come full circle. Pyne writes:

> In the early years the consensus among foresters was that forestry would be impossible if surface fire were tolerated. By the 1970s it was asserted with equal conviction that forestry and land management would be impossible if prescribed surface fires were excluded. So complete was the conversion that when threats to prescribed burning appeared, foresters—with the Forest Service in the lead—rushed to its defense.[51]

So great is the shift that today federal land managers employ fire more than any other tool to accomplish management objectives. Prescribed fire lies at the heart of the federal hazardous fuels reduction program and is an important tool in achieving a variety of land-management tool objects such as habitat restoration and range management. During the period of 2001–2008, for example, fire was used as a management tool on over 18 million federal acres.[52] But what about the use of fire on private lands, where it has always been chiefly associated with agriculture?

Early general acceptance of fire as a tool of agriculture has given way in the face of public health concerns about smoke pollution.[53] Smoke extends the geographic reach of concern from neighbors worried about fire risk itself to highly populated urban areas often far distant from burning fields. For example, smoke drifting from burning sugar cane in Louisiana can cause air-quality alerts in Houston and Galveston, Texas.[54] Such concerns pose a growing challenge to the use of fire as a land-management tool in agriculture. They also impact the use of fire on federal lands, where smoke management is a major component of prescribed fire training and where state smoke-management requirements may play an important role in its use.[55]

In summary, before European contact and for more than three centuries thereafter, fire was a widely used and generally accepted tool for land management in the United States. Concerns about fire grew during the last half of the nineteenth century, culminating in a national policy in opposition to the use of fire on federal lands that lasted until the 1970s. Federal policymakers and land managers (as well as state and local officials) now strongly advocate fire's use on public lands. Use and public support of fire on private lands declined overtime in the face of growing worries centered on the public health effects of smoke. This section deals with shifting ideas about a land-management tool; the next addresses change in how landscape types may be valued, using wilderness as an example.

Wilderness

What is wilderness? Wilderness, writes award-winning geographer David Lowenthal, "is not, in fact, a type of landscape at all, but a congeries of feelings about man and nature of varying import to different epochs, cultures and individuals."[56] William Cronon proclaims that wilderness

> is quite profoundly a human creation—indeed, the creation of very particular human cultures at very particular moments in human history. It is not a pristine sanctuary where the last remnant of an untouched, endangered, but still transcendent nature can for at least a little while longer be encountered without the contaminating taint of civilization. Instead, it is a product of that civilization.[57]

Noted environmental historian Roderick Nash agrees, writing:

> There is no specific material object that is wilderness. The term designates a quality (as the "-ness" suggests) that produces a certain mood or feeling in a given individual and, as a consequence, may be assigned by that person to a specific place. . . . The New World was . . . [a] . . . wilderness at the time of discovery because Europeans *considered* it such [emphasis in the original].[58]

Native Americans did not share this view of the same landscape. Indeed, the idea of wild or wilderness was not part of their thinking about the land.[59] Lowenthal, Cronon, and Nash make the point that the notion of wilderness is a cultural construct and that the attributes or values we assign to landscapes we call "wilderness" are likewise cultural constructs subject to change.

As a practical matter, Americans now generally consider wilderness to be at one end of a continuum based on the degree of human landscape manipulation. Congress adopted this definition in the Wilderness Act of 1964: wilderness is "an area where the earth and its community of life are untrammeled by man, where man himself is a visitor who does not remain."[60] Central cities occupy the other extreme, with villages, farms, ranches, timber-producing forests, and so forth occupying waypoints between the extremes. Ecologically, this view rests on popular thinking half a century ago, when wilderness was a place in which nature could pursue balance and equilibrium in her weaving of a fragile web of life. Philosophically, it rests upon a belief in the separateness of humans (at least in industrial and postindustrial societies) from all else on the planet. It is a shaky foundation.

A quick look reveals the difficulties with the popular conception of wilderness and its policy manifestation. Ecologists abandoned the notions of balance and equilibrium decades ago when they could not find them in nature.[61] Such terms and phrases as *harmony* and *delicate webs of life* have no scientific meaning or definition, but they remain popular precisely because every user may employ their own understanding. Philosopher J. Baird Callicott writes that "upon close scrutiny the simple, popular wilderness idea dissolves before one's gaze" because it perpetuates the "'man' and nature" dichotomy, is "woefully ethnocentric" since it ignores aboriginal peoples, and neglects landscape change through time.[62] Given what we now know about the degree of human impact on the landscape dating back thousands of years, the idea of there actually being lands "untrammeled by man" as called for in the Wilderness Act has no relation to lands of the United States. Consequently, our common understanding of wilderness is difficult to justify on scientific, philosophical, or historical grounds but in the policy realm at least, constructs do not need an objective justification, only acceptance.

While there may be a consensus on the meaning wilderness as a type of landscape, views regarding its value have sharply diverged over time. As I noted earlier in this chapter (also see the "Values and Federal Land Management" section of the introduction), Europeans first saw America's forests as a wilderness; as such, it was a place of evil, the home of Satan, not God. Here morality was threatened. Such views flowed from scripture, where the dominant portrayals of wilderness are negative. Biblical references point to wastelands, landscapes of banishment or trial rather than Edenic locations where one went to view God's wonders or works.[63] In this view wilderness was reviled and humans did God's will by bringing a transforming hand to such places. Civilizing wilderness was a moral imperative. Today, in stark contrast, many wilderness advocates turn this moral imperative on its head and strive to return landscapes to wilderness or protect remaining areas perceived to be wilderness. Nature and its most ideal physical manifestation—wilderness— are morally superior to humans and their manipulated landscapes.

In the minds of some people, wilderness became sacred space.[64] Two distinct routes to sacredness present themselves. In the first instance, Christians in particular began to think of wilderness as part of God's creation, or part of God's nature, and hence it took on a sacredness owing to its representing His work.[65] Its sacredness depended on its connection with God. The second path eliminates the God of western monotheistic faiths who hold that worship is for God alone. Instead it bestows sacredness based upon wilderness representing the unblemished work of a divine nature. As David Lowenthal wrote in 1964, "A new religion is in the making. Worshipers of nature exhort us from the pulpits of countless conservation societies and Audubon clubs. . . . Nature is wonderful. . . . Pay homage to it in the wilderness."[66] More recently, Cronon finds that "many environmentalists who reject traditional notions of the Godhead and who regard themselves as agnostics or even atheists nonetheless express feelings tantamount to religious awe when in the presence of wilderness."[67] Distinguished historian Donald Worster puts it this way: "Nature [has] . . . become the basis for a new (or rediscovered [pagan]) religion, a fathomless source of spirituality, complementary to or independent of traditional religion."[68] He adds that

> old notions that humans have been created especially in the image of God or that have been given dominion over all other forms of life or that . . . [the ideals of liberty and equality are] the exclusive province of *Homo sapiens*, have proved to be unsustainable. . . . [Nature is] worthy of respect, protection, and even worship.[69]

This is, of course, very different from believing that the hand of God can be seen in creation and that he seeks stewards not pillagers for its care. How might this view of nature and wilderness impact land management? Consider the Wildlands Project (renamed the Wildlands Network in 2008), a one-hundred-year effort to drastically reshape land use in the United States in service to nature.

The Wildlands Project is breathtaking in scope.[70] In outlining the project in 1992, cofounder Dave Foreman describes it as "a bold attempt to grope our way back to 1492. . . . We seek a path that leads to beauty, abundance, wholeness, and wildness."[71] The Wildlands Project seeks to re-create plant and animal distributions of that bygone time and return half of the United States to wilderness conditions that proponents describe as "vast landscapes without roads, dams, motorized vehicles, powerlines, overflights, or other artifacts of civilization, where evolutionary and ecological processes that present four billion years of Earth wisdom can continue."[72] Foreman's 50/50 (wilderness/nonwilderness) ratio represents a significant expansion of the 10/90 split regarding the appropriate amount of wilderness suggested by then–Sierra Club Executive Director David Brower in 1961 and reflects a growing confidence among wilderness advocates in their ability to influence land management.[73]

Reverence for nature, not science, drives the Wildlands Project. As I point out in the introduction, science has no way to determine if the landscape of some past time is preferable to that of today. The fact that we cannot return the landscape to 1492 (even if we could magically determine it was the ideal year) is not the issue for many Wildlands Project advocates. Instead the goal is to maximize wilderness and prevent human development as a way to protect nature in her idealized form. Writing in *Science*, Charles Mann and Mark Plummer call it "the most ambitious proposal for land use management since the Louisiana Purchase."[74] Yet this proposal pales in comparison to Roderick Nash's idea on protecting wilderness.

In the epilogue to the fourth edition of his classic book, *Wilderness and the American Mind*, Nash calls for returning the planet to conditions of "ten or fifteen thousand years ago, before herding and agriculture" so "humans are once again good neighbors in the biotic community."[75] In what he calls his "Island Civilization" people and their works are restricted to small areas so wilderness can dominate the Earth.

For Nash, wilderness represents the "other," everything on the planet but humans, who have become "cosmic outlaws."[76] His "Island Civilization" aims to establish what he considers an appropriate ethical relationship between humans and the "other," a "kind of ecocentrism [that] is not 'against' humans . . . [but that] transcends them and subsumes their interest in that of the larger whole."[77] Nature comprises this larger, perfect whole: the goddess whose defilement began with the advent of civilization, which he marks as the boundary between hunting and gathering on the one hand and agriculture and herding on the other.[78] He writes, "Civilization severed the web of life as humans distanced themselves from the rest of nature. Behind fenced pastures, village walls, and later, gated condominiums, it was hard to imagine *other living things as brothers or nature as sacred* [emphasis mine]."[79] Nash argues that in the last quarter of the twentieth century this "ecocentric or biocentric rationale for the meaning and value of wilderness has gained an impressive following among both philosophers and activists."[80] Such views have also generated substantial criticism.

Much of human history has been consumed by trying to escape the whims of an uncaring and unknowing nature: hunger, disease, cold, drought, insects, predators, floods, hurricanes, earthquakes, fire, and other aspects of the environment that kill, harm, and bring human suffering. In the face of nature past and present, many people, myself included, find it difficult to think of HIV as a brother (Nash) or to apply to it the concepts of liberty and equality (Worster). Ecologist Ramachandra Guha—whose comments on deep ecology, the philosophical foundation of bio- and ecocentrism, are widely read—makes the point directly. He labels as "specious nonsense" the idea of "equal rights of all species."[81] The notion of 'biocentric equality," he writes, elevates above all other environmental concerns "the protection of wild species and wild habitats and . . . [provides] . . . high sounding, self-congratulatory but nonetheless dubious moral claims for doing so."[82]

The ideas Nash and many other bio- or ecocentrists embrace represent what Cronon deems a "flight from history," a denial of our past and civilization and the romantic fantasy of urbanites disengaged from the actual landscape.[83] Lowenthal makes much the same point, arguing that "in concentrating on wilderness, we turn our backs not only on the rest of nature but on man himself."[84] If nature's defilement began with agriculture, then all the human advances that agriculture ultimately made possible by freeing people from a constant pursuit of sustenance—that is, science, medicine, written language, mathematics, technology, philosophy, and so forth—must be viewed with suspicion because they were made at the expense of a sacred nature and our biotic brothers and moral equals.[85]

I hasten to point out that critics such as Cronon, Lowenthal, Guha, and Callicott support landscapes containing large tracts of wild places and those where the human footprint lies lightly on the land. As I read them, they look to a gentler human touch and consideration of nonhuman biota rather than to a deified nature. At bottom, they are anthropocentric, not biocentric.

Critics notwithstanding, biocentrism adds to a list of values Americans variously assign to wilderness. Many people may find wilderness valuable for one or more of these attributes (this list is only suggestive):

- Stewardship of a landscape made by God;
- Spiritual renewal, a place to find God;
- Solitude and respite from civilization;
- Biological reserve, wildlife habitat, a source of biodiversity;
- Natural-resource-based recreation;
- Ecological benchmark;
- Fulfillment of primeval human need for wilderness;
- Scientific and educational opportunities; and
- Historical attributes.[86]

These values (and others) emerged over the course of the nineteenth and twentieth centuries.

Overall, public sentiment about wilderness has changed significantly over the years. In terms of federal land management, public officials face no significant pressure to reduce the size of the National Wilderness Preservation System while members of Congress regularly introduce legislation to expand it. At one stage or another, such legislation routinely meets resistance on the grounds that it would unnecessarily prevent development or use of valuable natural resources. Consequently, any bill that finally becomes law is the product of political horse-trading among members of Congress and between the legislative and executive branches. They reflect geographic compromises about what lands should be added to the system. The upshot is that in most years Congress adds acreage and, because of the compromises reached as part of those actions, they have withdrawn virtually no lands from the system.[87]

In these last two sections, I dealt with specific topics, fire and wilderness, in the context of changing societal attitudes and assigned values. In the next section, I look at change from the perspective of shifting settlement patterns.

Change in Attitudes with Change in Settlement

Where we live influences our views of federal lands and their management. Over the last century two broad changes in U.S. settlement patterns are of particular interest. First we became an urban nation. In 1910, some 71 percent of the population lived in nonmetropolitan areas, but by 2000 only 20 percent did so.[88] Moreover, at the end of the twentieth century 57 percent of us lived in metropolitan areas with populations greater than 1 million. As a people, we left the countryside for the suburbs. The overwhelming majority of the population now has no day-to-day experience with farms, ranches, working forests, mines, and other land- and natural-resource-based activities on which our lifestyles are wholly dependent. We separate product from place. When we think of food, we think of grocery stores not farms; wood comes from Home Depot or Lowe's, not forests and sawmills. We also separate product from people. How many Americans personally know a farmer, rancher, logger, miner, roustabout, or other person who makes an on-the-ground living in a primary industry? Because of the population shift to metropolitan areas over the last century our sense of nonmetropolitan landscapes—what they are and what they should be—comes from sources other than extensive firsthand knowledge.

Americans form impressions of rural landscapes directly and indirectly. We live away from the land but view it directly from airplanes and through car windows. Many millions of people seek out forests, lakes, rivers, mountains, deserts, canyons, and other nonmetropolitan locations for vacation each year drawn by a variety of resource-based recreational opportunities and landscapes where human artifacts take a back seat. Even here, however, our direct interaction with working landscapes and their inhabitants is fleeting as we return to our cattleless, mineless, loggingless home ground after a brief absence. Indirectly, we gain information via programs that flood cable networks. We see television programs on parks, pollution, and all manner of outdoor recreation activities as well as on work and survival in harsh environments. Coffee tables across America hold books with stunning pictures of various landscapes. News media offer us stories about places and land use. One can gorge on Google images. Combinations of such information sources help form our views of proper land management.

The second broad shift in settlement that took place in the twentieth century was the westward movement of people.[89] The West contained 5 percent of the nation's population in 1900, compared with 23 percent in 2000.[90] The Census Bureau reports that for the first half of the twentieth century, nine out of the ten fastest-growing states were in the West, while in the second half of the century, eight of the ten fastest-growing states were so located.[91]

Viewed another way, each western state except Montana and Wyoming rose in total population rank between 1900 and 2000, with California showing the greatest advance, moving from the twenty-fourth most-populous state in 1900 to number two by 1950 and number one in 2000.[92] These data also show that population growth in the West was uneven and, as I show in the next paragraphs, these differences color views of proper federal land management.

Like other regions, changes in western settlement patterns over the last century resulted in greatly increased urbanization. By 2000, 87 percent of people lived in metropolitan areas, making it the second most urbanized region behind the Northeast.[93] Coastal areas like Southern California and the San Francisco Bay Area drew most attention, but as the century wore on, large inland urban areas such as Albuquerque, Denver, Las Vegas, Phoenix, Salt Lake City, and Tucson grew rapidly, as have several smaller cities like Boise, Flagstaff, and Santa Fe, to name but a few. More so than their coastal counterparts, people in these inland urban areas are more tightly linked with federal lands if for no other reason than they are likely to see them every day. Commuters in these and other inland urban centers routinely look upon federally managed mountains, forests, or deserts while those in Southern California or San Francisco often do not. In many cases people moved to these inland urban locations in part because nearby federal lands offered desired attributes like outstanding scenery and recreational opportunities. They tend to support management policies that protect these conditions. While the urban population dominates numerically, rural residents and the change in their composition over time is at least as significant for federal land management.

Factors influencing movement to the rural West have changed over time. For most of our history farming, ranching, mining, logging, and related processing activities provided much of the economic basis for rural settlement in the West. People came to small towns and their environs to make their living in these industries or in support of them and their workers. Tourism, be it to national parks, national forests, or destination resorts, cannot be overlooked in the early years, but its role was less than that of extractive industries. The traditional narrow and often-uncertain economic base of the rural West coupled with its remoteness limited population growth until recent decades. Change began in the later part of the twentieth century. By that time the Interstate Highway System and state and county roads had greatly increased accessibility. The electric grid had reached most areas. Communication and information technology now linked the rural West to larger population centers. The rural West had become a viable alternative to cities and suburbs.

Remoteness overcome, residents outside rural areas began looking at them anew, for the West housed many desirable attributes, particularly a variety of environmental amenities. In nearby federal forests, parks, and deserts one could find nature, scenic beauty, and a multitude of outdoor recreation opportunities. Southwestern climates attract many people. Writing in *BioScience*, Andrew Hansen and his coauthors observe that "many newcomers speak of the 'one-hour rule': They want to work within an hour's drive of good fishing, hunting, skiing, and hiking."[94] To multiple environmental assets were added attributes like low population densities, low land prices (compared to urban and suburban areas), and the opportunity to become part of idealized visions of western landscapes. People came in large numbers because the rural West was increasingly viewed "more as a place to live [the new attractive force] than a place to make a living [the old attractive force]."[95]

Recent migrants form a mixed bag but loggers, miners, and cowboys are not among them. Retirees comprise a major share of the influx. Retirees bring money and help create the burgeoning service sector as well as opportunities in retail and construction that provide jobs for migrants still in the workforce. Other newcomers work in footloose professions that may only need Internet access, FedEx, and cell phone coverage to function. Second-home owners augment the infusion of retiree dollars and help fund similar economic activity as well as some rather unique economic opportunities. For example, Antler Ridge is a second-home development outside Missoula, Montana. One owner of a 200-acre parcel expressed his interest in wildlife by hiring a local contractor to install, monitor, and maintain web cameras over a bear den and bird nests. He received pictures of a bear emerging from its den on his Blackberry while in Paris.[96] In short, the overall economic base of the rural West now depends chiefly on amenities.[97]

New migrants frequently possess little practical understanding of the landscape they are entering while they routinely seek to re-create landscapes they fled (see box 2.1). In doing so they erode the very landscape characteristics that originally attracted them. They want gated communities, condos, golf courses, Costcos, medical facilities, restaurants, and all the other accoutrements of the suburbs they left behind. They build trophy homes and ranchettes. Together this creates demand for private land that traditionally supported land uses that were part of the romanticized western landscape. As economists Thomas Power and Richard Barrett put it, "If everyone wants to live amid open grazing lands with unobstructed views of the surrounding peaks, the open grazing land will soon disappear and the view will be blocked by new homes, which must be built ever taller to clear the roof lines of the homes that went before."[98] Those readers who have traveled the rural West over the last few decades can easily attest to Power and Barrett's observation.

In today's economy, revenues from cattle, crops, and timber cannot always compete with those to be gained from development.[99] So some landowners sell.[100] As a result, land use changes and nature recedes as development frag-

Box 2.1.   New and Old Residents in the Rural West

New arrivals bring different expectations and experiences from those of long-time residents. They extend into many aspects of living in the rural West. Larimer County sits in north-central Colorado. The two largest cities (Fort Collins, population 118,000 in 2000, and Loveland, population 50,608) lie in the east at the western edge of the Great Plains. Most of the county lies in the Rocky Mountain region and is federal land. Here most people live in small towns like Estes Park, population 5,413, or in unincorporated places, which accounted for 27 percent of the county's 251,226 people in 2000. These places draw new residents attracted by such places as Rocky Mountain National Park just outside Estes Park.

The county felt it useful to publish a "Code of the West" explaining to newcomers the differences between rural living and what they were likely accustomed to coming from urban or suburban places. It contains sixty specific admonitions organized under five headings: access, utilities, your property, mother nature, and agriculture. Among other things the county informs newcomers that: views may change; nature can be dangerous, be it from fires, landslides, floods, or wild animals; and farmers and ranchers need not alter their practices to please those objecting to smoke, smells, noise, or livestock invading one's property (Colorado has an open-range law, meaning it is your responsibility to fence animals out, not the rancher's responsibility to fence them in).

Source: www.larimer.org/planning/planning/code_of_the_west

ments habitat and hinders wildlife movement while increasing visual impacts of humans on the landscape. The webcam owner introduced above lamented that Antler Ridge is "almost some kind of housing subdivision, that isn't what I was looking for. I guess I wish I bought the whole thing up, and then I wouldn't have to worry."[101]

As the close-to-nature aspect of their landscape ideal fades on private lands, new arrivals look more to federal lands as repositories of nature and favor land-management policies that minimize resource development and use and favor shifting public lands even more toward being nature preserves. As I have shown throughout this chapter, however, society's judgments change, and present views and values are not final. As historian Joseph Taylor III cautioned, we should not be overly wedded to the current picture of the New West, pointing out that over the last 135 years observers have identified four or five other New Wests, one following another through time and space.[102]

Change in Attitudes with Change in Conditions

History's wheel continues to turn. In the summer of 2008, the price of petroleum fluctuated around 130 dollars per barrel. Consumers paid four dollars a gallon for gas, airlines parked planes to save fuel, General Motors announced the closure of several plants that produced vehicles with low miles-per-gallon ratings while laying off thousands of employees. Increased transportation costs raised prices of food and other products. All this impacted public attitudes on federal land management.

Polls in the summer of 2008 showed strong public support for development of oil and natural gas resources.[103] A CNN/Opinion Research poll found that 48 percent of respondents "strongly favor" drilling in "offshore U.S. waters" and another 25 percent "mildly favor" such action. A Pew Research Center for the People and the Press survey showed 60 percent of those polled favored developing new energy sources, compared with 34 percent who favored protecting the environment. In May 2008, 49 percent favored development and 42 percent opted for environmental protection. The same survey asked about drilling in the Arctic National Wildlife Refuge (ANWR) and found 50 percent favored drilling while 43 percent opposed. In January 2006, 44 percent favored and 47 percent opposed. Finally, a *Los Angeles Times*/Bloomberg poll offered respondents three choices:

1. Drilling is usually done in a way that harms the environment and should not be done in environmentally important areas; or
2. Drilling can be done safely and should be allowed in environmentally important areas with proper controls in place; or
3. The nation's energy needs are so pressing that drilling should be allowed even if environmentally important areas may suffer damage as a result.

Twenty-two percent of those polled chose option 1; 57 percent selected option 2; 12 percent opted for option 3; 10 percent were unsure. In August 2009, even though gas prices had fallen to around two and half dollars a gallon, an ABC/*Washington Post* poll found that 64 percent of respondents favored the government expanding oil and gas drilling, with 33 percent opposed. Powerful stuff.

Changed conditions had some politicians scrambling. On July 17, 2008, Nick Rahall (D–West Virginia), the chairman of the House Natural Resources Committee, which has jurisdiction over federal lands, announced, "On behalf of a number of freshman Democratic Members and in concert with the Democratic Leadership, I am pleased to bring to the floor the 'Drill Responsibly in Leased Lands Act' (H.R. 6515)—the Drill bill."[104] While the bill was cosmetic in that it did not lift development prohibitions on potentially energy-rich federal lands like ANWR or offshore areas, it was revealing that Chairman Rahall proudly announced: "As Democrats, we are pro-drilling." I must say that for many of us who have been involved in federal land management over the last thirty years, his statement comes as something of a surprise. H.R. 6515 came three days after President Bush lifted a 1990 executive order preventing development of federal offshore areas.[105]

In the public's eye, history's wheel turned again with the April 2010 blowout of British Petroleum's (BP) Deepwater Horizon rig in the Gulf of Mexico. The environmental and economic impacts of the blowout were extensive and received widespread media coverage over several months. Pollsters immediately began sampling public opinion. Results were mixed. For example, an ABC/*Washington Post* poll done in the period June 3–10 had 52 percent of those responding supporting increased oil and gas drilling, while 45 percent opposed.[106] An Associated Press/GfK poll of August 11–16 had 48 percent favoring increased drilling and 36 percent of respondents opposing. On the other hand, a Fox News/Opinion Dynamics poll of June 8–9 had 44 percent favoring increased offshore drilling and 48 percent opposing. A CNN/Opinion Research poll of June 10 found 49 percent favoring and 51 percent opposing increased drilling. This same poll revealed a significant decline in support for offshore drilling caused by the blowout. In June 2008, 73 percent of respondents favored increased offshore drilling. Events impact attitudes.

Changing conditions lead to shifting values and altered perceptions of what constitutes good land management, which in all cases must comport with existing law. Chapter 3 addresses questions of applying multiple societal interests in federal lands through the interaction of the three branches of the federal government, and looks at the matter of applying legal language to the landscape.

Notes

1. Michael Balter, "DNA from Fossil Feces Breaks Clovis Barrier," *Science* 320 (2008): 37.

2. See the September 1992 (volume 82, pages 343–568) issue of the *Annals of the Association of American Geographers*, devoted to the theme of the Americas before 1492; and Charles C. Mann, *1491: New Revelations of the Americas before Columbus* (New York: Vintage Books, 2006).

3. William Cronon, *Changes in the Land: Indians, Colonists and the Ecology of New England* (New York: Hill and Wang, 1983), 62–67.

4. See generally Mann, *1491*, and William Doolittle, "Agriculture in North America on the Eve of Contact," *Annals of the Association of American Geographers* 82 (1992): 386–401.

5. Karl Butzer, "The Americas Before and After 1492: An Introduction to Current Geographical Research," *Annals of the Association of American Geographers* 82 (1992): 345–68.

6. Doolittle, "Agriculture in North America on the Eve of Contact."

7. Michael Williams, *Americans and Their Forests: A Historical Geography* (New York: Oxford University Press, 1989), 32–49. For an early analysis of human impacts on the Earth, including Native American manipulation of forests, see Carl Sauer, "The Agency of Man on Earth," pp. 49–69 in *Man's Role in Changing the Face of the Earth*, ed. William Thomas Jr. (Chicago: Chicago University Press, 1956).

8. Mann, *1491*, 279.

9. Williams, *Americans and Their Forests*, 49.

10. *Broadcast fire* refers to burning as a means of altering the landscape to achieve a desired end. It is distinct from use of fire as a source of heat or in a manufacturing process. References to fire as a landscape management tool presuppose broadcast fire. Scholars have long acknowledged the role of fire as a land-management tool; see, for example, Omer C. Stewart, "Fire as the First Great Force Employed by Man," pp. 115–33 in *Man's Role in Changing the Face of the Earth.*

11. Of course fire had other uses: for example, a weapon of war, an insect repellant, and for ceremonial purposes. See Stephen Pyne, *Fire in America: A Cultural History of Wildland and Rural Fire* (Seattle: University of Washington Press, 1997 [1982]), 71–72.

12. The NPS has established a program of prescribed burning in the valley to reduce the threat of wildland fire.

13. Pyne, *Fire in America*, 84.

14. Cronon, *Changes in the Land*, 51.

15. Pyne, *Fire in America*, 133–34

16. See: H. C. Darby, "Clearing the Woodland of Europe," pp. 183–216 in *Man's Role in Changing the Face of the Earth.* Also see Clarence Glacken, *Traces on the Rhodian Shore: Nature and Culture in Western Thought from Ancient Times to the End of the Eighteenth Century* (Berkeley: University of California Press, 1967), 288–351, for a review of medieval forest clearing.

17. Cronon, *Changes in the Land*, 118.

18. Pyne, *Fire in America*, 144.

19. Roberta Robin Dods, "The Death of Smokey Bear: The Ecodisaster Myth and Forest Management Practices in Prehistoric North America," *World Archeology* 33 (2002): 475–87, quote at 477.

20. Roderick Nash, *Wilderness and the American Mind*, 4th ed. (New Haven, CT: Yale University Press, 2001), 86.

21. National Interagency Fire Center, "Fire Information—Wildland Fire Statistics," available at www.nifc.gov/fire_info/fire_stats.htm (accessed September 10, 2010).

22. D. W. Meinig, *The Shaping of America, Volume 2: Continental America 1800–1867* (New Haven, CT: Yale University Press, 1993), 222–30.

23. Langdon White, Edwin Foscue, and Tom McKnight, *Regional Geography of Anglo-America*, 5th ed. (Englewood Cliffs, NJ: Prentice Hall, 1979), 524. Williams, *Americans and Their Forests*, 193–230.

24. Pyne, *Fire in America*, 201.

25. Unless otherwise indicated, data in this description of the Peshtigo Fire are taken from W. E. Morton, *The Wisconsin Centennial Story of Disasters and Other Unfortunate Events 1848–1948* (Madison: Wisconsin State Centennial Committee, 1948), 14–20, available at www.wisconsinhistory.org/turningpoints/search.asp?id=1675 (accessed September 10, 2010).

26. Morton, *The Wisconsin Centennial Story*, 14.

27. National Interagency Fire Center, "Fire Information—Wildland Fire Statistics."

28. Pyne, *Fire in America*, 200.

29. Morton, *The Wisconsin Centennial Story*, 17.

30. Pyne, *Fire in America*, 204.

31. For a demographic and geographic overview of the United States in the twentieth century, see Frank Hobbs and Nicole Stoop, *Demographic Trends in the Twentieth Century* (Washington, D.C.: U.S. Census Bureau, 2002), available at www.census.gov/prod/2002pubs/censr-4.pdf (accessed September 10, 2010).

32. U.S. Forest Service, Forest Inventory Analysis, "Trend Data," slide 2, "Forest Area, 1760–2000," available at www.fia.fs.fed.us/ (accessed September 10, 2010).

33. Morton, *The Wisconsin Centennial Story*, 20.

34. By 1900, corn- and wheat-based agriculture was widely practiced in an area extending from central Oklahoma through eastern Kansas, Iowa, eastern South Dakota, and most of North Dakota. Additionally, a dense network of railroads extended from the center of the country to the east coast, thereby facilitating the growing understanding of the nature of the landscape among more and more people via direct contact.

35. The speech is available at www.presidency.ucsb.edu/ws/index.php?pid=29549 (accessed September 10, 2010).

36. Gifford Pinchot, *The Fight for Conservation* (Garden City, NY: Harcourt Brace, 1910), as reprinted in Roderick Nash, ed., *The American Environment*, 2nd ed. (Reading, MA: Addison-Wesley, 1976), 60.

37. Pinchot, *The Fight for Conservation*, 60.

38. James Young and Charlie Clements, "Range Research: The Second Generation," *Journal of Range Management* 54 (2001): 115–21.

39. Jan van Wagtendonk, "The Evolution of National Park Service Fire Policy," *Fire Management Notes* 42 (1991): 10–15.

40. The FS did make allowances for burning slash piles and litter under special circumstances, as well as burning some cleared areas and using fire in the construction of fuel breaks intended to halt fire spread.

41. The Fish and Wildlife Service, for example, traces its use of prescribed fire to the 1930s; available at www.fws.gov/fire/who_we_are/history/shtml (accessed September 10, 2010).

42. Agreements or not, Pyne notes that after a bad fire season private landowners would revert to light burning as a means of protecting their land; see Pyne, *Fire in America*, 107.

43. Henry Graves, "A Policy of Forestry for the Nation," a statement of a policy presented before Forestry Conferences of 1919, U.S. Department of Agriculture Circular 148, Office of the Secretary, December 1919, 6.

44. Over time *Paiute* has also been spelled *Piute*. The tribes call themselves Paiute so that is the spelling I have adopted herein.

45. The following account of light burning is taken from Pyne, *Fire in America*, 100–122, unless otherwise noted. The Paiute tribe occupied the region centered on northern California and southern Oregon and used light burning in the forests to maintain desired conditions.

46. Aldo Leopold, "Piute Forestry vs. Forest Fire Prevention," pp. 68–70 in *The River of the Mother of God and Other Essays by Aldo Leopold,* eds. Susan Flader and Baird Callicott (Madison: University of Wisconsin Press, 1991 [1920]). At the time he wrote this, Leopold was assistant district forester with the Forest Service in the Southwest. In 1924 he would acknowledge that fire played a role in maintaining grasses on some southwestern landscapes, which in turn had limited erosion. Overgrazing and fire exclusion resulted in replacement of grasses and brush by various woody species that were ineffective in preventing erosion. See Aldo Leopold, "Grass, Brush, Timber, and Fire in Southern Arizona," *Journal of Forestry* 22 (1924): 1–10.

47. 16 U.S.C. §521.

48. FS leadership so objected to controlled burning that in 1927 they went so far as to deny states fire-suppression monies authorized by the Clarke-McNary Act (16 U.S.C. 2101) enacted three years earlier. They modified their position in 1932. See Pyne, *Fire in America*, 115.

49. Pyne, *Fire in America*, 114–15

50. Jan van Wagtendonk, "The History of and Evolution of Wildland Fire Use," *Fire Ecology Special Issue* 3 (2007): 3–15.

51. Pyne, *Fire in America*, 121.

52. Department of the Interior and Department of Agriculture, *Healthy Forests Report—FY 2008 Accomplishments,* 2009, available at www.forestsandrangelands.gov/reports/documents/healthyforests/2008/healthy_forests_report_fy2008.pdf (accessed September 11, 2010).

53. Interestingly, in focus groups, citizens from the inland Northwest differentiated between smoke from prescribed fires and that from agricultural burning and were more tolerant of the former. See Brad Weisshaupt, Matthew Carroll, and Keith Blatner, "Using Focus Groups to Involve Citizens in Resource Management—Investigating Perceptions of Smoke as a Barrier to Prescribed Forest Burning," pp. 178–85 in *The Public and Wildland Fire Management: Social Science Findings for Managers,* ed. S. M. McCaffrey, General Technical Report NRS-1, Newtown Square, PA, USDA, Forest Service, Northern Research Station, 2006. Also see Jonathan Yoder, David Engle, and Sam Fuhlendorf, "Liability, Incentives, and Prescribed Fire for Ecosystem Management," *Frontiers in Ecology and the Environment* 2 (2004): 361–66.

54. "Smoke from Louisiana Leads to Health Warning," *Houston Chronicle*, March 8, 2001, 20.

55. For example, see Cary Blake, "Regulations Cloud Opportunities Spark Outlook for California Rice Industry," *Western Farm Press* (online exclusive), March 31, 2008, available at http://westernfarmpress.com/regulations-cloud-opportunities-spark-outlook-california-rice-industry-0 (accessed September 11, 2010). Ben Nicholson, "Flaming Out: Will Chapter 481 Extinguish Agricultural Burning in the San Joaquin Valley?"

McGeorge Law Review 35 (2004): 561–68. David Whitman, "Fields of Fire," *US News and World Report*, September 3, 2001, 10. Estimates of the extent of agricultural burning are not readily available; however, in 1999 the Agricultural Air Quality Task Force opined that some 9 million acres (3 percent) of harvested cropland is burned annually (compare this to the 2.7 million acres of public land treated with prescribed fire in 2008). Another 2 million acres adjacent to cropland are burned annually to accomplish weed and pest control and the maintenance of drainage ditches. See Agricultural Air Quality Task Force, *Air Quality Policy on Agricultural Burning: Recommendations to U.S. Department of Agriculture*, November 10, 1999, available at www.airquality.nrcs .usda.gov/aaqtf/Documents/Old_Archives/2000/Policy/Burning%20Policy.htm (accessed September 11, 2010).

56. David Lowenthal, "Is Wilderness 'Paradise Enow?' Images of Nature in America," *Columbia University Forum* 36 (1964): 34–40.

57. William Cronon, "The Trouble with Wilderness," pp. 69–90 in *Uncommon Ground: Rethinking the Human Place in Nature*, ed. William Cronon (New York: W. W. Norton, 1995).

58. Roderick Nash, *Wilderness and the American Mind*, revised ed. (New Haven, CT: Yale University Press, 1967), 1 and 7.

59. Roderick Nash, *Wilderness and the American Mind*, 4th ed., xiii. For third-world critiques of the wilderness idea related to the views of indigenous peoples, see Ramachandra Guha, "Radical American Environmentalism and Wilderness Preservation: A Third World Critique," *Environmental Ethics* 11 (1989): 71–83; Ramachandra Guha, "Deep Ecology Revisited,"pp. 271–79 in *Wilderness Debate*, eds. J. Baird Callicott and Michael Nelson (Athens: University of Georgia Press, 1998); Arturo Gomez-Pampa and Andrea Kaus, "Taming the Wilderness Myth," pp. 293–313 in *Wilderness Debate*; and Fabienne Bayet, "Overturning the Doctrine: Indigenous People and Wilderness—Being Aboriginal in the Environmental Movement," pp. 314–24 in *Wilderness Debate.*

60. *The Wilderness Act*, Public Law 88-577. 16 U.S.C. 1131.

61. John Briggs et al., "Why Ecology Needs Archaeologists and Archaeology Needs Ecologists," *Frontiers in Ecology and the Environment* 4 (2006): 180–88.

62. J. Baird Callicott, "The Wilderness Idea Revisited," in *Wilderness Debate*, 348.

63. For a detailed analysis of wilderness and the Bible that seeks to identify the value of wilderness and nature to Christianity, see Susan Bratton, *Christianity, Wilderness, and Wildlife: The Original Desert Solitaire* (Scranton, PA: Scranton University Press, 1993), and John Nagel, "The Spiritual Value of Wilderness," *Environmental Law* 35 (2005): 955–1003.

64. Cronon, "The Trouble with Wilderness," 73. Also see Linda Graber, *Wilderness as Sacred Space* (Washington, D.C.: Association of American Geographers, 1976).

65. I am a Christian and write from that perspective.

66. Lowenthal, "Is Wilderness 'Paradise Enow?'" 34.

67. Cronon, "The Trouble with Wilderness," 80.

68. Donald Worster, "Epilogue: Nature, Liberty, and Equality," pp. 263–72 in *American Wilderness: A New History*, ed. Michael Lewis (Oxford: Oxford University Press, 2007), quote at 268.

69. Worster, "Epilogue," 267.

70. The December 1992 issue of *Wild Earth, Special Issue* (hereafter *Wild Earth*) described the project in detail. Advocates view their work as a series of incremental steps taking perhaps a century to complete. The plan is moving forward aggressively on a number of fronts. See the project website at www.twp.org (accessed September 13, 2010).

71. Dave Foreman, "Around the Campfire," *Wild Earth*, inside front cover.

72. *Wild Earth*, 4 and 15.

73. David Brower, introduction to *Wilderness America's Living Heritage*, ed. David Brower (San Francisco: Sierra Club, 1961), vii.

74. Charles Mann and Mark Plummer, "The High Cost of Biodiversity," *Science* 260 (1993): 1868. The current manifestation of the Wildland Project, the Wildlands Network, heavily emphasizes conservation biology in its land-management proposals but service to nature remains the driving principle. In the fall 2009 newsletter, *Wild Connections*, executive director Margo McKnight echoes the goals of the Wildland Project's founders, writing: "The ultimate result will be a continentally scaled network of biologically diverse and resilient wildlands, roamed freely by the full suite of native species once present," available at www.twp.org:80/cms/File/wc_fall09.pdf (accessed September 13, 2010).

75. Nash, *Wilderness and the American Mind*, 4th ed., 383.

76. Nash, *Wilderness and the American Mind*, 4th ed., 386.

77. Nash, *Wilderness and the American Mind*, 4th ed., 386.

78. Nash, *Wilderness and the American Mind*, 4th ed., xii.

79. Nash, *Wilderness and the American Mind*, 4th ed., xii–xiii.

80. Nash, *Wilderness and the American Mind*, 4th ed., 388.

81. Guha, "Deep Ecology Revisited," 276.

82. Guha, "Deep Ecology Revisited," 277.

83. Cronon, "The Trouble with Wilderness," 80.

84. Lowenthal, "Is Wilderness 'Paradise Enow?'" 40.

85. See generally Jared Diamond, *Guns, Germs, and Steel: The Fates of Human Societies* (New York: W. W. Norton, 1999).

86. There have been many attempts to list and categorize the attributes of wilderness. See generally *The Wilderness Act*, 16 U.S.C 1131–1136; John Nagel, "The Spiritual Value of Wilderness"; H. Ken Cordell, John Bergstrom, and J. M. Bowker, *The Multiple Values of Wilderness* (State College, PA: Venture Publishing, 2005); and Michael Nelson, "An Amalgamation of Wilderness Preservation Arguments," pp. 154–98 in *Wilderness Debate*, in which the author summarizes thirty separate arguments.

87. In thirty-one of the forty-four years between 1965 and 2008, laws were enacted expanding the National Wilderness Preservation System.

88. Hobbs and Stoop, *Demographic Trends in the Twentieth Century*, 33. Metropolitan areas are considered to be the sum of central cities and suburbs, as defined by the Census Bureau.

89. Scholars from economics, geography, history, law, sociology, and other perspectives have examined the New West. Representative works include: William Travis, *New Geographies of the American West* (Washington, D.C.: Island Press, 2007); Philip

Jackson and Robert Kuhlken, *A Rediscovered Frontier: Land Use and Resource Issues in the New West* (Lanham, MD: Rowman & Littlefield, 2006); Douglas Booth, *Searching for Paradise: Economic Development and Environmental Change in the Mountain West* (Lanham, MD: Rowman & Littlefield, 2002); Thomas Power and Richard Barrett, *Post-Cowboy Economics: Pay and Prosperity in the New American West* (Washington, D.C.: Island Press, 2001); Charles Wilkinson, *The Eagle Bird: Mapping the New West* (Boulder, CO: Johnson Books,1999); William Riebsame, ed., *Atlas of the New West* (Boulder, CO: Center for the American West, University of Colorado, 1997); and John Baden and Donald Snow, eds., *The Next West: Public Lands, Community, and Economy in the American West* (Washington, D.C.: Island Press, 1997).

90. Hobbs and Stoops, *Demographic Trends in the Twentieth Century,* 19.

91. Hobbs and Stoops, *Demographic Trends in the Twentieth Century,* 26.

92. Hobbs and Stoops, *Demographic Trends in the Twentieth Century,* 29.

93. Hobbs and Stoops, *Demographic Trends in the Twentieth Century,* 40.

94. Andrew Hansen et al., "Ecological Causes and Consequences of Demographic Change in the New West," *BioScience* 52 (2002): 151–62, quote at 152.

95. Jackson and Kuhlken, *A Rediscovered Frontier,* 2.

96. Karl Vick, "Closed-Door Deal Could Open Land in Montana," *Washington Post,* July 5, 2008, A1, A5.

97. The production and processing of food, energy, minerals, and timber remains important in many towns, counties, and states but these activities no longer dominate the economic landscape.

98. Power and Barrett, *Post-Cowboy Economics,* 148.

99. Stephanie Pincetl, "Conservation Planning in the West, Problems, New Strategies and Entrenched Obstacles," *Geoforum* 37 (2006): 246–55.

100. Not every sale means immediate development. Nontraditional buyers of ranch land, for example, include investors, developers, conservation organizations, and individuals who may continue ranching activities although they are not ranchers themselves (they will hire a manager or lease the operation to a nearby rancher). See Hannah Gosnell, Julia Haggerty, and William Travis, "Ranchland Ownership Change in the Greater Yellowstone Ecosystem, 1990–2001," *Society and Natural Resources* 19 (2006): 743–58.

101. Vick, "Closed-Door Deal Could Open Land in Montana," A5.

102. Joseph Taylor III, "The Many Lives of the New West," *Western Historical Quarterly* 35 (2004): 141–55.

103. All polling data reported here are taken from www.pollingreport.com/energy .htm (accessed July 18, 2008, and November 19, 2009).

104. Rahall statement on Drill Act, available at: http://resourcecommittee.house .gov/index.php?option=com_contents&task=viewed&id=40litemid=27 (accessed July 18, 2008).

105. This action would not, in and of itself, open these areas to leasing, as congressional action would also be required. The White House, July 14, 2008, "Fact Sheet: Allowing Offshore Exploration to Help Address Rising Fuel Costs," available at www .whitehouse.gov/news/releases/2008/07/print/20080714-7html (accessed July 18, 2008). The Obama administration announced its offshore drilling plan on March 31, 2010. It

adopted many of the ideas suggested by the Bush administration toward the end of its term by opening large, previously off-limits, areas off the east coast to exploration and development. See Department of the Interior, "Secretary Salazar Announces Comprehensive Strategy for Offshore Oil and Gas Development and Exploration," press release, March 31, 2010, available at www.doi.gov/news/pressreleases/index.cfm?pagenum=8 (accessed September 14, 2010). Also see John Broder, "Obama to Open Offshore Areas to Oil Drilling for the First Time," *New York Times*, March 31, 2010, A1, available at www.nytimes.com/2010/03/31/science/earth/31energy.html?_r=1 (accessed September 14, 2010).

106. All polling data are taken from www.pollingreport.com/energy.htm (accessed July 18, 2008, November 19, 2009, and September 13, 2010).

3

Laws, Regulations, Policies, and Courts

Sources of Management Direction

When in doubt mumble. . . . The vague, contradictory, and problematic
language found in public land law drives and perpetuates many conflicts
and often turns them into prolonged and complicated legal battles.

—Martin Nie

CHAPTER 1 CONSIDERS THE WHAT AND WHERE OF FEDERAL LANDS. Chapter 2 looks
at changing societal attitudes toward the federal lands, their resources, and
their management. This chapter examines the mechanisms that link the two.

We are a nation of law. The Constitution provides that Congress makes
laws, the executive administers them, and the judiciary assures it does so as
Congress intended. Of course, this general framework contains flexibility.
Congress can and does pass conflicting and vague laws; the executive can and
does interpret legislation in different ways; and judges can and do creatively
read statutory language and executive branch implementations thereof on
their way to reaching conclusions that may differ from court to court. All told,
this means there are several ways to look at the land-management morass we
have created. This chapter briefly looks at the routinely intertwined congressional, executive, and judicial avenues of influence on land management as
well as the difficulties in applying legislative language to the landscape.

Congressional Influence

Federal land management rests upon a cumulative effect of laws, bills passed
by Congress and signed by the president (box 3.1 outlines the congressional

Box 3.1.   Congressional Committees and Federal Land Management

Multiple congressional committees have jurisdiction over one or more facets of federal land management. A dichotomy exists between authorizing committees (those that determine management goals and direction) and appropriation committees (those that determine annual agency budgets). In addition there are committees that oversee laws not specifically directed at federal lands but that nonetheless significantly impact their management, such as the National Environmental Policy Act. Most congressional actions begin in subcommittees that have their own subject matter. The content of proposed legislation may touch the jurisdiction of more than one subcommittee or full committee.

Concerning authorizing committees of the 112th Congress, in the House of Representatives the Natural Resources Committee oversees federal land management. The Energy and Mineral Resources Subcommittee covers mineral and energy production on federal lands, and thus the Bureau of Land Management and the Forest Service are particularly interested in its deliberations. The Fisheries, Wildlife, Oceans, and Insular Affairs Subcommittee looks after wildlife resources and has specific jurisdiction over the Fish and Wildlife Service. The Bureau of Land Management, Forest Service, and National Park Service come under the authority of the National Parks, Forests, and Public Lands Subcommittee that also oversees the National Wilderness System, the Wild and Scenic Rivers System, and the National Trails System.

The Senate charges two committees with responsibilities for federal land management: the Committee on Energy and Natural Resources and the Committee on Environment and Public Works. The Committee on Energy and Natural Resources divides its work among the Energy Subcommittee (energy development on public lands), the National Parks Subcommittee (National Park Service, National Wilderness System, Wild and Scenic Rivers System, and the National Trails System), and the Public Lands Subcommittee (Bureau of Land Management, Forest Service, mining and minerals development). The Subcommittee on Water and Wildlife of the Environment and Public Works committee oversees the Fish and Wildlife Service.

On the appropriations side, parallelism exists between the House and Senate Appropriations committees. Each has an Interior, Environment, and Related Agency subcommittee with authority over the budgets of all four major federal land managing agencies.

The organization of Congress, with its multiple and overlapping jurisdictions coupled with committee and subcommittee chairs generally opposed to changes that would lessen their influence over legislation, stands as an impediment to cutting the Gordian Knot. It can be overcome, however, which is one reason I recommend the creation of a new and empowered public land law review commission.

committee structure wherein most of these laws arise). The U.S. Code contains such laws. The House of Representatives issues the code every six years with updates between the major revisions. It contains fifty titles organized by subject. Titles 16 (Conservation), 30 (Mineral Lands and Leasing), and 43 (Public Lands) contain most legislation relevant to public land management. Each title holds dozens of chapters, which have various numbers of subchapters, which may be further divided into sections. Not all the laws contained in these titles affect federal lands; for example, chapters 62 and 62A of Title 16 relate to the conservation of African and Asian elephants, respectively, while Title 43, chapter 39, deals with abandoned shipwrecks. Conversely, statutes of vital importance to federal land management can be found outside these three titles. One finds the National Environmental Policy Act in Title 42 and the Administrative Procedures Act in Title 5. No matter where one may find them, however, hundreds of laws govern management of our public lands.

From the universe of statutes, the land-management bureaus identify which apply to fulfillment of their particular responsibilities. Recent tallies are:

- BLM lists 140 statutes applying to the agency;[1]
- FS finds 155 such statutes;[2]
- FWS counts 164 "natural resource laws";[3] and
- NPS identifies 22 major laws plus those establishing individual national park system units.[4]

Impressive as these totals may be, there is more on the legislative front as Congress also uses the appropriations process to direct federal land management.

"If it ain't in the budget, it ain't." A longtime NPS employee passed that bit of wisdom on when I first went to work for the deputy director in the early 1980s. Existing law may authorize federal agencies to do all manner of things. If, however, Congress does not provide money in an agency's budget to accomplish the task, then it will not be done. Funding reflects congressional priorities. For example, the Land and Water Conservation Fund Act of 1965 authorized spending $900 million annually for federal land-managing agencies to acquire recreational lands (chiefly privately owned tracts surrounded by federal lands) and provide matching grants to state and local governments in support of outdoor recreation.[5] In the more than forty years since passage, Congress fully funded the program only twice (1998 and 2001). In most years appropriations were less than half the authorized amount. Dramatic fluctuation in year-to-year funding is common and reflects shifts in priorities. It also introduces uncertainty into the agencies' land-acquisition programs, adding another twist in one strand of the Gordian Knot.

Congress uses the appropriations process in other ways to direct management of federal lands. Directions may take the form of riders on appropriation bills, earmarks within the bills, and conference report language. Members attach riders to appropriations bills that must pass to fund government operations. Using a rider means its substance will not be debated and voted upon based on its own merits; instead, it becomes flotsam in the budgetary current that sweeps it into law. Martin Nie, in his excellent book on governing western public lands, notes the long history of these riders going all the way back to 1897, when Congress used one to pass the Forest Service Organic Act.[6] Riders provide a means of cutting the Gordian Knot regarding a particular matter since they may take the form of compelling an action while prohibiting administrative or judicial appeals and exempting the action from compliance with (usually) environmental or procedural laws. They can be controversial but members of both parties use them.

Earmarks are another means whereby Congress directs land management using the power of the purse. Earmarks specify that a given sum be dedicated to achieving a particular task: conducting a study, doing a plan, building a facility, or some other activity. Many observers deride earmarks as pork, monies delivered to their home state by powerful politicians. Beneficiaries see it otherwise. Some members of Congress defend the practice, arguing that they know better than federal agencies where the greatest needs are at a local level. Other members decry it, claiming it subverts rational decision-making by shielding the favored projects from competition for limited funds. In any event, earmarking remains a bipartisan enterprise and may be found in legislation itself or in accompanying report language, as I describe in the next paragraph.

When budget conferees meet to iron out differences between House and Senate versions of the budget each year they issue a conference report. It can play a major factor in management actions. For example, the *Conference Report for the Fiscal Year 2001 for Interior and Related Agencies Appropriations Act* (P.L. 106-291) contains the following language:

> The Secretaries [of Agriculture and Interior] should also work with the Governors on a long-term strategy to deal with wildland fire and hazardous fuels situation. . . . The managers [of the appropriations bills in House and Senate] expect that a collaborative structure, with the states and local government as full partners, will be the most efficient and effective way of implementing a long-term program. . . . The managers direct the Secretaries to engage the Governors in a collaborative structure to cooperatively develop a coordinated, National ten-year comprehensive strategy with the states as full partners in the planning, decision-making, and implementation of the plan.

The language had profound effects on the federal fire program and public land management.

The direction resulted in extensive negotiations between the federal government, states, tribes, and counties that produced management direction in *The 10-Year Comprehensive Strategy* in 2001, *A Collaborative Approach for Reducing Wildland Fire Risks to Communities and the Environment: 10-Year Comprehensive Strategy Implementation Plan* in 2002, and a revised implementation plan in 2006.[7] It spawned creation of the national-level Wildland Fire Leadership Council, composed of federal, state, tribal, and county representatives, that provides guidance to the overall federal fire program. It gave rise to numerous state and regional cooperative entities. This report language directly affects the operation of the federal hazardous fuel reduction program. At the DOI, from 2001 through 2009, the bureaus treated some 9.6 million acres using 1.6 billion appropriated dollars.[8] Removal of hazardous fuels lessens the risk of wildland fire to people and communities, reduces fire severity and undesirable impacts to multiple components of the physical environment, and increases the opportunities for allowing desired fires to continue to burn. The hazardous fuels program is arguably the single most significant contemporary public land-management activity.

Executive Influence

The executive branch weaves many strands of the Gordian Knot within the boundaries prescribed by law. Presidents pass direction to cabinet secretaries, who pass direction to assistant secretaries and bureau heads, who pass it on to various elements within bureaus. Guidance comes in many forms: cascading executive direction, regulations, rules, departmental and bureau manuals, handbooks, memos, and guidance letters, among others. At every level, the responsible official typically adds more detailed direction, thus adding to the Knot's complexity.

Among the many forms guidance may take, regulations and formal rules represent the executive branch's chief means of translating policy and management decisions into operational direction. Regulations appear in the *Code of Federal Regulations* (CFR) while bureaus (and other divisions of the executive branch) publish preliminary and final rules in the *Federal Register*. CFR Title 36 contains the regulations of the NPS and the FS while Titles 43 and 50 hold BLM and FWS regulations, respectively. The applicable chapters in these three titles collectively cover some 2,500 pages.[9] Rules and regulations carry the force and effect of law and are reviewable in the federal courthouse. More often than not, however, the courts have held that handbooks, manuals, directives, memos, and similar instruments with their voluminous directions are not fodder for judicial oversight.[10] As a consequence, policies and management direction inculcated into regulations and rules have greater permanence than those contained in other forms of guidance.

While a portion of the body of direction remains relatively fixed in time, shifts routinely occur when the White House changes parties. The Carter administration, for example, was the first to produce a single comprehensive guide for managing the national parks. It published *Management Policies* in 1978. Presidents Reagan (1988), Clinton (2001), and Bush (2006) each subsequently revised *Management Policies* to reflect their interpretation of the mission and purpose of the national parks. Such change, however, is not preordained. The Bush administration incorporated nearly all of the Clinton administration's September 2001 *National Fire Plan* into its *Healthy Forest Initiative* announced in August 2002. Conversely, it replaced the so-called Roadless Rule for the national forests finalized by the Clinton administration nine days before it ended. The rule applies to nearly one-third of national forest land. The Roadless Rule controversy effort deserves a closer look because it illustrates multiple aspects of the Knot's complexity: changes occurring with shifts in administration, interplay between the executive and judicial branches, and conflicting decisions between individual courts.

Today's roadless area inventory of 58.5 million acres in the national forests arises chiefly from actions taken in response to the passage of the Wilderness Act in 1964.[11] The act established 9.1 million acres of statutory wilderness upon passage. It directed federal land-managing agencies to examine their lands to identify candidate wilderness areas for future congressional designation as wilderness. In response, the FS launched a Roadless Area Review Evaluation (RARE I) in 1967. It completed a follow-on study (RARE II) in 1979, but the courts held that neither effort complied with the National Environmental Policy Act (NEPA).[12] Nonetheless, roadless areas had been identified and how to manage them consistent with existing law and policy became a matter of concern.

Throughout the 1970s, 1980s, and 1990s, management of roadless areas was handled within the context of planning for the particular national forest of which they were a part. On October 13, 1999, President Clinton directed the secretary of agriculture to develop regulations for the long-term protection of roadless areas. Six days later a notice of intent to prepare an environmental impact statement (EIS) for approaches to protecting the areas appeared in the *Federal Register*. The draft EIS and proposed rules followed in May 2000 and the final EIS in November 2000.[13] On January 12, 2001, eight days before the end of the Clinton administration, the Forest Service published a final rule in the *Federal Register* (see box 3.2 for a description of roadless area characteristics as described in the Clinton Roadless Rule).[14] Given the vast extent of the lands involved (30 percent of the nation's national forests) and the major

---

Box 3.2.   Roadless Area Characteristics and Values

According to the Clinton Roadless Rule, roadless areas contain "high quality or undisturbed soil, water, and air; sources of public drinking water; diversity of plant and animal communities; habitat for threatened, endangered, proposed, candidate, and sensitive species and for those species dependent on large, undisturbed areas of land; primitive, semi-primitive non-motorized, and semi-primitive motorized classes of dispersed recreation; reference landscapes; natural appearing landscapes with high scenic quality; traditional cultural properties and sacred sites; and other locally identified unique characteristics." It is fair to note that most of these characteristics and values are not unique to roadless areas.

Source: 66 Federal Register, January 12, 2001, 3245.

---

departure from past practice regarding their management, these were amazingly short timeframes.[15]

The rule addressed roadless area management from two perspectives: permissible activities and the procedures to determine them in the future. The final rule "prohibits road construction, reconstruction, and timber harvest in inventoried roadless areas because they have the likelihood of altering and fragmenting landscapes, resulting in immediate long-term loss of roadless area values and characteristics."[16] It goes on to note:

> Under this final rule, management actions that do not require the construction of new roads will still be allowed, including activities such as timber harvesting for clearly defined limited purposes [enhancement of species habitat, restoration or maintenance of ecosystem characteristics, or reduction of wildland fire risk], development of valid claims of locatable minerals, grazing of livestock, and off-highway vehicle use where specifically permitted.[17]

As for altering these prohibitions through future planning, Pamela Baldwin, a legislative attorney at the Congressional Research Service, read the Clinton-era rule to mean that

> while other possible restrictions on use of the roadless areas would be developed as part of the planning process. . . . The prohibitions and restrictions of the rule are not subject to reconsideration, revision, or rescission in subsequent project decisions or land and resource management plan amendments or revisions.[18]

Hence, absent a rule change, local and regional forest managers could strengthen, but not relax, the rule's land-use restrictions as part of future public planning efforts. The rule established some 58 million acres of de facto wilderness via executive action in spite of the fact that no Congress had added more than 9 million acres to the system in any year since initial passage of the Wilderness Act (the only exception was 1980 when the 96th Congress declared 60 million acres in Alaska as wilderness as part of the Alaska National Interest Lands Conservation Act).

The rule altered thirty years of land-management planning practice by having its land-management requirements replace those developed through extensive and public planning processes done at local and regional levels. The Forest Service argued that the national rulemaking was needed so that officials could consider the "whole picture" and not fear the emergence of cumulative harmful national impacts on roadless areas resulting from local or regional planning.[19] It further argued that a national standard was needed to avoid controversies, appeals, and lawsuits centered on roadless area management decisions arising from local and regional plans, controversies that were costly in terms of dollars and in relations with "communities of place and communities of interest."[20] Alas, the rule did not reduce controversy as the FS had hoped.

Reaction to the final rule was swift and divided. The major fault line separated those who favored maximizing protection of roadless area characteristics and values versus those seeking greater balance among possible land uses or consideration of factors beyond attributes assigned to roadless areas. These philosophical and value-based positions played out chiefly as support of, or opposition to, the rule's shift to a national land-management standard. Interests favoring managing roadless areas to maximize protection of their characteristics and values supported the national standard. Those seeking a broader perspective did not. An important factor influencing the positions of state and county executives proved to be the amount of roadless acreage within a state. In reviewing the public reaction to the proposed rule that preceded the final rule, the FS notes, "In general, those Western States with the greatest roadless acreage (for example, Idaho, Montana, Nevada, Utah, and Wyoming) tended to generate the greatest number of negative comments from Governors, agencies, and officials."[21] These officials were concerned about the rule's impact on access to state lands, its effects on communities and commodity industries, and the consequences for rural lifestyles. Conversely, "public officials from areas with larger urban populations generally supported the proposed rule because of their expressed desire for recreation opportunities, protection of water quality, and undisturbed landscapes."[22] The final rule garnered opposition from seven states; they and others moved quickly into courthouses in six different federal judicial districts. Addressing concerns with the rule fell to the Bush administration and the courts.

The first act of the Bush administration was to call time out. Because of provisions of the Congressional Review Act, the Roadless Rule could not become effective before March 13, 2001.[23] Nonetheless, it was covered by a blanket sixty-day hold on implementing all not-yet-effective regulations issued by the White House.[24] The effective date for Roadless Rule implementation was later pushed back to May 12, 2001. The new administration found concerns raised by states, tribes, and local communities persuasive. On May 4, 2001, the Secretary of Agriculture, Ann Veneman, declared that the administration would conserve roadless area values but the department would review the rule to address those concerns. On June 7, the chief of the Forest Service wrote:

> The Forest Service is committed to protecting and managing roadless areas as an important component of the National Forest System. The best way to achieve this objective is to ensure that we protect and sustain roadless values until they can be appropriately considered through forest planning.[25]

Following the secretary's declaration and the chief's letter, the Forest Service asked for public input on a series of management issues that would inform whatever changes to the Roadless Rule it should consider.[26] The request came on July 10, 2001. Thus, the management issue was not whether or not roadless areas would be protected but how such protection was to be accomplished and how it would be done in concert with other public policy matters that impact national forest management.

By this time court decisions had begun to impact implementation of the Clinton Roadless Rule. The Kootenai Tribe of Idaho had sued in the U.S. district court in Idaho to enjoin the rule. On April 5, 2001, the court agreed with the tribe and stopped implementation of the rule.[27] The decision was appealed to the Ninth Circuit Court of Appeals, which reversed the district court's decision, a judgment that led to the rule becoming effective on April 14, 2003, for the first time. That situation did not last long because on July 14, 2003, the U.S. district court for Wyoming, acting on a suit brought by the state, declared the rule to be unlawful and issued a permanent injunction against it.[28] That decision was then appealed to the Tenth Circuit Court of Appeals. The court agreed to hear the case on May 11, 2004, but subsequently found the case to be moot because the Clinton rule had been replaced by one produced by the Bush administration.[29] The appeals court did not find that the Wyoming district court had erred in throwing out the Clinton rule.

The Bush rule, announced by the Forest Service on May 13, 2005, differed significantly from the Clinton rule.[30] It removed the national standard and returned to the traditional approach of using local and regional planning to set the direction for roadless management. In part, the FS summarizes the rule this way: "Under this final rule . . . management requirements for inventoried roadless areas would be guided by individual land-management plans until and *unless these management requirements are changed through a State-specific rulemaking* [emphasis mine]."[31] Yet the rule does not simply return matters to their status prior to the Clinton rule. The state-specific rulemaking provision sets the Bush rule apart from previous practice by providing a means to address concerns arising from a multitude of differing state-level conditions. The rule provides that:

> the Governor of any State or territory that contains National Forest System lands may petition the Secretary of Agriculture to promulgate regulations establishing management requirements for all or any portion of National Forest System inventoried roadless areas within that State or territory. Any such petition must be submitted to the Secretary of Agriculture not later than November 13, 2006.[32]

The rule neither increases nor decreases the protections for roadless areas already contained in existing plans.[33] Instead it offers governors a method to address concerns within their state. In doing so, protections could be changed. The secretary may accept or reject the petition.

As with the Clinton rule, reaction to the Bush rule was swift, divided, and again involved the federal courts. The governors of North Carolina, South Carolina, and Virginia welcomed the rule as an opportunity to protect resources and were the first to submit petitions to the secretary.[34] Reaction was mixed among western states. The states of California, Oregon, New Mexico, and Washington joined with environmental organizations in asking the federal district court in Northern California to overturn the Bush rule and reinstate the Clinton rule.[35] Alaska, Idaho, and Wyoming, however, joined the case as supporters of the Bush rule. The federal district court, beginning on September 20, 2006, and ending with a final injunction on February 7, 2007, struck down the Bush rule as violating the NEPA and the Endangered Species Act and ordered the Forest Service to abide by the Clinton rule. Its decision was appealed to the Ninth Circuit Court of Appeals. On August 5, 2009, the Ninth Circuit upheld the district court in rejecting the Bush rule and reinstating the Clinton rule.[36] The Obama administration supported that decision. It was, however, not the final word, simply another twist in a strand of the Gordian Knot, for the issue remained before the Wyoming federal district court within the Tenth Circuit Court of Appeals.

On August 20, 2008, the Wyoming court set aside the Clinton Roadless Rule for the second time, finding it violated the NEPA and the Wilderness Act. The Wyoming court did not mince words regarding the decision of the Northern California court, particularly by requiring a return to the Clinton rule. It writes:

The court is disturbed, and frankly shocked at the fact that a Magistrate Judge essentially re-instituted a policy [the Clinton rule] that was not properly before that Court, and especially in light of the fact that an Article III judge had already [July 14, 2003] ruled that the re-instituted policy was promulgated in violation of law [NEPA and the Wilderness Act].[37]

The Wyoming court's decision was appealed to the Tenth Circuit Court of Appeals. The appeal was argued on March 10, 2010, and the court issued its opinion on October 10, 2011. It found that in promulgating the rule the Forest Service's action was not "arbitrary, capricious, an abuse of discretion, or otherwise not in accordance with the law," hence it reversed the lower court and upheld the Clinton rule.[38]

Like the Bush administration before it, the Obama administration addressed the roadless issue through executive action shortly after its inception. It favored the Clinton rule and quickly transferred decision-making authority from the undersecretary for natural resources at the Department of Agriculture and the chief of the Forest Service, where it historically resided, to the secretary of agriculture. Secretary Tom Vilsack reserved to himself the "authority to approve or disapprove road construction or reconstruction and the cutting, sale, or removal of timber in those areas" identified as roadless.[39]

This interplay among the courts, between the courts and the executive branch, and between administrations with unlike views of federal land management illustrates the Gordian Knot at its finest.

The Roadless Rule conundrum illustrates the expanded role of the courts in federal land management, a theme picked up in the following two sections.

Judicial Influence

"By any measure," writes law professor Robert Keiter, "the federal courts have become a major institutional presence on public land and natural resource issues."[40] The role of the courts changed over the last several decades owing chiefly to citizen suit provisions that Congress inserted into virtually all environmental and land-management legislation passed since the mid-1960s. A "veritable explosion of litigation" resulted.[41] While anyone may take advantage of these provisions, environmentalists have made the greatest use of the courts to achieve their land-management goals. The usual court action sought by litigants is the issuance of an injunction prohibiting the federal land-management action they oppose.

I awoke on March 3, 2009 (when I was writing the first draft of this chapter) to find a front-page story in the *Washington Times* about a line in the 2009 omnibus spending bill directing the Army Corps of Engineers to build a bridge on the Tamiami Trail in Everglades National Park "immediately and without further delay." Thus, Congress overturned an injunction by a federal judge preventing construction prior to compliance with environmental laws.[42] While congressional action of this kind is unusual, the sort of judicial action prompting it has become commonplace.

Federal judges have issued environmental injunctions for some 125 years. The first came in an 1884 Northern California case, *Woodruff v. Bloomfield*, in which the judge ruled in favor of farmers over miners in the latter's use of hydraulic mining methods to extract gold. Over time, injunctions have become even more useful in stopping projects as some courts have lowered the standard for their issuance. In November 2008, the Supreme Court addressed such changes in their opinion in *Winter v. Natural Resources Defense Council*.[43]

The issue in *Winter v. Natural Resources Defense Council* was the Navy's use of midrange active sonar in training exercises off the coast of southern California. The Natural Resources Defense Council and others argued use of the sonar harmed marine mammals within 2,200 yards of its source and sought an injunction against training unless the Navy shut down the sonar to prevent harm to the mammals. The district court and the Ninth Circuit Court of Appeals agreed. The Supreme Court reversed the lower courts in part because it found them to have inappropriately lowered the threshold for issuing a preliminary injunction.

To succeed in their pursuit of a preliminary injunction, plaintiffs must meet multiple requirements. Of necessity they must convince the court that absent the requested injunction the plaintiffs will likely suffer irreparable injury. In *Winter* the lower courts issued or affirmed an injunction against the Navy based on the possibility of irreparable harm. Justice John Roberts, in writing for the Supreme Court majority, noted, "The 'possibility' standard is too lenient. This Court's frequently reiterated standard requires plaintiffs seeking preliminary relief to demonstrate that irreparable injury is *likely* in the absence of an injunction [emphasis in the original]."[44] He went on to write that even if the plaintiffs had met the irreparable injury test they would fail to meet other criteria for a preliminary injunction—balance of harms and the overall public interest—and he faulted the lower courts' work here. After reviewing the record, the Supreme Court's majority concluded that shutting down naval exercises is of greater harm to national defense and the public interest therein than is any environmental damage the training may cause.

Justice Roberts refers to the testimony of senior naval officers and how they pointed out the importance of moving forward with the training. He does not find the lower courts' conclusions to the contrary persuasive. Put differently, Roberts rejects the courts' assertions that they know more about training for naval warfare than do senior naval officers. The same question can be asked about science and land management. This brings me to my next topic, judicial deference to agency expertise (see also the discussion on Yosemite Valley in the introduction).

Judges face dueling scientists and other experts nearly every time a federal land-management issue comes before them. Few jurists are trained as ecologists, geologists, geographers, foresters, biologists, hydrologists, or in other relevant scientific fields, or have any experience in land or natural-resource management. On the other hand, federal land-managing agencies have thousands of personnel with applicable scientific training and extensive experience in land and resource management. For their part, plaintiffs rarely have a large scientific staff but may enlist academic and think-tank scientists to bolster their case. In considering judicial influence on the Gordian Knot, the question becomes: "Under what circumstances should judges substitute their opinions (and those of plaintiffs) for those of the agency?"

Deference to agency expertise varies among the courts, but has generally waned over the last few decades. For example, federal judge William Dwyer of the Western District of Washington rejected what was widely hailed in the scientific community as the state-of-the-art study of spotted owls and old-growth forests in the Pacific Northwest and then essentially used a series of orders to put himself in charge of forest service lands in Oregon and Washington for some five years.[45] Dwyer was a nonscientist, having spent over thirty years as a trial lawyer before his appointment to the federal bench. *Resources for the Future* scholar George Hoberg concludes that Dwyer's actions represent "perhaps the most extreme case of judicial intervention into environmental policymaking."[46] Dwyer's court falls within the Ninth Circuit Court of Appeals, which upheld his rulings on appeal in the 1990s. A recent decision by that court, however, would have reined in Dwyer's ability to substitute his judgment for that of the Forest Service.

The Ninth Circuit Court of Appeals wields a good deal of authority over federal lands by virtue of the fact that most federal lands fall within its jurisdiction.[47] Absent reversal by the Supreme Court, its findings are binding on district court judges in nine western states. Thus, its July 2008 decision in *Lands Council v. McNair and the United States Forest Service* (*Lands Council II*) signals a return to greater judicial deference to agency expertise.[48]

The *Lands Council II* decision is important on multiple fronts: it establishes a deferential standard for judicial review of Forest Service decisions and by extension all other federal land-management agencies; it overturns previous jurisprudence within the Ninth Circuit that improperly extended the ability of courts to second-guess agency actions; and, as a unanimous en banc decision, it does not leave much wiggle room for future plaintiffs hoping to have the courts substitute their judgments for those of the agencies.[49]

The case began with environmental plaintiffs seeking an injunction to prohibit the selective logging of some 3,800 acres (the Mission Brush Project) in the Idaho Panhandle National Forest. The trial court denied the motion, but the decision was reversed by a three-judge panel of the Ninth Circuit on appeal. Several Ninth Circuit judges were troubled by that decision and the appeals court convened an eleven-judge panel to review that ruling. The panel made it clear what it was about in the first sentence of its ruling: "We took this case en banc to clarify some of our environmental jurisprudence with respect to our review of actions of the United States Forest Service."

The *Lands Council II* court specifically rejects the idea that the federal judges should substitute their judgment for that of the agency. They write that "in essence, Lands Council asks this court to act as a panel of scientists. . . . This is not the proper role for a federal appellate court."[50] The court makes the point that judges are not scientists and are limited in their review to questions regarding Forest Service compliance with the law. Judges cannot choose between dueling groups of scientists. If the Forest Service (and by extension all other federal land-managing agencies) reasonably explains why its scientific positions are reliable, then judges are not free to accept scientific arguments offered by plaintiffs. The panel finds that:

> Thus, as non-scientists, we decline to impose bright-line rules on the Forest Service regarding particular means that it must take in every case to show us that it has met the NFMA's [National Forest Management Act] requirements. Rather, we hold that the Forest Service must support its conclusions that a project meets the requirements of the NFMA and relevant Forest Plan with studies that the agency, in its expertise, deems reliable.[51]

They go on to note, "When specialists express conflicting views, an agency must have discretion to rely on the reasonable opinion of its own qualified experts even if, as an original matter, a court might find contrary views more persuasive."[52] In another notable portion of the decision, the court held that the mere fact that a project may cause environmental harm does not require the issuance of an injunction. Noting that the Supreme Court "has instructed us not to exercise [our] equitable powers loosely or casually whenever a claim of 'environmental damage' is asserted," they reemphasize the need for the trial court to engage in a balance-of-harms analysis.[53]

The trial court must balance the harms caused by going forward with the project against those resulting from halting the project. In this case the Lands Council argued that the loss of trees was an environmental harm and habitat change could harm the flammulated owl. In contrast, the Forest Service identified harms associated with no action—for example, catastrophic wildland fire, increased tree morality and ill health stemming from insect infestation and disease, and job loss. In this particular case, the court found that the balance of harms did not clearly tip in the plaintiffs' favor. It went on to clarify that in the Ninth Circuit "we decline to adopt a rule that *any* potential environmental injury *automatically* merits an injunction [emphasis in the original]."[54]

In the end, the Ninth Circuit affirmed the district court's denial of a preliminary injunction halting the project. The decision came some five years after the Forest Service published a draft EIS for the project.

We apply laws, rules, regulations, and court opinions to an ever-changing landscape. In doing so, the Knot gains complexity. The next section looks at some of the aspects of the Knot that emerge when moving from the halls of Congress and courtrooms to the landscape we live upon and to its management.

Moving from Law to the Landscape

When all is said and done, law, regulation, and policy declare that on the land we can do some things "here but not there." The trick is figuring out just where *here* and *there* are located. A purpose of the Endangered Species Act, for example, is "to provide a means whereby the ecosystems upon which endangered species and threatened species depend may be conserved."[55] Further, it directs the secretary of the interior to identify "critical habitat" for listed species; hence, ecosystems and critical habitat link the ESA with the land in words, but where are we to find them on the landscape? The ESA offers little help in answering such questions, offering no guidance regarding ecosystems and limited help on critical habitat.

About critical habitat, the ESA directs that in general it "shall not include the entire geographical area which can be occupied." Instead it means "specific areas" within occupied (at the time of listing) landscapes plus "specific areas" beyond those landscapes deemed "essential to the conservation of the species."[56] How does one find these areas and then subsequently identify specific lands wherein some management actions are permitted and others prohibited? It boils down to maps (see box 3.3).

The Clean Water Act (CWA) offers another opportunity to look at applying the language of the law to the physical environment. Intended to protect the nation's waters, the statute creates multiple permitting programs to help accomplish its goal. But even the seemingly straightforward task of looking at the landscape and saying, "Yes, I see a water body where the law applies, or no, that is not a place where a permitting program pertains" has occupied federal land managers, advocates, private landowners, land users, state and local governments, judges, and others for decades. I turn briefly to the specific

---

Box 3.3.   On Maps and Ecological Boundaries

All maps are edited collections of information. They leave out the overwhelming majority of geographic data about the area they depict. In preparing maps, researchers pick through vast amounts of imperfectly known spatial information and select a small subset to use in map creation. They blend the different individual distributions of selected variables into map boundaries using particular criteria and techniques. Different researchers approaching the same problem would not use the same set of variables or blending techniques and would produce a different set of boundaries. Ecological boundaries on maps are not usually visible on the landscape. That is, the boundaries on maps used to declare the "here but not there" component of moving the law to the landscape are most often geographic fictions.

---

cases of protecting northern spotted owls and implementation of section 404 of the CWA to better illustrate the difficulties in moving the law to the land.

Northern Spotted Owls

The northern spotted owl emerged from ornithological obscurity in the 1970s to become a central focus in federal land management in the 1980s, a focus that remains in place to the present day. The extent of the owl's range, coupled with the valuable resources thereon, first attracted the spotlight. Home comprises the coniferous and mixed coniferous-hardwood forests southward from British Columbia through western Washington and Oregon and into northwestern California as far south as San Francisco.[57] It especially favors late-successional old-growth forests that often also contain valuable timber resources. Some of these forests are already protected within national parks and wilderness areas, but most lie on national forest and BLM lands otherwise designated for multiple use. Owl researchers have long recognized logging-caused habitat change as a major factor in the decline of the owl population, so protection of the owl ran headlong into concerns for human well-being caused by owl-related threats to the forest products industry. Noted students of the owl R. J. Gutierrez and George Barrowclough write: "The Northern Spotted Owl is one of the most studied birds in the world because conservation of its habitat has enormous economic ramifications. Indeed, virtually every conservation or major scientific finding that affects the owl's conservation has been controversial."[58] Many observers boil the conundrum down to "Owls v. Jobs," which translates to how much land would be placed off limits to logging and where it would be.[59]

A quick tour of major events helps place the issue into perspective. During the 1980s the Forest Service put out a series of management and guidance documents along with accompanying NEPA compliance documents.[60] Environmentalists routinely challenged these documents in the courthouse and by 1989 had essentially halted all timber sales in the Pacific Northwest.[61] Congress, seeking a way to resolve the regional land-management gridlock, called for a scientifically credible approach to protecting the owls. In 1989 it directed the four land-managing agencies to establish the Interagency Science Committee (ISC) to develop such a plan, which the ISC issued in 1990.[62] In addition, the Agriculture and Merchant Marine Committees in the House of Representatives commissioned a report by four noted scientists (nicknamed the "Gang of Four"). They delivered it in 1991.[63] In 1990 the FWS listed the owl as threatened under the ESA.[64] It published a final rule in 1992 identifying the owl's critical habitat as well as a draft final recovery plan.[65] None of these actions calmed the waters.

The owl conundrum took on a new perspective when President Clinton assumed office. To fulfill a campaign promise he convened a forest summit to address the owl problem. He established another group, the Forest Ecosystem Management Assessment Team (FEMAT), to provide scientifically and legally defensible land options to protect the owl but went beyond them to involve all other species inhabiting old-growth forests. The FEMAT ultimately involved some 600 specialists from the natural and social sciences.[66] The FEMAT developed ten options in ninety days.[67] The administration selected option 9, which called for some 77 percent of the region's 25 million acres of federal forests to be reserved.[68] It became the basis for the Northwest Forest Plan (NFP), jointly issued by the departments of Agriculture and Interior in 1994. Timber interests and environmentalists alike went to the courthouse, where the NFP was ultimately ruled as legally sufficient.[69] Activity continues. In May 2008 the FWS published the *Final Recovery Plan for the Northern Spotted Owl* and a dozen environmental groups challenged it in federal court.[70] On September 2, 2010, the court directed the FWS to revise the 2008 plan.[71]

The efforts cited in the last two paragraphs had several common characteristics, including: the guiding law—the ESA—had not changed, the participants were respected practitioners of their professions, each adopted procedures and methods to analyze and integrate information in the preparation of their recommendations, they sought to use the best available science, and they produced maps identifying areas that should be managed in particular ways. That is, they presented their views of what constituted the "here but not there" in federal land management. All the maps differed, illustrating the difficulty of tying the law to the landscape.

The groups posited multiple kinds of land-management zones. For the ISC, four categories of Habitat Conservation Areas (HCAs) formed the core of areas to be protected for spotted owls.[72] Using a complex iterative procedure, the ISC identified 162 HCAs chiefly on federal lands in California, Oregon, and Washington in addition to HCAs on state and private lands.[73] The federal HCAs occupy some 7 million acres and range in size from less than 1,000 acres to well over 100,000 acres.[74] HCAs were to be no more than 12 miles apart. The ISC termed the lands between HCAs "matrix lands." These were unreserved lands where timber harvesting would be permitted providing that at least 50 percent of the remaining timber be at least 11 inches in diameter at breast height and have a 40 percent canopy cover—the so-called "50-11-40 rule." The ISC effort produced tens of thousands of miles of boundaries to identify the "here but not there" of owl management and timber harvest. Scholars generally regard the ISC report as a landmark study.

The Gang of Four set out to map late-successional old-growth forests within the owl's range. Gang of Four member Jerry Franklin describes the process this way:

> When the team agreed to map and grade the old-growth forest, no one was sure exactly how that could be done. Success depended on the biologists, silviculturists, hydrologists and other experts in the field—government employees and researchers that knew the land—exchanging information with each other. These professionals came together in a common place, brought their materials, and took two weeks to map, grade, and evaluate alternatives for the old-growth forests. Approximately 125 to 150 people came together to work on this issue. People were arranged according to geography—the table at one end of the room was the Mt. Baker National Forest staff and the next one was the Gifford Pinchot staff and the next one was the Mt. Hood staff, and so forth. Each working table was geographically arranged in relation to its neighbors so participants could look at what was going on at the other table and see how well their work fit together.[75]

The effort created a new set of boundaries. It produced three categories of late-successional old-growth forests labeled LS/OG1, LS/OG2, and LS/OG3 (all with their own boundaries) plus lands termed "Owl Additions," which were added to meet the criteria the ISC used to create HCAs.

In explaining their 1992 designation of critical habitat, the Fish and Wildlife Service staff make several salient points. "Comparison," they say, "of the maps that have been developed over the past few years underscores the limitations that exist in trying to identify habitat to be protected or preserved for this or any other forest species."[76] They note the differing assumptions and purposes used by groups authoring the maps as well as the constantly changing nature of information. For example, the ISC estimated total federal, state, and private lands within HCAs to be 7.7 million acres, but within two years, the FWS indicated HCAs totaled 8.1 million acres.[77] In preparing their critical habitat determination, the FWS proposal went from 11.6 million acres in their first published draft to 6.9 million acres in the final rule as state and private lands as well as federal lands in national parks and wilderness areas were removed from the proposed designation. By this time, no reader will be surprised to learn that boundaries and acreage appearing in the FWS's Draft Recovery Plan, the work of the FEMAT, and the 2008 *Recovery Plan* all differ. Cutting the Gordian Knot in the face of changing physical, scientific, political, and judicial landscapes poses multiple issues, which brings me to the matter of wetlands.

Wetlands

Wetlands, as a landscape feature, took on new land-management importance with passage of the Clean Water Act in 1972 with its objective "to restore and maintain the chemical, physical, and biological integrity of the Nation's waters."[78] To achieve that goal, the act generally prohibits (without a permit) the discharging of pollutants into "navigable waters," which the act defines to mean "the waters of the United States, including the territorial seas."[79] Pollutants include dredge and fill material not associated with a point source. Under section 404 of the act, the U.S. Army Corps of Engineers (Corps) has authority (with Environmental Protection Agency oversight) to issue permits regarding deposition of such materials and to determine where its permitting authority extends on the landscape.

Until passage of the CWA there was a direct nexus between legal language, judicial interpretation, and the landscape. Justice Scalia, writing for the plurality in *Rapanos v. United States*, notes that "for a century prior to CWA, we [the Court] had interpreted the phrase 'navigable waters of the United States' in the Act's predecessor statutes to refer to interstate waters that are 'navigable in fact' or readily susceptible of being rendered so."[80]

This view represents a plain reading of the language of the law and is easily understandable by the public as it makes sense when applied to the land. By defining the phrase *navigable waters* as it did, however, the CWA created a situation that "for over thirty years . . . has taxed the legal system's collective wits."[81] This occurred because it permitted the lower courts and the Corps to begin a series of ever-more-inventive judicial and regulatory interpretations of "waters of the United States" that had less and less in common with the actual landscape and with public understanding of landscape features like wetlands.[82] The public's collective wits were challenged every bit as much as the judiciary's.[83]

A glance at the landscape features the Corps considers "waters of the United States" helps explain how the Gordian Knot has grown to its present proportions. In addition to the more traditional understanding of "waters of the United States," the Corps includes: "intermittent and ephemeral streams, drainage ditches, mudflats, sandflats, sloughs, wet meadows, playa lakes, and the tributaries to any of the above."[84] "Waters" includes wetlands adjacent to any of the above, with *adjacent* meaning bordering, contiguous to, or neighboring, whether or not they may be separated from these features by natural or manmade barriers. Until struck down by the Supreme Court in 2001, the Corps also claimed CWA regulatory authority over isolated wetlands based on their status as habitat for migratory waterfowl.[85] The plurality in *Rapanos* found that the Corps' idea of what constitutes "waters of the United States" includes

> virtually any parcel of land containing a channel or conduit—whether man-made or natural, broad or narrow, permanent or ephemeral—through which rainwater or drainage may occasionally or intermittently flow. On this view, the federally regulated "waters of the United States" include storm drains, roadside ditches, ripples of sand in the desert that may contain water once a year, and lands that are covered by floodwaters once every 100 years.[86]

They conclude that the Corps "has stretched the term 'waters of the United States' beyond parody."[87] The plurality in *Rapanos* point to the need for common sense in interpreting statutory language on the landscape; land cannot be construed to be "waters."

Justice Stevens, in his dissent (joined by Justices Breyer, Souter, and Ginsburg), does not look to the landscape for guidance on what may constitute "waters of the United States." Instead he defers to Corps expertise. He faults the plurality and Justice Kennedy for their failure to accept the Corps' position, finding that "the Corps' resulting decision to treat these wetlands as encompassed within the term 'waters of the United States' is a quintessential example of the Executive's reasonable interpretation of a statutory provision."[88] Such judicial deference regarding the interpretation of landscape descriptors was not always the case. In 1975, the Federal Court of the District of Columbia rejected the Corps' traditional interpretation of "waters of the United States" as described by Justice Scalia. Their decision in *Natural Resources Defense Council v. Callaway* launched the Corps and the lower courts on their creative views of the term.[89] Congressional clarity in drafting statutory language on these and many other environmental and public land-use statutes would have saved society a great deal of time and energy as well as financial and emotional capital.

It is time for the rubber to meet the road. So far I have illustrated the Gordian Knot from several perspectives, outlined its complexity and the sources thereof, and sketched the attributes of the public lands whose rational management it confounds. What I suggest we do about it is the subject of the next chapter.

Notes

1. U.S. Department of the Interior, Bureau of Land Management, *Fiscal Year 2007 President's Budget: Budget Justification* (Washington, D.C.: Department of the Interior, 2006), III-1 through III-19. Many statutes are common to all bureaus, for example, the Endangered Species Act.

2. U.S. Department of Agriculture, Forest Service, *Fiscal Year 2008 President's Budget: Budget Justification* (Washington, D.C.: Department of Agriculture, 2007), 18-1 to 18-21.

3. Fish and Wildlife Service, Office of Congressional and Legislative Affairs, "Digest of Federal Resource Laws" (Washington, D.C.: Fish and Wildlife Service, 2010), available at www.fws.gov/laws/Lawsdigest.html (accessed September 14, 2010).

4. National Park Service, "Laws and Related Material," available at www.nature.nps.gov/RefDesk/index.cfm (accessed September 14, 2010).

5. 16 U.S.C. 4601–4. See Carol Hardy Vincent, *Land and Water Conservation Fund: Overview, Funding History, and Current Issues* (Washington, D.C.: Congressional Research Service, 2006).

6. Martin Nie, *The Governance of Western Public Lands* (Lawrence: University of Kansas Press, 2008), 184.

7. Respectively, the 2001, 2002, and 2006 reports are available at www.westgov.org/wga/initiatives/fire/final_fire_rpt.pdf; www.westgov.org/wga/initiatives/fire/implem_plan.pdf; and www.fs.fed.us/news/2006/releases/12/10-year-strategy-december-2006.pdf (accessed September 14, 2010).

8. The totals are for fiscal years and include treatments on BLM-, FWS-, and NPS-managed lands as well as tribal lands. See U.S. Department of the Interior, *Department of the Interior Budget Justifications and Performance Information, Fiscal Year 2011, Wildland Fire Management* (Washington, D.C.: Department of the Interior, 2010), 39, available at www.doi.gov/budget/2011/data/greenbook/FY2001_WFM_Greenbook.pdf (accessed September 14, 2010).

9. I calculated the total from the Internet versions of the *Code of Federal Regulations*, accessed on September 9, 2008. I am unaware of a corresponding page count for the *Federal Register* since they simply accumulate over time. It would, I suspect, total many thousands if anyone undertook to count them.

10. Robert Glicksman and George Cameron Coggins, *Modern Public Land Law in a Nutshell* (St. Paul, MN: Thomson-West, 2006), 84.

11. Bill Supulski, "Forest Service Update: Status of Roadless Rule," briefing paper, Forest Service, Washington, D.C., October 23, 2009, available at www.fsx.org/

pdf/2009-10-23_roadless_update.pdf (accessed September 15, 2010). Copy on file
with the author. The 58.5 million roadless inventory acreage is 31 percent of the FS
land base and 2 percent of the U.S. land base.

12. Robert Glicksman, "Traveling in Opposite Directions: Roadless Area Management under the Clinton and Bush Administrations," *Environmental Law* 34 (2004): 6.

13. Pamela Baldwin, *The National Forest System Roadless Area Initiative—Update
of May 18* (Washington, D.C.: Congressional Research Service, 2001), CRS Report
RL30647.

14. *Federal Register* 66, no. 9 (January 12, 2001): 3244.

15. I recall standing with a BLM manager in southern Arizona near the Mexican
border while he explained that it took him the better part of a year to do all the NEPA
work required to reduce hazardous fuels on a tract of less than 50 acres.

16. *Federal Register* 66, no. 9 (January 12, 2001): 3244.

17. *Federal Register* 66, no. 9 (January 12, 2001): 3250.

18. Baldwin, *Roadless Area Initiative,* 6.

19. *Federal Register* 66, no. 9 (January 12, 2001): 3246.

20. *Federal Register* 66, no. 9 (January 12, 2001): 3253.

21. *Federal Register* 66, no. 9 (January 12, 2001): 3249.

22. *Federal Register* 66, no. 9 (January 12, 2001): 3249.

23. The sixty-day delay in implementation occurred because it was a major rule
and subject to provisions of the *Congressional Review Act*, Public Law 104-121, 5
U.S.C. §§ 801 *et seq.*

24. Baldwin, *Roadless Area Initiative,* 8.

25. *Federal Register* 66, no. 132 (July 10, 2001): 35919.

26. *Federal Register* 66, no. 132 (July 10, 2001): 35918–20. In brief, the FS sought
input on the following questions: What is the appropriate role of local forest planning? What is the best way to work with states, tribes, local communities, and individuals? How should inventoried roadless areas be managed to provide for healthy
forests? How should communities and private property near inventoried roadless
areas be protected from natural events that may occur on adjacent federal lands?
What is the best way to implement the laws ensuring states, tribes, organizations,
and citizens have reasonable access to their property? What are the characteristics,
environmental values, social and economic considerations that should be considered
in evaluation roadless areas? What specific activities should be expressly prohibited or
allowed for roadless areas when in forest plans or amendments? Should inventoried
roadless areas selected for future protection though local forest plan revisions be
proposed to Congress for wilderness status or managed under the forest plan? How
can the FS work effectively with interests having strongly competing views? They also
had a "miscellaneous" category inviting input on any item of the respondent's choice.

27. Russ Gorte et al., *Federal Lands Managed by the Bureau of Land Management
(BLM) and the Forest Service (FS): Issues for the 110th Congress—Update of May 9*
(Washington, D.C.: Congressional Research Service, 2008), 18. Also see: Forest Ser-
vice, *Roadless Rule Timeline—2005,* available at www.fs.usda.gov/Internet/FSE_DOC-
UMENTS/stelprdb5057688.pdf (accessed September 15, 2010).

28. Gorte, *Federal Lands Managed by the Bureau of Land Management,* 18.

29. Gorte, *Federal Lands Managed by the Bureau of Land Management*, 18.

30. *Federal Register* 70, no. 92 (May 13, 2005): 25653–62.

31. *Federal Register* 70, no. 92 (May 13, 2005): 25653.

32. *Federal Register* 70, no. 92 (May 13, 2005): 25661.

33. For example, 24 million of the 58.5 million inventoried roadless acres were off-limits to road construction under forest plans in effect in 2000. See *Federal Register* 70, no. 92 (May 13, 2005): 25659.

34. U.S. Department of Agriculture, "USDA Accepts First Three State Petitions for Conserving Roadless Areas in National Forests," press release 0212.06, Washington, D.C., June 21, 2006.

35. *California v. U.S. Department of Agriculture*, 459 F. Supp. 2d 874 (N.D. Cal. 2006).

36. *California v. U.S. Department of Agriculture*, 575 F.3d 999 (9th Cir. 2009). See Monica Voicu, "At a Dead End: Need for Congressional Direction in the Roadless Area Management Debate," *Ecology Law Quarterly* 37 (2010): 478–524. Also see Kristina Alexander and Ross Gorte, *National Forest System Roadless Area Initiatives* (Washington, D.C.: Congressional Research Service, 2009), CRS Report RL30647, and Kristina Alexander and Ross Gorte, *National Forest System (NFS) Roadless Area Initiatives* (Washington, D.C.: Congressional Research Service, 2011).

37. *Wyoming v. U.S. Department of Agriculture*, 570 F. Supp. 2d at 1352. As quoted in Alexander and Gorte, *National Forest System Roadless Area Initiatives* (2009), 16.

38. *State of Wyoming v. the United States Department of Agriculture*, nos. 08-8061 and 09-8075, quote at 19.

39. U.S. Department of Agriculture, Office of the Secretary, *Secretary's Memorandum 1042–154*, May 28, 2009. The memorandum is reauthorized each year: see U.S. Department of Agriculture, "Agriculture Secretary Vilsack Renews Interim Directive Covering Roadless Areas in National Forests," press release no. 0223.11, May 31, 2011.

40. Robert Keiter, *Keeping Faith with Nature* (New Haven, CT: Yale University Press, 2003), 34.

41. Jeanne Nienable Clarke and Kurt Angerbach, "The Federal Four: Change and Continuity in the Bureau of Land Management, Fish and Wildlife Service, Forest Service, and National Park Service, 1970–2000," pp. 35–54 in *Western Public Lands and Environmental Politics*, 2nd ed., ed. Charles Davis (Boulder, CO: Westview Press, 2001), quote at 47.

42. The judge acted in a suit brought by the Miccosukee Tribe, who live in the Everglades and describe the project as an "environmental bridge to nowhere." The $212 million bridge is intended to increase water flow in the Everglades National Park. According to the article, no one took credit for inserting the language into the bill.

43. *Winter v. Natural Res. Def. Council, Inc.*, 518 F.3d 658, 703 (9th Cir.), 129 S. Ct. 365. (2008). Justice Roberts wrote for the majority, which included Justices Scalia, Kennedy, Thomas, and Alito, with Justices Breyer and Stevens concurring in part and dissenting in part and Justices Ginsburg and Souter dissenting.

44. 129 S. Ct. 365, quote at 2 in the Court's Slip Opinion, available at www.supremecourt.gov/opinions/08pdf/07-1239.pdf (accessed September 16, 2010).

45. The 1990 report of the Intergovernmental Committee of Scientists: see the discussion of spotted owls in the next section. George Hoberg, *Science, Politics, and*

U.S. Forest Law: The Battle over the Forest Service Planning Rule (Washington, D.C.: Resources for the Future, 2003), discussion paper 03-19.

46. Hoberg, *Science, Politics, and U.S. Forest Law,* 12.

47. The Ninth Circuit hears cases from Alaska, Arizona, California, Hawaii, Idaho, Montana, Nevada, Oregon, and Washington.

48. *Lands Council v. McNair (Lands Council II),* 537 F.3d 981 (9th Cir. 2008) (en banc).

49. The en banc panel consisted of eleven members of the Ninth Circuit. It vacated *Ecology Center, Inc. v. Austin,* 430 F.3d 1057 (9th Cir. 2005), which had provided the jurisprudence for judges substituting their judgments for those of agency experts, and reversed the decision of the three-judge appellate panel that had reversed the trial court's denial of a preliminary injunction to halt the Mission Brush Project. The *Lands Council* is a collective term for two organizations, the Lands Council and the Wild West Institute, while Ranotta McNair is the Idaho Panhandle National Forest Supervisor (the national forest in which the challenged project is located).

50. The opinion in *Lands Council II* is available at www.ca9.uscourts.gov/datastore/opinions/2008/07/02/0735000.pdf (accessed September 16, 2010). The page references in the endnotes reflect the pagination on that website. *Lands Council II,* 8244.

51. *Lands Council II,* 8254.

52. *Lands Council II,* 8265.

53. *Lands Council II,* 8274.

54. *Lands Council II,* 8274.

55. *Endangered Species Act,* Public Law 93-205. 16 U.S.C. § 1532.

56. 16 U.S.C. § 1532(5)(A).

57. U.S. Fish and Wildlife Service, "Endangered and Threatened Wildlife and Plants; Determination of Critical Habitat for the Northern Spotted Owl," *Federal Register* 57, no. 10 (January 15, 1992): 1796.

58. R. J. Gutierrez and George Barrowclough, "Redefining the Distributional Boundaries of the Northern and California Spotted Owls: Implications for Conservation," *The Condor* 107 (2005): 182–87, quote at 182, references omitted. For a detailed examination of the differing values and their interplay in the policy arena regarding spotted owls and their habitat, see Alston Chase, *In a Dark Wood: The Fight over Forests and the Tyranny of Ecology* (Boston: Houghton Mifflin, 1995).

59. The issue has always been far more complex than the logging versus owls issue, although timber harvesting was certainly a major factor in the decline of spotted owl numbers and its cessation within critical habitat areas was called for by many scientists.

60. The Forest History Society has a very useful website containing multiple documents on the northern spotted owl as well as a detailed timeline, available at http://foresthistory.org/ASPNET/Policy/northern_spotted_owl/timeline.aspx (accessed September 16, 2010). Also see the timeline in Bruce G. Marcot and Jack Ward Thomas, *Of Spotted Owls, Old Growth and New Policies: A History since the Interagency Scientific Committee Report,* Forest Service, Pacific Northwest Research Station, General Technical Report PNW-GTR-408, 1997, table 1. Federal lands contain over 90 percent of northern spotted owl habitat with the greatest concentration being in national forests (>70 percent), the BLM (>10 percent) and the NPS (<10 percent). See *ISC Report,* cited in note 62, pages 14–15.

61. See, generally, Katharine Hammond, Liana Reilly, and Heidi Binko, eds., "The Northwest Forest Plan Revisited," *Yale Forest Forum Review* 5 (2002).

62. Public Law 101–121, § 318. J. W. Thomas et al., *A Conservation Strategy for the Northern Spotted Owl: A Report of the Interagency Scientific Committee to Address the Conservation of the Northern Spotted Owl* (Portland, OR: U.S. Department of Agriculture Forest Service; U.S. Department of the Interior, Bureau of Land Management, Fish and Wildlife Service, and National Park Service, 1990).

63. Norman Johnson et al., *Alternatives for Management of Late-Successional Forests in the Pacific Northwest,* a report to the United States House of Representatives; Committee on Agriculture, Subcommittee on Forests, Family Farms, and Energy; and the Committee on Merchant Marine and Fisheries, Subcommittee on Fisheries and Wildlife, Conservation and the Environment (Corvallis, OR: Department of Forest Resources, Oregon State University, 1991).

64. U.S. Fish and Wildlife Service, "Endangered and Threatened Wildlife and Plants; Determination of Threatened Status for the Northern Spotted Owl," *Federal Register* 55 (1990): 26114–94.

65. Fish and Wildlife Service, "Endangered and Threatened Wildlife Habitat and Plants: Determination of Critical Habitat for the Northern Spotted Owl," *Federal Register* 57, no. 10 (January 15, 1992): 1796–1838. Fish and Wildlife Service, "Draft Final Recovery Plan for the Northern Spotted Owl" (Portland, OR: U.S. Fish and Wildlife Service, 1992).

66. See Jack Ward Thomas et al., "The Northwest Forest Plan: Origins, Components, Implementation Experience, and Suggestions for Change," *Conservation Biology* 20 (2006): 277–87, and Marcot and Thomas, *Of Spotted Owls, Old Growth, and New Policies.*

67. J. W. Thomas et al., *Viability Assessments and Management Considerations for Species Associated with Late-Successional and Old-Growth Forests of the Pacific Northwest* (Portland, OR: U.S. Forest Service, 1993).

68. Marcot and Thomas, *Of Spotted Owls, Old Growth, and New Policies,* figure 1.

69. Brendon Swedlow, "Scientists, Judges, and Spotted Owls: Policymakers in the Pacific Northwest," *Duke Environmental Law and Policy Forum* 13 (2003): 187–278.

70. U.S. Fish and Wildlife Service, *Final Recovery Plan for the Northern Spotted Owl* (Portland, OR: U.S. Fish and Wildlife Service, 2008), available at www.fws.gov/ecos/ajax/docs/recovery_plan/NSO%20Final%20Rec%20Plan%20051408_1.pdf (accessed September 17, 2010). On November 24, 2008, Earthjustice, representing twelve environmental groups, asked the Federal District Court for the District of Columbia to declare the 2008 recovery plan in violation of the Administrative Procedures Act (case no. 1:08-cv-01409-EGS). The Earthjustice complaint is available at http://earthjustice.org/our_work/cases/2003/northern-spotted-owl-critical-habitat (accessed September 17, 2010).

71. Earthjustice, "Judge Orders U.S. Fish and Wildlife Service to Revise 2008 Spotted Owl Recovery Plan and Critical Habitat Designation," press release, September 2, 2010, available at http://earthjustice.org/news/press/2010/judge-orders-u-s-fish-and-wildlife-service-to-revise-2008-spotted-owl-recovery-plan-and-critical-habitat-designa (accessed September 17, 2010).

72. Categories were based on blocks of land that could protect: (1) twenty or more nesting pairs; (2) less than twenty nesting pairs; (3) blocks for individual pairs; and

(4) smaller blocks. See Thomas et al., *A Conservation Strategy for the Northern Spotted Owl*, appendix Q, table Q1.

73. The ISC describes the mapping process this way: "A map was created to represent a unique 'solution' with a specific distribution of habitat blocks of various sizes. This map was then evaluated, to the extent possible, by applying both personal judgment (using site-specific knowledge) and quantitative evaluation of specific components of the standards and guidelines (see appendix O). Any conclusions drawn from these tests that failed to confirm specific properties of the map (for example, the size or location of management areas) were used to redraw and refine the map. The new map was then similarly tested until a solution was reached that met all criteria specified in the standards and guidelines. We drafted and tested maps for at least 10 iterations using this method. Each iteration was drafted, tested, and adjusted until all map properties were confirmed or explained and the process was considered final." Thomas et al., *A Conservation Strategy for the Northern Spotted Owl*, 13.

74. Thomas et al., *A Conservation Strategy for the Northern Spotted Owl*, appendix Q, especially table Q7.

75. Hammond, Reilly, and Binko, "The Northwest Forest Plan Revisited," 14.

76. U.S. Fish and Wildlife Service, "Determination of Critical Habitat for the Northern Spotted Owl," *Federal Register* 57 (1992):1796–1838, quote on 1810.

77. U.S. Fish and Wildlife Service, "Determination of Critical Habitat for the Northern Spotted Owl," table 3, and Thomas et al., *A Conservation Strategy for the Northern Spotted Owl*, table Q7.

78. *Federal Water Pollution Control Act Amendments of 1972*, commonly termed the *Clean Water Act of 1972*, Public Law 921500, 33 U.S.C. §§ 1251–1387 (2000), quote at § 1251. I must note that the phrase "chemical, physical, and biological integrity" lacks scientific meaning or measure; it is purely a political statement.

79. 33. U.S.C. § 1362 (7).

80. *Rapanos et ux. v. United States*, 547 U.S. 715 (2006). The Supreme Court has addressed the geographic reach of section 404 of the CWA in three cases, of which *Rapanos* is the most recent. *United States v. Riverside Bayview Homes, Inc.* (474 U.S. 121 [1985]) was the first, followed by *Solid Waste Agency of Northern Cook County v. United States Army Corps of Engineers* (531 U.S. 159 [2001]). The *Rapanos* decision is sometimes described as 4-1-4. Justice Scalia wrote what is labeled the "plurality opinion"; it was joined by Justices Alito, Thomas, and Roberts, hence the first "4." The plurality argued for overturning the lower court's decision and to remand the case back to the court using guidance from the Supreme Court's findings. They used a plain reading of the statute to conclude that the Corps had badly overreached its authority. Justice Kennedy agreed with the remand, but did not agree with the plurality's stricter interpretation of the CWA with respect to its spatial reach. Kennedy's opinion is the "1." The second "4" comprises the dissent authored by Justice Stevens and joined by Justices Souter, Ginsburg, and Breyer. The dissenters deferred to agency expertise and accepted the Corps' expansive geographic interpretation of its jurisdiction.

81. Jamison Colburn, "Waters of the United States: Theory, Practice, and Integrity at the Supreme Court," *Florida State University Law Review* 33 (2007): 8.

82. The Corps' initial interpretation of "waters of the United States" held to the traditional view. In *Natural Resources Defense Council v. Callaway* (392 F. Supp. 685, Washington, D.C., 1975), however, the U.S. Court for the District of Columbia ruled this too narrow a view and so launched the processes that increasingly decoupled the law from the landscape.

83. The *U.S. Army Corps of Engineers Wetlands Delineation Manual*, Wetlands Research Program Technical Report Y-87-1, U.S. Army Corps of Engineers Waterways Experiment Station (Vicksburg, MS: Wetlands Regulation Center 1987), available at www.wetlands.com/regs/tlpge02e.htm (accessed November 28, 2011), guides the placing of lines indicating the beginning or ending of a statutory wetland on the ground. On page 9, the manual defines wetlands as "those areas that are inundated or saturated by surface or ground water at a frequency and duration sufficient to support, and that under normal circumstances do support, a prevalence of vegetation typically adapted for life in saturated soil conditions. Wetlands generally include swamps, marshes, bogs, and similar areas." The Corps defines a nonwetland as "any area that has sufficiently dry conditions that indicators of hydrophytic vegetation, hydric soils, and/or wetland hydrology are lacking. As used in this manual, any area that is neither a wetland, a deepwater aquatic habitat, nor other special aquatic site" (appendix A). In 2004 the General Accounting Office (now the Government Accountability Office [GAO]) issued a report highlighting the confusion within the Corps of Engineers (COE) itself regarding the identification of wetlands; see GAO, "Waters and Wetlands: Corps of Engineers Needs to Evaluate Its District Office Practices in Determining Jurisdiction," GAO-04-297 (Washington, D.C.: General Accounting Office, 2004), available at www.gao.gov/new.items/d04297.pdf (accessed November 28, 2011).

84. Scalia, *Rapanos*, 5. The pagination of quotes from *Rapanos* reflects that in the slip opinion, available at www.epa.gov/owow/wetlands/pdf/Rapanos_SupremeCourt .pdf (accessed September 17, 2010).

85. *Solid Waste Agency of Northern Cook County v. U.S. Army Corps of Engineers* (SWANCC), 531 U.S. 159 (2001).

86. Scalia, *Rapanos*, 3.

87. Scalia, *Rapanos*, 15.

88. Stevens, *Rapanos*, 2, of dissent.

89. *Natural Resources Defense Council v. Calloway*, 392 F. Supp. 685 (D. D.C. 1975). The courts have issued a variety of opinions regarding wetlands, some holding that the Corps has a wide sway and others being far more restrictive.

4

Toward Cutting the Gordian Knot

The significant problems we have cannot be solved at the same level of thinking with which we created them.

—Albert Einstein

IN THIS CHAPTER I BRIEFLY EVALUATE PREVIOUS SUGGESTIONS for reform offered by other observers, describe and discuss seven specific recommendations for congressional action, point out where Congress has recently taken hesitant steps in the directions I suggest, and make a specific recommendation for management action by the president.

By and large, Congress created the Gordian Knot. Over the years, Congress badly mishandled its responsibilities for providing a coherent legislative basis for managing our public lands. It did so by passing well-intended but poorly thought out and poorly written legislation. It blurred the distinction between multiple-use lands and conservation lands. It punted difficult decisions to the courts and federal land managers, with often unexpected and detrimental results. The courts, for example, drove the NEPA's analytic requirements to depths and details Congress never envisioned. During legislative debate, the NEPA supporter Senator Scoop Jackson was asked on the floor of the Senate how long an environmental impact statement would be. He responded no more than "ten pages." Twenty years later, a wag is said to have claimed that was a misquote, that Jackson must have actually said "ten pounds."[1] When members passed the Endangered Species Act in 1973 they had in mind protecting bald eagles and grizzly bears, not obscure plants and rodents. Had they known how their work would be interpreted by the courts and used as a tool to thwart human use of the land, the act would never have passed.[2] The bulk of the burden for cutting the Gordian Knot falls upon Congress.

Evaluating Previous Reform Proposals

In the introduction I sketched a variety of suggestions to improve federal land management that encompass a wide array of approaches, including divestiture, bureaucratic reorganization, shifting management emphasis to protection of ecosystems and the environment, reshaping land law or amending the constitution, and altering funding sources. Some of these ideas contain useful components that others do not. I look at each approach in turn.

One category of proposals would resolve the federal land-management problem by ridding the federal government of federal lands in whole or in significant part. Adherents of this general view argue that the lands managed by federal agencies suffer from unnecessary environmental degradation and from fiscally irresponsible management. They posit that shifting control of land to various mixes of state, regional, and private-sector entities would result in improved environmental quality and more rational allocation of resources chiefly by employing market forces in land-use decision-making. It would end an outdated federal paternalism toward a fully mature West. I agree that improving environmental quality and management efficiency as well as moving decision-making closer to people most impacted by land management are laudable goals. As I explain in the following paragraphs, however, I find the idea of the national divesture of public lands a poor approach to achieving them.

Would private ownership improve environmental quality? I have serious doubts. First is the problem of fragmentation of the landscape for management proposes. Private ownership would replace current comprehensive planning and management actions coordinated over very large swaths of the landscape with thousands of separate, uncoordinated, and ad hoc geographically limited measures to the detriment of a host of large-scale land-management tasks such as wildland firefighting and habitat management. A second doubt concerns money. Fighting fires, managing habitat, controlling erosion and invasive species, and many other land-management activities are expensive, to say nothing of the cost of supporting pertinent research. For fiscal year 2010 alone, for example, Congress appropriated some $11.1 billion to operate the four federal land-management agencies.[3] The private sector is unlikely to commit a comparable level of funding to land management in part because the commitment would not necessarily yield a significant financial reward. A third area of concern centers on the degree to which private owners are committed to, or capable of, sound stewardship. While many private landowners practice excellent stewardship, others do not for a variety of reasons, such as lack of understanding or desire, short-term thinking about the land, or insufficient resources. Finally there is the matter of accountability. Federal land managers are responsible to departmental officials, regulatory agencies, Congress, and the public for their management of our 627 million acres of federal land. All manner of governmental and nongovernmental interests inspect the managers' work regarding environmental quality. With a transfer of ownership to the private sector, most of this oversight ends or becomes far less influential in future land-management decisions. In view of the foregoing, I cannot see how divestiture of federal lands to private owners would improve the lands' environmental quality; indeed I submit that just the opposite would occur.

What about the proposition that private ownership would lead to more rational decision-making? This idea leans heavily on the thought that market forces would drive private-sector decision-making. In most cases private landowners would primarily react to market signals when determining how to use their newly acquired land.[4] Profit maximization and practicability would be the principal drivers in land management and in some sense that can be described as more rational decision-making since the process is clear and the measures quantifiable. Under this approach, however, multiple use gives way to profit-driven land use, which would eliminate those activities not yielding sufficient financial return regardless of their overall desirability. Many users of what are now public lands would find themselves shut out or shut off as the new private-sector owners decided their favored activities did not yield sufficient revenue and would not be permitted. Private ownership would be accomplished to the detriment of the public interest in balanced land management that seeks to assure accommodation of multiple interests.[5]

Does state ownership avoid the flaws associated with private ownership? In part, yes. Certainly it would lessen issues associated with management fragmentation of the landscape. In general, state management would reflect the desires of the citizens to a far greater degree than would private-sector ownership. In some cases, however, the power of particular special interests would be magnified at the expense of other legitimate land-management possibilities and the views of an unorganized public. Given their influence in California politics, for example, one can easily envision environmental organizations successfully pushing state managers to exclude or significantly restrict (beyond current practice) logging, grazing, and extractive uses as well as recreational activities on former federal lands throughout the state to achieve their land-management goal of protecting nature from human impacts.[6] In states where political power is more evenly distributed among competing special interests, disparate influence would be less of a problem.[7] Under these circumstances balanced land-use decisions would be far more likely to occur than under private-sector ownership.

What about states possessing the interest and capital needed to provide for good stewardship? States have the interest; they do not have the capital. At the end of the first decade of the twenty-first century, public land states in the West are running large deficits. They are cutting expenditures for basic services and programs and laying off state workers. In this fiscal climate, natural-resource management cannot hope to successfully compete for limited state monies. Education, police, and social services, for example, are among those state-funded activities having superior claims on state dollars. One might argue that upon assuming management responsibility the monies that now flow to the federal treasury would come to the states instead, and indeed they would, but the amounts involved vary dramatically by state.[8] Like all revenues, other program areas would make claims on these monies and, as I just noted, many would have a higher priority than natural-resource management. The likely outcome of state ownership is a reduction of resources available for land-use management to the detriment of good stewardship.

Despite the flaws with the divestiture of federal land, giving a greater voice in federal land management to people most impacted by land-use decisions is long overdue. Kootenai National Forest, for example, surrounds the town of Libby, Montana. Management decisions on the forest impact its residents every day while having no observable effect on someone in Boston or Memphis or Los Angeles. Residents of states, counties, and local communities where federal lands dominate the landscape have far more at stake environmentally, economically, and socially in their management than do people living where such lands are far away. Management should reflect that truth by giving more weight to the views of those most affected. Transferring public lands to states or regional entities is a way of doing that, but not the best way.

Eliminating federal ownership in favor of regional bodies, as Kemmis suggests, falls short of good public policy because it stills the voices of those beyond the region. The BLM manages much of the land in northern Nevada, where one finds the town of Winnemucca. While the views of the town residents should carry more weight than those of New Yorkers, the thoughts of New Yorkers should nonetheless be considered. Federal management offers the best opportunity to provide for broad societal input. The trick lies in developing a mechanism to elevate the role of those most directly affected by land-use decisions without completely shutting out the views of people with less at stake. Federal ownership offers the best avenue to achieve that end because only it provides a means for the inculcation of views from across the country.

Finally, for me, our public lands are part of our national inheritance—the natural resource equivalent of the Declaration of Independence and the Constitution; divestiture would diminish the nation.

A second approach to reform emphasizes a revised suite of management organizations and redistribution on federal lands among them. I fundamentally agree with this view because successful restructuring would simplify management, resulting in improved stewardship and management efficiency. Change, however, must avoid the arcane. Recall from the introduction that O'Toole proposed a complex, trust-based management scheme that does not pass the simplification test. O'Toole would establish market and nonmarket trusts to comanage federal lands in place of the traditional bureaus and thus create a Byzantine management structure. He introduces new pathways to conflict by adding additional land-management goals and by creating new entities able to bring suit over management actions they oppose. Further, he seeks to build a management foundation based in part on nebulous ideas coming from the errant view that ecosystems are valid land-management units. The Knot tightens.

In the introduction I also noted that Fairfax and Nelson each propose major reorganization of existing land-management bureaus. Nelson would eliminate the Forest Service and the Bureau of Land Management and dispose of about 80 percent of current federal lands. The National Park Service and Fish and Wildlife Service would manage the remaining federal estate. As I explained in the preceding paragraphs, I believe transfer of federal lands to nonfederal entities is inappropriate. Fairfax would eliminate all the existing bureaus in favor of a new entity modeled after the BLM because of its record of cooperation with state and local officials. The new organization would focus on providing outdoor recreation. I concur with Fairfax on the need for federal agencies to work in close partnership with state, tribal, and local officials, and that provision of outdoor recreation plays a more prominent role today than in times past. I do not agree, however, that recreation should become the focus of federal land management. In chapter 1, I discuss the multiple benefits society obtains from federal lands, many of which lie outside the realm of recreation. A recreation-based management mandate for a single new federal land-management agency would lessen the ability of society to capture all that the lands may provide.

A third category of ideas on reforming federal land management involves protecting ecosystems as landscape units or "the environment" writ large. These suggestions would take us in a variety of wrong directions. For their part, ecosystems are but geographical and ecological fictions lacking intrinsic characteristics of any kind and thus they offer us neither anything concrete to manage nor any coherent standards by which we could judge management effectiveness.[9] Conversely, environment encompasses everything on the landscape and it is well beyond human capabilities to manage everything on our federal lands.

Consider the following reform ideas centered on ecosystem and environmental protection I presented in the introduction. Keiter would make ecosystem health and the prevention of ecosystem impairment the cornerstone of public land management. He calls for protection and restoration of species diversity on an ecosystem basis. Gildor wants to amend the Constitution to "preserve, protect, and promote the environment," while Schmaltz seeks a constitutional guarantee of "the right of citizens . . . to the continuing integrity, diversity, and viability of the environment and existing ecosystems." Such language would lead to land-management chaos. I look first at ecosystem protection and then at environmental protection as cornerstones of federal land management.

When determining the validity of government actions, the courts routinely determine if the action in question is arbitrary or capricious. If so, the court overturns it. Because everything about ecosystems is fundamentally arbitrary and capricious, how can the courts rationally determine if government actions to protect ecosystems as landscape units are justifiable? Keiter's ecosystem health and nonimpairment standards have no objective measures. For some people, human manipulation of the environment via logging, dam-building, or many other activities diminishes ecosystem health yet the disturbed ecosystem provides home and habitat for many species previously unable to occupy the now-altered space. So is it really "unhealthy" or just presently configured in a way someone dislikes? On the matter of impairment, one person's impaired ecosystem is another's golf course. Ecosystem health and impairment lie in the eye of the beholder. How is the court to judge?

Continuing, Schmaltz wishes to protect the "integrity, diversity, and viability of the environment and existing ecosystems." There are no such things as "existing ecosystems" as actual entities on the landscape whose "integrity, diversity, and viability" the law or management can protect. The supposed characteristics of integrity, diversity, and viability are entirely subjective notions. Ecologists and other scholars cannot objectively say what constitutes a viable ecosystem. They cannot say when a supposed ecosystem became itself or how much change must occur before it turns into a different ecosystem. What, then, is the meaning of *viability*? Even if we could make such a determination, there is no scientific basis for keeping the old ecosystem in preference to that which replaced it. *Viability* has no substantive meaning and neither does *ecosystem integrity* or *diversity*. How is the court to judge?

If ecosystem protection cannot pass the arbitrary and capricious test, what about "the environment," since it certainly exists? The difficulty here lies in a different direction but the questions of arbitrariness and capriciousness still arise. With ecosystems, the management subject lacks tangible substance and the judicial question lacks a port from which to begin an inquiry. With the environment, the manager has real things to manage—soil, species habitat, plants, animals, and so forth—but the court is nearly as far out at sea as before. The problems here are priorities and impact of management actions on nontargeted environmental components.

How does a land manager protect everything in the landscape? Any action a manager takes to shield one component of the environment will *always* adversely impact something else. Vegetation management, for example, favors newly welcomed species at the expense of those it seeks to displace. Given this reality, should there be a hierarchy of environmental components to be protected? Is soil more important than water? Is preventing erosion more important than avoiding the introduction of nonnative plants that may be the most effective in doing so? Given that the environment constantly changes, what are managers supposed to protect the environment from? Should they treat change caused by natural processes differently than those of human origin? Why or why not? By now you can create your own list of questions that managers and the courts could face; it takes little imagination to generate one of substantial length.

With protection of "the environment," as with ecosystem protection, the courts have no basis for making decisions. Everything cannot be of equal importance, but the courts are ill equipped to prioritize environmental components for protection purposes or to assess tradeoffs. Yet under these reform proposals, they will be asked to do so. I can only conclude that proposals elevating the protection of ecosystems or the environment to the top of the federal land-management legal pyramid would drastically magnify the size and complexity of the Gordian Knot rather than cut through it.

What about the ideas of Freyfogle and Schlickeisen I presented in the introduction? Freyfogle would solve the problem by dissolving the dichotomy between public and private land and replace it with collective land management for the nation. The predictable results of such moves to collectivism are an expansion of rules, regulations, administrative processes, litigation, and general confusion, as it would overturn two centuries of public and private property law. For his part, Schlickeisen sees all "living natural resources" as the "common property of all people" and wants the Constitution to assure that they are "conserved and maintained for the benefit of all the people." It takes little imagination to anticipate the land-management pandemonium resulting from these two approaches. I find no redeeming qualities in these ideas.

Another proposed way of reforming federal land management looks through the lens of funding. Fretwell sees the congressional appropriations process as hamstringing sound federal land management by conditioning funding on the provision of constituent services at the expense of scientific management. She suggests various means to fund land management, at least in part, outside the appropriations process to give land managers greater independence. Encouraging managers to obtain funds other than via congressional appropriations makes a good deal of fiscal sense, especially if managers are free to apply them to locally agreed-upon priorities. Presently, the NPS applies entrance fees paid at individual parks to funding-deferred maintenance projects not covered by congressional appropriations. Moreover, fees and excise taxes collected from hunters and fishermen when they buy everything from fishing lures to shotgun shells is funneled back into wildlife-management programs. Congress would continue, however, to use the appropriations process as one tool to direct policy and land-management actions regardless of the amounts they provide. Moreover, funding diversity would not resolve the conflicting policies and unclear congressional intent that lie at the heart of the Gordian Knot.

The Way Forward

How does the public want its lands managed? In chapter 2, I show that public attitudes regarding federal land management are complex, changing through time and circumstance, and containing multiple viewpoints depending on an individual's personal preferences and situation. Overall, however, I posit that the general public seeks balance and accommodation among the many values and benefits it associates with (and derives from) public lands. Irrespective of one's leanings regarding the appropriate weighting of various kinds of land uses—be it wilderness, logging, recreation, energy and mineral production, wildlife habitat, scenic preservation, watershed protection, or grazing—I am persuaded that most Americans would agree that management should be efficient, effective, transparent, and done with a substantial amount of public input. So what to do? Since Congress created the Gordian Knot, the solution lies there.

Congress should:

1. Reaffirm the fundamental public land-management categories of multiple use on the one hand and protected areas on the other and clarify management priorities and dominant uses on lands in those two categories. In particular, it should clarify that multiple-use lands remain available for a wide variety of human uses and not be allowed to morph into de facto protected lands. As a corollary, it should cease the practice

of geographically overlapping management designations such as having Yosemite Valley being managed as part of a national park as well as part of the wild and scenic river system.

2. Review judicial interpretations of existing law to see if they accurately reflect contemporary congressional intent and priorities and make changes as needed.

3. Examine the validity of decades-old laws because in many cases the underlying science has been eclipsed by new findings, and, as a corollary, determine if old laws are capable of addressing new issues like climate change or, in the alternative, do new issues require new legislation.

4. Reduce the role of the federal courts in public land management. Implementation of the three recommendations above will achieve part of this much-needed reform. Additional tasks include eliminating excessive opportunities for judicial appeal of publicly approved plans via a bonding requirement and establishing a high bar regarding judicial deference to agency expertise.

5. Abolish the Forest Service and redistribute the land it presently manages among the BLM (multiple-use lands), the FWS (high-value wildlife habitat), and the NPS (wilderness and other protected lands). As a corollary, Congress should consider taking advantage of the considerable land-management expertise within many tribes by enabling them to become off-reservation land managers of public lands.

6. Establish a management mechanism giving greater weight to local and regional voices in land-management decision-making.

7. Create a new public land law review commission to address these six action areas and make recommendations to Congress that require an up or down vote.

Turning to the executive branch, the president should end the involvement of the Office of Management and Budget in land-management activities. I consider each action area in turn.

Reaffirm Management Categories and Clarify Priorities

The fundamental distinction between protected or special-use lands and multiple-use lands began at the end of the 1800s. The "protected" category rests on the determination that particular characteristics of a landscape are so outstanding that their conservation must trump other uses. It began with the national parks and emphasized protection of the special attributes for human benefit. Congress established Yellowstone National Park in 1872. The year 1890 saw establishment of Yosemite, Sequoia, and General Grant (later incorporated into Kings Canyon) national parks, and Mt. Rainier became a park in 1899. The act creating Yellowstone set the land "apart as a public park or pleasuring-ground for the benefit and enjoyment of the people" and called for management that "shall provide for the preservation, from injury or spoliation, of all timber, mineral deposits, natural curiosities, or wonders within said park" while permitting the construction of roads and visitor accommodations.[10] By 1916 Congress had established a dozen national parks and determined that a single agency was needed for their management and so created the National Park Service. The NPS Organic Act called for the new organization to "promote and regulate the use" of these areas to fulfill their purpose, which the act defined as "to conserve the scenery and the natural and historic objects and the wild life therein and to provide for the enjoyment of the same in such manner and by such means as will leave them unimpaired for the enjoyment of future generations."[11] The law gives the secretary of the interior wide latitude to actively manage the parks to provide for visitor use tempered by the need to conserve the natural resources that gave rise to the area's being designated a national park in the first place.

In 1964 Congress added a new dimension to the "protected area" category. In passing the Wilderness Act, it declared that portions of the landscape were worthy of protection simply because the works of humans were not visible.[12] The act was to "secure for the American people of present and future generations the benefits of an enduring resource of wilderness." It followed language in the NPS Organic Act by calling for their management "for the use and enjoyment of the American people in such manner as will leave them unimpaired for future use as wilderness." Unlike the NPS Organic Act, however, the Wilderness Act drastically restricts human use in order to protect essential wilderness characteristics. Subsequently, Congress placed most of the land in the western national parks into the national wilderness system, thereby moving such land beyond the use and enjoyment (at least through direct interaction and experience) of the overwhelming majority of park visitors.[13] From a land-management perspective, Congress elevated nature protection above human use and enjoyment of natural landscape elements for most national park land.

On the other hand, the multiple-use idea recognizes that the land contains numerous attributes beneficial to society and that there is value in obtaining as many as is reasonable. In 1891, Congress passed the Forest Reserve Act authorizing the president to establish forest reserves on public land. The Organic Act of 1897 provided the first congressional management guidance for the reserves. Public forests were to be established to "improve and protect the forest" or "for the purpose of securing favorable conditions of water flows, and to furnish a continuous supply of timber for the use and necessities of the citizens of the United States."[14] Sixty years later the Multiple-Use Sustained-Yield Act (MUSYA) of 1960 declared that the national forests (as they were now called) "shall be administered for outdoor recreation, range, timber, watershed, and wildlife and fish purposes" and management was to continue providing for mineral use.[15] Multiple use and sustained yield of renewable resources were to guide management and the act defined each term.

> Multiple use means: The management of all the various renewable surface resources of the national forests so that they are utilized in the combination that will best meet the needs of the American people; making the most judicious use of the land for some or all of these resources or related services over areas large enough to provide sufficient latitude for periodic adjustments in use to conform to changing needs and conditions; that some land will be used for less than all of the resources; and harmonious and coordinated management of the various resources, each with the other, without impairment of the productivity of the land, with consideration being given to the relative values of the various resources, and not necessarily the combination of uses that will give the greatest dollar return or the greatest unit output.
>
> Sustained yield of the several products and services means the achievement and maintenance in perpetuity of a high-level annual or regular periodic output of the various renewable resources of the national forests without impairment of the productivity of the land.

The MUSYA specifically acknowledges that "the establishment and maintenance of areas of wilderness are consistent with the purposes and provisions of this Act." Multiple use and sustained yield has always been predicated upon wise use and good stewardship.

Congress reaffirmed the importance of multiple use and sustained yield in the Federal Land Policy and Management Act (FLPMA) of 1976, which codified the concepts as the basis for administration of Bureau of Land Management lands.[16] It called for:

> The public lands be managed in manner that will protect the quality of scientific, scenic, historical, ecological, environmental, air and atmospheric, water resource, and archeological values; that, where appropriate, will preserve and protect certain public lands in their natural condition; that will provide food and habitat for fish and wildlife and domestic animals; and that will provide for outdoor recreation and human occupancy and use.

It goes on to require that "the public lands be managed in a manner which recognizes the Nation's need for domestic sources of minerals, food, timber, and fiber from the public lands." The FLPMA adopts the definitions of multiple use and sustained yield spelled out in the MUSYA with some adjustments. Whereas the MUSYA speaks of renewable resources, the FLPMA adds consideration of nonrenewable resources and appends the modifier "permanent" to the MUSYA's requirements to prevent resource impairment. As a practical matter, the MUSYA and the FLPMA combine to create virtually identical multiple-use and sustained-yield management mandates for the BLM and the FS.

But the protection principle is evident in the FLPMA too, and it confounds good management by conflating management categories. Congress acknowledged that BLM lands contain areas (other than wilderness) whose attributes are such that particular management attention must be given to their protection. The FLPMA established "areas of critical environmental concern" containing "important historic, cultural, or scenic values, fish and wildlife resources or other natural systems or processes" requiring protection from irreparable damage. Congress continued this pattern in the Omnibus Public Lands Act of 2009 when it codified the National Landscape Conservation System in the BLM and added over 1.2 million acres to various conservation management categories, bringing the total to some 27 million acres of BLM lands.[17] Thus, under the overall umbrella of multiple use and sustained yield, there exists a subset of management directives closer to the protected area category best associated with the NPS and, to a slightly lesser degree, the Fish and Wildlife Service. How does this mixed message facilitate good management? This mixing of the two mandates further complicates the Gordian Knot. The straightforward solution is for Congress to shift management responsibility for wilderness and other specially protected areas from the BLM to the NPS.

Meanwhile, Congress continues to chip away at the universe of lands available for multiple use and sustained yield without any apparent understanding of the overall land-management implications of doing so.[18] The Omnibus Public Lands Management Act of 2009, for example, placed an additional 1.5 million acres of BLM and FS land into the national wilderness system. As I describe in chapter 1, the federal lands provide Americans with a wide range of benefits. Some of these accrue only from protected lands; others come only from multiple-use lands; neither category offers society a full range of benefits, so it is essential that Congress should reaffirm the traditional multiple-use/protected-area duality and clarify management priorities within each of them.

Part of management clarification should include dispensing with multiple designations for the same tract of land. The idea that land should be managed for multiple use *but . . .* , or that a place should be managed as a national park *but . . .* , needlessly gets in the way of efficiency and effectiveness. Overlaying multiple designations on the same land not only complicates management of supposedly multiple-use lands but also thwarts good management of already protected lands. I return to the example of Yosemite Valley first discussed in the introduction. The public receives its full measure of benefit from the land within the boundaries of Yosemite National Park by virtue of the land being in Yosemite National Park. It gains nothing when Congress places some of Yosemite's acres into additional land-management categories by, for example, designating them as wilderness or within a wild and scenic river corridor.[19] The public can, however, lose a great deal.

In 1987 Congress declared eighty-one miles of the Merced River in Yosemite National Park to be within the Wild and Scenic River System, including the portion flowing through Yosemite Valley. Yosemite Valley had long been the subject of detailed NPS management planning culminating with the widely accepted overarching Yosemite Valley Plan, issued in 2000. The Wild and Scenic Rivers Act (WSRA), however, mandates a separate comprehensive management plan for wild and scenic river corridors.[20] As I discussed in the introduction, the NPS also produced the WSRA-required Merced River Plan in 2000. In a series of court actions lasting (to date) from 2000 to 2009, the federal district court for the Eastern District of California and the 9th Circuit Court of Appeals agreed with the environmental plaintiffs that the original Merced River Plan and the revisions done to comply with court decisions violate the WSRA and the NEPA.[21] In the summer of 2009, in compliance with the court direction, the NPS began anew to gather public comments and prepare additional NEPA documentation with an expectation that a new Merced River Plan would be available in the fall of 2012.[22]

The WSRA designation resulted in an enormous waste of management resources without palpable benefits to the public or to the land. By 2012, twenty-five years will have passed since the Merced River flooded. Twenty-two years will have elapsed since the NPS published the first Merced River Plan and the Yosemite Valley Plan (whose full implementation is in suspended animation pending final approval of the Merced River Plan). Countless thousands of hours of NPS staff time have been consumed by the effort, hours that could have been far more productively spent on everything from resource management to enhancing the visitor experience. And it is a fair bet that the plaintiffs will again go to court in 2012 in order to continue their efforts to limit public visitation to the incomparable valley. By overlaying a Wild and Scenic Rivers designation on the Merced River in Yosemite Valley, Congress succeeded only in providing a route for special interests to thwart sound management of one of the nation's most outstanding natural areas at public expense. It should rescind such overlays.

Review Judicial Interpretations for
Consistency with Congressional Intent

What about judicial interpretations of laws guiding federal land management; do they reflect congressional intent and priorities? For decades, legal scholars and others have written about court decisions impacting federal land management. They produced a rich literature with no end in sight whose review is far beyond the purpose of this book. Nonetheless, a brief look at how the courts have interpreted two statutes—the NEPA and the ESA—may be worthwhile (also see the discussion of northern spotted owls, roadless areas, and wetlands in chapter 3).

The idea behind the NEPA was and remains straightforward. It requires that a "major federal action significantly affecting the quality of the human environment" be accompanied by an analysis of those impacts so they may be factored into decision-making.[23] The NEPA is a process statute, not requiring the adoption of the most environmentally benign (assuming one can be identified) alternative, but only that the effects of action be taken into account. The NEPA also includes creation of the president's Council on Environmental Quality (CEQ), which Congress directed to develop regulations implementing the act. The regulations appeared in 1978.[24] In the four decades since its enactment, the courts have adjudicated the meaning of all the operative words in the NEPA directive noted above as well as regulatory phrases like "cumulative impact" and "effects."[25] Thousands of NEPA cases have reached the federal courts, including several coming to the Supreme Court.[26] Over time, the suits have claimed that ever more analysis was required to satisfy the NEPA, leading the agencies to make NEPA documents look like data dumps in order to prevent adverse court decisions. The ten-page environmental impact statement said to have been envisioned by Senator Jackson at the NEPA's passage has morphed into NEPA document packages routinely running hundreds of pages for a given federal action. In his dissent in the 9th Circuit Court of Appeals decision in *Ecology Law Center v. Austin,* Judge McKeown observes that the court found to be inadequate an administrative record that included a more than 1,900-page Final Environmental Impact Statement, 150 detailed maps, and 20,000 pages of background information.[27] Little wonder observers point to the courts as the driving force expanding NEPA analysis beyond Congress' original intent and far beyond what is reasonable to inform responsible land-management decision-making.

The courts can reach some puzzling conclusions when agencies seek to rein in excessive analysis. Consider the 9th Circuit Court of Appeals' 2007 ruling in *Sierra Club v. Bosworth,* in which the plaintiffs sought to prevent use of a categorical exclusion to satisfy NEPA requirements before removing hazardous fuels from small tracts of public lands.[28]

CEQ regulations specify three possible levels of analysis to satisfy the NE-PA's requirements. An agency must use an environmental impact statement when it believes significant impacts are likely. When it is unsure if the impacts will be significant, it must prepare an environmental assessment to make that determination. The third option is use of a categorical exclusion (CE) to meet its NEPA responsibilities. The CEQ defines a CE in the following way:

> "Categorical exclusion" means a category of actions which do not individually or cumulatively have a significant effect on the human environment and which have been found to have no such effect in procedures adopted by a Federal agency in implementation of these regulations (Sec. 1507.3) and for which, therefore, neither an environmental assessment nor an environmental impact statement is required.[29]

The purpose of a CE is to reduce delays and costs when an agency knows from past experience that a category of projects will not significantly affect the quality of the human environment.

As part of his Healthy Forest Initiative, President Bush called for a streamlining of processes to facilitate timely removal of excess fuel from public land to reduce the damage from unwanted wildland fire. Allowing agencies to promptly fulfill the NEPA's analytic requirements was an obvious target for reducing delays. Consequently, the Forest Service and the Department of the Interior, in close consultation with the CEQ, prepared a categorical exclusion for hazardous fuels projects of limited size that met other criteria.[30] The Sierra Club sued the Forest Service (Dale Bosworth was chief of the FS at the time), arguing that the FS should have prepared at least an environmental assessment of the categorical exclusion. The district court rejected its argument but the 9th Circuit overturned that decision on appeal.

The 9th Circuit's decision in *Sierra Club v. Bosworth* is difficult to comprehend. The departments prepared the categorical exclusion at issue with the active participation and specific approval of the CEQ. The parameters of the CE flowed from a review of over 3,000 hazardous fuels projects and some 39,000 public comments. Nonetheless, the 9th Circuit threw it out. The court found that the Forest Service must at least do an environmental assessment of the categorical exclusion. In essence, the 9th Circuit ruled that it knew more about the Council of Environmental Quality's regulations than the council itself did. The ruling put the 9th Circuit at odds with the 7th Circuit Court of Appeals, as well as two federal district courts that all held that a CE, by definition, does not significantly impact the human environment so it is self-evident that an EA or EIS is unnecessary when proposing a new CE.[31] The split between the circuit courts of appeals can be resolved either by the Supreme Court or Congress.

The NEPA's judicial and regulatory maze has prompted numerous calls for reform. From 2001 to 2005 the executive branch and Congress formed four task forces with the intent of improving the NEPA's functioning through regulatory or statutory changes.[32] Yet substantive change remains elusive. On the one hand, some see the NEPA as "America's environmental magna carta," while others view it as "an old law that may no longer fit the times" and whose paperwork demands "done to respond to the threat [of environmentalists'] litigation has thwarted land managers' ability to be good stewards of the public's land."[33] Longtime CEQ general council Dinah Bear writes, "To avoid, at best, an ossified, mechanical approach to NEPA process . . . much work needs to be done."[34]

The NEPA may be "America's environmental magna carta" but the Endangered Species Act is the "pit bull of environmental law." Congress passed the ESA "without significant discussion or debate" intending to protect grizzly bears, bald eagles, and other megafauna held in high regard as symbols of America.[35] They did not intend to create a litigation dynamo by requiring the protection of plants, animals, and insects on public and private land alike that no one ever heard of or cared about. In his legislative history of the ESA, attorney Shannon Peterson notes that one reason the pit bull emerged is that:

> no one anticipated how it might interfere significantly with economic development or personnel [sic] property interests. . . . The timber industry, other natural resource industries, and private property groups declined to fight the law in 1973 because they failed to see how it might affect them. . . . Members of Congress also failed to anticipate many of the act's consequences.[36]

Public policy professor Martin Nie expands on Peterson's point, finding that "the environmental community . . . [has] continued to use the ESA as a political battering ram, legal monkeywrench, and tool for institutional disruption."[37] The WildEarth Guardians amply illustrate Nie's point.

In the summer of 2007 they filed petitions to list 681 little-known species with the Fish and Wildlife Service. Ann Carlson, a FWS biologist, said, "This was not envisioned by the act and is not helpful to us at all because it takes an enormous amount of resources to look at this."[38] These results occur because the courts, largely beginning with the Supreme Court's 1978 decision in the snail-darter Tellico dam case, have interpreted the ESA as largely overriding other factors in making land-use decisions (see the discussion of northern spotted owls in chapter 3).[39] If, in 1973, Congress had foreseen where the courts would take the ESA, the law would never have passed.

The courts, of course, deal with the law as written (and how they interpret it) so it is up to Congress to revise the ESA if actions like that of WildEarth Guardians or court-directed federal land management like that associated with northern spotted owls is not how they wish the ESA to function today. Likewise it is up to Congress to update and clarify the NEPA unless they agree with the 9th Circuit's finding in *Ecology Law Center v. Austin* that a 1,900-page Final Environmental Impact Statement supported by 20,000 pages of background information and 150 maps does not meet congressional intent.

Court decisions are not the only vexing aspect of major laws impacting federal land management today as the decades old science on which they rest has now been rejected outright or called into serious question by new understanding. With respect to the ESA, for example, marine biologist Deborah Brosnan notes that "the science has since moved on" from where it was in 1973.[40] Indeed, the veracity of species concept itself now draws considerable attention in the scientific community.[41]

Evaluate Laws in Light of New Scientific Understanding

Evolving scientific developments impact laws influencing federal land management in two ways. On the one hand, they can undermine the assumptions on which major pieces of environmental legislation rest. On the other hand, they raise new issues that existing legislation never intended to address. In the first instance, for example, the demise of the equilibrium paradigm in ecology removes a basic scientific assumption behind major environmental statutes. Writing in 1994, law professor Dan Tarlock observes:

> Modern environmental law's contributions to the legal system, which are based on the paradigm, include the National Environmental Policy Act of 1969, the Endangered Species Act of 1973, the Wilderness Act of 1964, and parts of the Clean Water Act such as section 404. In the twenty-five years since it has been enshrined in environmental law, the equilibrium paradigm has been rejected in ecology.[42]

In the second instance, the characteristics of the newly emerging issue of climate change pose a challenge to its sensible consideration under statutes written prior to its recognition. I look at each of these two areas in turn and note that Congress has yet to deal with either side of this coin.

In the 1960s the equilibrium concept remained a major theme in American ecology, as it had been for many years. It posited that nature was in balance and traveled with a corollary holding that human actions upset that balance to the detriment of humans and nature alike. The equilibrium idea made its way into legislation in several guises. The NEPA, a basically anthropocentric law at its inception, nonetheless contains a congressional statement that "it is the continuing policy of the Federal Government . . . to use all practicable means and measures . . . to create and maintain conditions under which man and nature can live in productive harmony."[43] The Wilderness Act protects wilderness areas as places "untrammeled by man," to create, at least in part, places intended as refuges where nature can pursue equilibrium unfettered by human interference (see chapter 2 for a more detailed discussion of wilderness). For its part, the ESA requires land managers (public or private) to protect the ecosystems on which threatened or endangered species depend.

In the years since those laws were passed, ecologists have abandoned the equilibrium concept in favor of nonequilibrium (see the discussion in chapter 2). Scholars now widely accept that the landscape is in constant flux, endlessly perturbed by natural and human actions so that there is no balance, no equilibrium, no harmony, no "way to be" in nature. In addition, scholars have come to more fully appreciate that humans have impacted virtually the entire planet so the notion that an undisturbed nature exists somewhere is unrealistic. A basic *scientific* assumption of the NEPA and the Wilderness Act is no longer valid. Does this matter to Congress? Should it matter?

What about the ESA? A landscape that constantly changes, as opposed to one in or seeking equilibrium, cannot be held constant or fossilized. With the ESA, one defines an ecosystem to conform to the needs of a single species. The ecosystems so defined rarely stay in a fixed location for extended periods of time because the biotic components of the landscape comprising that ecosystem constantly shift due to a variety of causes (e.g., wildland fire, plant diseases, insect outbreaks, introduction of exotic species, drought, human use of the landscape, and so forth). Scholars fully understand that now, but we did not in 1973 when the ESA was passed (see the discussion of northern spotted owls in chapter 3). How do you apply a law that calls for something that cannot be done?

What about the question of applying old laws to new policy questions revealed by scientific advancement? It is in the arena of climate change that we have seen perhaps the greatest evolution of scientific thinking impacting land management and the law. It is not my purpose here to argue a case for or against anthropocentric causation of climate change. Suffice it to say that climate is, as always, changing and that the majority of the scientific community involved in its study attribute a significant portion to the observed change over the last century to human activity, particularly carbon dioxide emissions. They further argue that the rate of change over the last century is unusually rapid and will lead to a variety of harmful alterations in environmental conditions. As a result, this line of thinking holds that humans across the planet need to take quick action to reduce anthropocentric activities contributing to atmospheric warming.

Many holders of this view seek to prod governmental action by using the federal courts. As Georgetown law professor Richard Lazarus notes, "The only thing accumulating these days as fast as greenhouse gas emissions in the atmosphere are climate change lawsuits in federal and state courts."[44] This is in spite of Chief Justice Roberts writing, "This Court's standing jurisprudence simply recognizes that redress of grievances of the sort at issue here [global warming] 'is the function of Congress and the Chief Executive' not the federal courts."[45] The NEPA and the ESA are among the statutes plaintiffs use in the courthouse to address climate change.[46]

In terms of applying these two laws to climate change the relative science in a nutshell is: the atmosphere receives greenhouse gases (GHGs) from innumerable sources (both natural and human) across the planet; it already contains sufficient GHGs to put it on a path for continued warming for decades; individual emission sources make vanishingly small contributions to global GHG levels; it is impossible to trace particular emissions to particular impacts; and there is no baseline to use to judge the significance of individually sourced impacts even if they could be determined.

Congress did not foresee such a scientifically complex and borderless issue as global warming when enacting the NEPA or the ESA. No one should be surprised, therefore, that significant scientific difficulties arise when seeking meaningful application of these decades-old laws to the current question of climate change. It is beyond reason, for example, to imagine that any particular federal land-management action requiring NEPA compliance would have a measurable impact on global climate. Yet the 9th Circuit Court of Appeals has already ruled that the NEPA's cumulative impact analysis requirements mean the Federal Highway Traffic Safety Administration must do such an analysis as part of a rulemaking on light-truck fuel-economy standards.[47] Remarkably, the court made its ruling despite the fact that the proposed ruling would actually reduce greenhouse gases! In this case, the law trumped the science. The Center for Biological Diversity, an organization that thrives on suing federal land managers, brought the suit.

As with the NEPA, the science gives no comfort to those seeking to invoke the ESA to advance their position on climate change despite the claim by Mark Clayton, the Center for Biological Diversity's policy director, that the ESA provides a "firm legal foundation for challenging global warming pollution."[48]

Consider the case of polar bears, which the FWS listed as endangered in 2008 as a result of climate-change-induced habitat change. Sections 7 and 9 of the ESA provide the normal vehicles for challenging federal land-management actions under the act. Section 7 prohibits federal agency actions that would "jeopardize the continued existence of any endangered species or threatened species or result in the destruction or adverse modification or habitat of such species." The notion that timber-harvesting in Colorado, building a new lodge in a national park in California, or burning hazardous fuels in a wildlife refuge in Arizona, or any of a myriad of other individual federal land-management actions, would adversely impact polar bear habitat lacks scientific merit. For its part, section 9 makes it illegal to "take any such species," meaning harming an individual polar bear in my example. Again, no one can make a plausible scientific case that a federal land-management action like those just noted can harm a specific bear.

The unmistakable conclusion here is that, as a matter of science, the NEPA and the ESA are totally unsuited for addressing concerns about climate change and efforts to apply them in that context can only result in a further tightening of the Gordian Knot. Congress can and should prevent such an occurrence.

Reduce the Role of the Courts

The federal courts generally play far too great a role in public land management. In their review of federal land-managing agencies from 1970 to 2000, political science professor Jeanne Nienaber Clarke and writer Kurt Angerbach find that:

> although citizen suits traditionally have been an integral component of our political system and our democracy, it is hard to escape the conclusion that they have been greatly overused in the past ten to twenty years. Judicial micromanagement represents both "the death of common sense" and the failure to find "common ground" in public lands management.[49]

Courts routinely undermine or reverse publicly vetted decisions made by experienced land managers supported by expert staff. Congress enables this situation by enacting vague, conflicting, and poorly crafted legislation that permits the courts to make their own interpretations as part of their ordinary judicial function. While some judges exercise self-restraint—recognizing they do not have the requisite knowledge, understanding, or experience to become a de facto land manager—others show no such hesitancy. Implementing the three recommendations I presented above would go a long way toward getting management decisions out of the courthouse, but those changes will take time so more immediate action is needed.

Judges do not initiate cases, so who is it that comes to the courthouse and why do they do so? Plaintiffs are most likely to be entities that do not get their way during the public review and comment phase of the management decision-making process. States, counties, tribes, corporations, environmental groups, and others all seek court intervention. That avenue should be open to all in a democratic society. Nonetheless, as a general matter, the courts should not serve as a highway to overturn actions agreed upon in publicly approved plans or via other open and transparent processes in service to private agendas. Government plaintiffs can make a prima facie case that the public interest motivates their suit. Other plaintiffs cannot so readily make the same claim. Corporate or business plaintiffs generally are pursuing a change in order to obtain financial benefit. Environmental interests—the most frequent courthouse visitors—routinely use the courts to advance their philosophical goals.

As discussed in the introduction, a nature-first philosophy pervades the environmental movement (also see chapter 2 for a look at the Wildlands Project). That worldview calls for the prevention or minimization of human impacts on nature without regard to human well-being. Little wonder then that even the most cursory examination of the websites of most large and small environmental organizations reveals a litany of court actions taken to prevent, halt, or delay some form of active land management.

One reason environmental organizations flock to federal courts is that they bear little of the overall cost of their action. Filing a suit is cheap; defending it or addressing the consequences of court decisions can be very costly. Government agencies must expend limited funds and staff resources on litigation-related activities instead of on good land management, beneficial research, and public outreach. Taxpayers see dollars diverted away from responsible management of their lands: a campground not built, culverts not cleaned of debris, a road not repaired, hazardous fuels not removed, energy not developed. The private sector, their employees, and state and local governments watch as profits and their associated taxes, jobs, and payrolls vanish and unproductive expenses are incurred in order to stand down from already-approved projects. Congress should level the playing field and in doing so reduce the role of the courts in land management.

Congress can require plaintiffs seeking to halt or delay land-management actions identified in publicly vetted plans, rulemakings, and other transparent processes to post a high-value bond to be forfeited in the event they do not prevail in the courts. One judge has already done so. In December 2005 federal district court judge Donald Molloy ordered three environmental groups, the Alliance for Wild Rockies, the Ecology Center, and the Native Ecosystems Council, to post a $100,000 bond as part of their suit to prevent logging in Butte Creek Basin in Montana.[50] The amount was 25 percent of the estimated cost of delay-caused lost government revenues.

Tribal lands offer another guide to the use of bonds when plaintiffs oppose agency decisions. The NEPA applies to lands held in trust by the Bureau of Indian Affairs (BIA) for tribes or individual tribal members as well as to our public lands. Consequently, actions such as timber harvesting require the preparation of an environmental assessment or environmental impact statement on tribal as well as national forest or BLM lands. Further, in all cases the sufficiency of the NEPA work may be challenged before the applicable body. Unlike the proposed sale on public lands, however, those objecting to the sale on tribal lands must comply with BIA regulations providing that the appellant may be required to post a bond.[51] The regulations stipulate:

> If a person believes that he/she may suffer a measurable and substantial financial loss as a direct result of the delay caused by an appeal, that person may request that the official before whom the appeal is pending require the posting of a reasonable bond by the appellant adequate to protect against that financial loss.
>
> In those cases in which the official before whom an appeal is pending determines that a bond is necessary to protect the financial interests of an Indian or Indian tribe, that official may require the posting of a bond on his/her own initiative.[52]

The BIA regulations provide a model easily adapted to public lands.

Congress can take a second action to lessen the role of the courts. In earlier examples, I showed that judicial deference to agency expertise varies. Rather than leave that decision to the courts themselves, Congress can enact legislation spelling out a judicial standard for deference to agency expertise. A high, but not insurmountable, bar would create certainty among agency decision-makers as well as judges and significantly increase the efficiency and effectiveness of public land management.

Eliminate the Forest Service and Realign Lands and Agencies

The current number and alignment of our land-management bureaus limits the ability of land managers to effectively and efficiently oversee the federal estate. The present patterns emerged piecemeal from a century of poorly coordinated decisions done to address problems of earlier days. Unfortunately, the pattern creates significant problems for today. I begin with the obvious clumsiness of assigning federal lands to two cabinet departments. For many years observers have questioned the wisdom of having the Forest Service in the Department of Agriculture while the other three bureaus call the Department of the Interior home.[53] At its establishment, when trees were often thought of in terms of crops, perhaps it made some sense to locate the FS among other agricultural agencies. No more. Keeping the FS in the Department of Agriculture can no longer be justified using arguments tied to good land management. The only forces forestalling a shift to the DOI are inertia, the congressional committee power structure, and those who benefit from it. A proper administrative location, however, is not the basic question involving the Forest Service.

The fundamental issue regarding the Forest Service is its continued existence. A look at the mission statements of the BLM and the FS reveals them to be nearly identical (chapter 1). They are both multiple-use agencies. There is no need for two when one can do the job. One might argue that Congress should fold the BLM into the FS. Alas, that runs afoul of the widespread understanding that, in the words of Roger Sedjo, director of forest economics and policy at Resources for the Future, "the reputation of the forest service is in dismal disarray." He further notes that "so serious have been the weaknesses of the system that for decades there have been calls for numerous organizational and institutional changes."[54] In contrast, Sally Fairfax, professor of forest policy at the University of California–Berkeley, finds "BLM's experience in collaborative management . . . far more appropriate as a point of departure for addressing issues of the twenty-first century."[55] Her point is especially apt because future management of all public lands should emphasize collaborative management, giving a primary role to local and regional interests most impacted by management decisions. Congress should dissolve the Forest Service.

With dissolution of the Forest Service the question becomes what to do with the 193 million acres it manages. As a general matter, multiple-use lands should go to the BLM, lands designated as having particular value as a wildlife habitat should enter the FWS refuge system, and wilderness or other protected areas should shift to the NPS. There is an additional point to be made regarding the organizations managing public lands.

Why not allow tribes who successfully manage their own lands to manage nonreservation lands adjacent to tribal lands? Over the years some tribes have established track records for good multiple-purpose forest management: for example, economic development, environmental protection, and cultural values promotion.[56] Many tribes have long occupied their lands, a longevity that can build an understanding of, and affinity for, a landscape not easily gained by other means.

Congress has already enacted legislation linking tribal forests with adjacent BLM and FS forestlands. The Tribal Forest Protection Act authorizes a tribe that identifies needed projects on adjacent or nearby BLM or FS lands to petition the appropriate secretary to enter an agreement allowing the tribe to conduct the appropriate management action.[57] Congress only has to take the next step and turn loose tribal expertise to accomplish management goals for public lands by acting as surrogates for one of the federal agencies when a tribe has a track record of successful land management. Such tribes include: the Mescalero Apache in New Mexico, the White Mountain Apache in Arizona, the Colville and the Yakama in Washington, the Confederated Salish and the Kootenai in Montana, and the Confederated Tribes of Warm Springs in Oregon. More creatively, Congress could authorize tribes to provide staff and on-the-ground management support for federal management trusts proposed in the next section.

Increase Role of Local and Regional Residents in Decision-Making

Since the 1990s, frustration with the Gordian Knot spurred development of multiple efforts to give greater voice to those most impacted by decisions regarding federal lands and private lands affected by federal law. Generally traveling under the banner of cooperative conservation, these efforts focus on bringing all stakeholders together to pound out consensus agreements on land-management matters. Regarding federal lands, Congress specifically sanctioned the work of one such effort—that of the Quincy Library Group—in 1998 (see box 4.1).[58] Two years later it gave additional momentum to locally based management of federal lands with the establishment of the Valles Caldera Trust to manage the newly created Valles Caldera National Preserve

---

Box 4.1.   The Quincy Library Group

President Clinton's Secretary of Agriculture, Dan Glickman, said, "The collaborative approach used by the coalition, the Quincy Library Group, is a model for the West and the entire nation."

Frustration with management gridlock on Lassen, Plumas—part of the Tahoe National Forests in Northern California—led a group of local environmentalists, timber interests, local governments, and others to collaboratively devise a management plan that eventually became embodied in the Herger-Feinstein Quincy Library Group Forest Recovery Act included within the fiscal year 1999 omnibus spending bill passed in October 1998.

By 2009, however, litigation by national environmental groups and foot-dragging by the Forest Service had so stymied implementation of the act that the present Quincy Library Group chairman, Bill Coates, said, "Some of us don't think collaboration is getting us anywhere. . . . I want to see performance on the ground . . . and not 5,000 years of process."

As I note later in the chapter, collaboration without the other reforms presented here will not cut the Gordian Knot.

Sources: The Glickman quote is from Michael McCloskey, "Local Communities and the Management of Public Forests," *Ecology Law Quarterly* 25, no. 4 (1999): 625, note 5; and the Coates quote is from Red Lodge Clearing House (Natural Resource Law Center of the University of Colorado Law School), available at: http://rlch.org/content/view/238/36/ (accessed November 2, 2011).

in New Mexico.[59] Bruce Babbitt, President Clinton's secretary of the interior, created advisory councils consisting of multiple stakeholders for BLM grazing districts as part of his Rangeland Reform 94 initiative, and collaborative conservation figured prominently in the administration of George W. Bush. [60]

Criticism of collaborative conservation generally centers on matters of "accountability and legitimacy," according to political scientists David Sousa and Christopher Klyza.[61] Several questions arise. What is the mechanism for selecting participants? Are they representative of the broader community? How does the effort comport with the law? Presently, the greatest obstacle to efforts to give greater voice to those most affected by federal land management through collaborative conservation is "the labyrinth of the green state—the existing laws and structures created over the last hundred years."[62] Answering the questions observers pose and overcoming identified obstacles, not surprisingly, requires congressional action.

Congress can take several important steps to move decision-making closer to the "communities of place." To overcome legal objections, Congress can establish boards, trusts, or other mechanisms and sanction their decision-making role. Likewise, Congress can establish the mechanism for the selection of members of the collaborative body to address concerns about representation. They did both with the establishment of the Valles Caldera Trust (see box 4.2). The more complex question is how these empowered collaborative conservation entities would interact with the established land-management agencies under my assumption of maintaining federal control of existing public lands. Two general models already exist, the Presidio Trust and the Valles Caldera Trust. They need not be the only approaches Congress considers in the future.

With the Presidio Trust, Congress assigned primary responsibility for the management of land within the boundaries of an existing federal unit to a newly created entity. Congress established the Golden Gate National Recreation Area (GGNRA) as a unit of the National Park System in San Francisco

---

Box 4.2.   Valles Caldera National Preserve

Congress added 89,000 acres of the Valles Caldera in New Mexico to the federal estate in 2000. The privately owned land had been part of the Baca land grant dating to the 1820s. Over time, livestock grazing and timber harvesting were major land uses. Nonetheless, the landscape remained highly attractive and legislation approving some $100 million to buy the land passed by unanimous consent in the U.S. Senate and by a vote of 377–45 in the House.

in 1972. At the time it targeted the Presidio, a U.S. Army post of some 800 buildings plus open space, for transfer to the National Park Service and inclusion in GGNRA should the Army determine it no longer needed the base. The Army did so in 1989 and finally withdrew in 1994. In 1996 Congress created the Presidio Trust to manage the area.[63] Congress required the secretary of the interior to transfer administration of the Presidio to the trust. The trust "shall" manage the area "in accordance" with the purposes stated in the legislation creating the GGNRA and its general management plan, which the NPS prepares.[64] Here, Congress gives administrative jurisdiction of a portion of federal land to a local board while directing this board, not the federal land manager, to be responsible for meeting congressional priorities and those cascading management objectives identified in a publicly vetted plan covering the overall land-management unit. The board carries out its functions in "consultation with the Secretary" and submits an annual report to Congress (as does the Valles Caldera Trust).

The Presidio Trust helps us on at least four fronts. For people most impacted by land-management actions, it moves decisions closer to home. It places decisions in the hands of interests Congress believes are best able to make them. People living at a distance remain involved via Congress specifying management purposes and priorities as well as requiring that overall management plans be subject to national public review and comment and remain in the purview of the federal land-managing agency (the NPS). It further helps by short-circuiting current agency chain-of-command review and approval processes.[65]

The Valles Caldera Trust grows out of congressional desire "to establish a demonstration area for an experimental management regime" for the newly established Valles Caldera National Preserve.[66] Congress wanted to try something other than business-as-usual, so it declined to assign management of the newly acquired lands to either the Forest Service or the National Park Service, managers of adjacent federal lands.[67] As new federal lands, the preserve had no publicly reviewed management plan or any administrative infrastructure available. The trust began from scratch on all possible fronts: no approved plans, no administrative or land-management staff, no facilities, and no pencils. It remains a work in progress.

A trust, or any other congressionally authorized collaborative conservation administrative structure, will still be subject to pressure from the same interests that would seek to influence management regardless of who is making decisions. Consequently, collaborative conservation entities will not, in and of themselves, untie the Gordian Knot. Their effectiveness requires congressional action of the kind I describe earlier in this chapter so as to free them from what Sousa and Klyza call the "the labyrinth of the green state."

Movement to locally and regionally based collaborative federal land management generates an extensive "to do" list. For example:

1. Determine the criteria for establishing the geographic reach, composition, and administrative responsibilities of collaborative groups;
2. Decide which lands are best suited for collaborative management (multiple-use areas are better suited to collaborative management than are wilderness areas);
3. Create more experimental management structures;
4. Identify those functions, like fire-fighting and research, best done at the national level; and
5. Establish functioning collaborative conservation entities.

To say shifting federal land-management responsibilities toward local collaborative conservation entities as well as the other recommendations I make is a tall order is a great example of understatement. The next section suggests a way to proceed in addressing the recommendations I make.

Create and New and Empowered
Public Land Law Review Commission

I join with others in recommending that Congress establish a new public land law review commission as the way to guide cutting the Gordian Knot.[68]

Addressing the comprehensive changes I suggest requires the sort of effort Congress normally avoids, but such an outcome is not preordained. Success requires Congress to rise above protection of committee turf, special-interest pressures, and agency resistance, and to ignore the inevitable demagogy of those who currently benefit from the Gordian Knot if the public is to see more effective and efficient federal land management. A proven way for Congress to deal with highly charged issues is via creation of a commission and giving teeth to its recommendations.

The Budget Control Act of 2011 provides the most recent example of Congress charging a select group of people (twelve of its own members) to devise solutions to substantively difficult and politically divisive problems, in this case the nation's massive budget deficit.[69] What makes the act particularly significant is it requires the group to produce its recommendations by a fixed date and that Congress must accept or reject them in total, up or down with no amendments. If the group cannot agree on recommendations or if Congress rejects them or if the president does not sign the approving legislation, then the act triggers politically unpalatable automatic government budget cuts. In other words, the act pushes the group toward compromise, precisely what is required if we are to cut the Gordian Knot.

The Base Realignment and Closing Commissions date from 1988. They identify military bases for closing and consolidation. The commissions emerged from a decades-long effort to improve the effectiveness and efficiency of the military by eliminating bases and operations that had accumulated over the years but were no longer needed. The political pressures to keep unneeded bases open were preventing streamlining, so Congress eventually appointed a commission whose members were nominated by the president and confirmed by the Senate to make recommendations that Congress had to accept or reject as a package.

Congress has previously used commissions to address federal land policy. In 1964 it created the last Public Land Law Review Commission but its pace and resulting congressional action are not good models for today's needs. It took the group six years to publish its report, *One-Third of the Nation's Land.* It took another six years for Congress to pass significant legislation—the Federal Land Policy and Management Act—stemming from its work. Twelve years is three presidential terms or six Congresses and is much too slow. In creating a new commission, Congress should provide deadlines and assure appropriations. It should also give substance to its findings by providing that Congress will take up-or-down votes on packages of recommendations.[70] Doing so will also have the advantage of attracting the best possible talent for work on the commission since such duties often require the sacrifice of a good deal of personal time and energy. While a commission is the best vehicle available, it must be robust and its findings must carry more than hortatory weight.

Like many observers of federal land management, I lay the fundamental blame for the Gordian Knot at the feet of Congress. I have, however, noted at various points in this book congressional actions that offer some hope for the future. The next section outlines a few of them.

Glimmers of Congressional Hope

Many members of Congress have expressed frustration with the current federal land-management milieu, especially as it relates to wildland fire. Initially they reacted on a case-by-case basis. In August 2002, for example, exasperation with environmentalist litigation blocking needed hazardous fuels treatments in the Black Hills of South Dakota prompted Congress to pass the following legislation:

Due to the extraordinary circumstances present here, actions authorized by this section shall proceed immediately and to completion notwithstanding any other provision of law including, but not limited to, NEPA and the National Forest Management Act (16 U.S.C. 1601 et seq.). Such actions shall also not be subject to the notice, comment, and appeal requirements of the Appeals Reform Act (16 U.S.C. 1612 (note), Pub. Law No. 102—381 sec. 322). Any action authorized by this section shall not be subject to judicial review by any court of the United States.[71]

Thus, Congress directed immediate management action and forbade any further administrative or judicial appeals under any provision of law. The following year it restricted application of the NEPA and the CWA in restoring burned areas in the Flathead and Kootenai National Forests.[72] Not satisfied with a case-by-case strategy, Congress passed the more comprehensive Healthy Forest Restoration Act (HFRA) with large bipartisan majorities that President Bush signed into law in December 2003.[73]

On the question of hazardous fuels treatments, the HFRA had much to say. It required a collaborative—federal, state, tribal, and local—approach to identifying and prioritizing areas for fuels treatments. While providing fuels treatments must be in compliance with environmental laws, it stipulated that only one alternative to the proposed treatment be analyzed in order to comply with the NEPA. This ended a favored litigation technique of plaintiffs who routinely argued that the NEPA required the consideration of multiple alternatives. The HFRA halted the practice of court-shopping by requiring that suits be filed in the district court that geographically coincided with the challenged treatment. It further required courts to balance the short-term and long-term effects of not doing the project against the short-term and long-term effects of doing the project. With the HFRA, Congress clearly seeks to diminish the role of the courts in federal land management while stressing collaboration, at least with respect to fire. Many of the key policy components of the HFRA have broad application in the world of federal land management.

Energy is another area that has attracted congressional attention. The Energy Policy Act of 2005 created a presumption that a categorical exclusion would satisfy NEPA requirements for the issuance of oil and gas exploration and development permits under specified circumstances.[74] As I described in the introduction, the act also required an assessment of the cumulative impact of various land-use restrictions on the availability of oil and gas resources beneath federal lands. Here Congress recognizes that its actions have cumulative adverse impacts and it can benefit from an evaluation of their extent.

Over the years, Congress has made several attempts to rectify the land-management problems it has created through hasty and sloppy work. The ESA, the NEPA, and wetlands provisions of the Clean Water Act, for example, have been subjects of countless hearings and members have introduced numerous bills to fix deficiencies. While some minor improvements occurred, Congress has been unable to muster the political will to make desperately needed major improvements. A new teeth-bearing public land law review commission would go a long way to overcoming this pervasive problem.

What about the executive branch? Throughout this book I have concentrated on actions by Congress to cut the Knot, yet the executive branch can take steps to unravel the Knot here and there. The next section looks at some of these.

Executive Branch Actions

I hope that by this time you, the reader, are convinced that Congress must wield the sword that cuts the Gordian Knot. Without congressional action the best the executive branch can do is to gnaw at the Knot. Departmental and agency executives can conduct further reviews with an eye toward increasing effectiveness and efficiency. For example: does the department or agency have too many or too complex planning requirements; are all the current management layers, power centers, and committees needed; and does process and procedure substitute for actual land management? While executives routinely conduct reviews of this kind, those of us who have worked in departments and agencies generally would agree that the job is far from complete, that there remains too much administrivia and too many self-inflicted wounds. Perhaps the greatest wound originates in the Executive Office of the President (EOP).

The Office of Management and Budget grew out of the Bureau of the Budget established in 1921 within the Treasury Department. It moved to the EOP in 1939 and became the OMB in 1970. The addition of a management component to the office's portfolio creates a significant land-management wound (see box 4.3). The president can close the wound by removing the management function from the Office of Management and Budget because the organization is substantively incapable of guiding land management, for reasons I point out below.

The president's 2010 budget provides for 528 total full-time positions for the OMB.[75] Of those, approximately ten people serve in the Interior Branch (which covers the BLM, the FWS, and the NPS, plus the Bureau of Indian Affairs, the Minerals Management Service, the Office of Surface Mining, and the Office of the Secretary, which includes legislative affairs, the solicitors office, and public affairs). There are another ten OMB staffers in its Agriculture Branch (which oversees all programs and organizations in the Department of Agriculture, including the Forest Service plus the Office of the Secretary). Typically, the OMB assigns one or two staff members to an agency. Even if one generously grants that these individuals have high levels of relevant education and experience, it is humanly impossible for one or two people to have the body of knowledge, expertise, understanding, and skills equivalent to the thousands of scientists, professional land managers, and other career staff em-

---

Box 4.3. Office of Management and Budget Mission Statement

The Office of Management and Budget's predominant mission is to assist the president in overseeing the preparation of the federal budget and to supervise its administration in executive branch agencies. In helping to formulate the president's spending plans, the OMB evaluates the effectiveness of agency programs, policies, and procedures, assesses competing funding demands among agencies, and sets funding priorities. The OMB ensures that agency reports, rules, testimony, and proposed legislation are consistent with the president's budget and with administration policies.

In addition, the OMB oversees and coordinates the administration's procurement, financial management, information, and regulatory policies. In each of these areas, the OMB's role is to help improve administrative management, to develop better performance measures and coordinating mechanisms, and to reduce any unnecessary burdens on the public.

Source: www.whitehouse.gov/omb/organization_role/ (accessed October 23, 2009)

---

ployed by an agency. Equally, they do not have a policy understanding matching that of the senior political appointees. Yet because of the power granted to the OMB by presidents beginning with its establishment in 1970, the OMB and its staff exercise significant authority regarding federal land management.

The OMB weighs in on a variety of land-management actions. In shaping the budget it may direct a cabinet officer to shift money between agencies. Who knows best where to allocate appropriated dollars, a cabinet officer and his or her departmental and agency budget shops plus agency heads and their professional staff, or one or two OMB staffers? The OMB staff plays a key role in determining program performance measures.[76] Who knows best how to determine program success, a cabinet officer plus agency heads and professional staff, or one or two OMB staffers? The OMB staff plays a role in negotiating agreements with states, tribes, and local government partners. Again, who knows best? The OMB must approve proposals for rules and regulatory actions guiding federal land management. If the president's political team at a cabinet department signs off on a proposal being consistent with the president's agenda, why do career OMB staff have veto power over their decision? The solution is for the president to strip the *M* from the OMB as it impacts management of public lands.

The OMB can perform legitimate functions in service to better government. Overall budget formulation (its original task), coordinating congressional testimony across agencies and departments, and assuring consistent policies regarding such things as procurement are among them. A substantive role in managing public lands is not such a function.

Final Thoughts

In this chapter I have set out specific recommendations for cutting the Gordian Knot and suggested a mechanism for moving forward with their consideration. I hope you agree with some of them. I do not expect anyone would agree with all of them. Likewise I hope no one would disagree with all of them. The best I can hope for is that you, the reader, find the arguments reasonable (even those you disagree with) and that they deserve further analysis and thought.

Notes

1. Jack Ward Thomas and Alex Sienkiewicz, "The Relationship Between Science and Democracy: Public Land Policies, Regulation and Management," *Public Land and Resources Law Review* 26 (2005): 51.

2. For a history of the ESA, see Shannon Peterson, *Acting for Endangered Species* (Lawrence: University of Kansas Press, 2002).

3. Committees on Appropriations, U.S. Senate and U.S. House of Representatives, "FY 2010 Conference Summary: Interior Appropriations," summary, October 27, 2009. The BLM received $1.1 billion; the FS $2.8 billion; the FWS $0.5 billion; the NPS $2.7 billion; wildland fire management received $3.5 billion; and the Land and Water Conservation Fund $0.5 billion (available at www.doi.gov/budget/2010/data/pdf/Interior_FY10_Conference_Summary.pdf [accessed September 17, 2010]).

4. The Property and Environment Research Center and its director, Terry Anderson, have a lengthy track record of publishing quality materials on free-market environmentalism, which lays out the theoretical underpinning of using markets to promote good environmental stewardship as well as providing real-world examples of its application to private and state-owned lands. Their work can be found at www.perc.org.

5. One can envision covenants and restrictions passing with the title to the land; however, they would be unlikely to accommodate changing societal views regarding resource values, especially those for which markets are nonexistent or poorly developed.

6. One only has to look at environmentalists' success in preventing leasing for offshore oil development in California state waters for some four decades despite the actual environmental record of such development as well as the significant financial benefit the state would obtain from such leases and subsequent production.

7. As a general matter this would include the inland states and Alaska.

8. See table 7 in chapter 1 for a glance at the state-by-state differences in revenues.

9. In their review of the ecosystem concept, Pickett and Cadenasso note that an ecosystem is independent of space or "narrow assumptions," and may be constantly changing in "composition, content, or the processing of nutrients and energy." Use of "the ecosystem" in public discourse is but "a shallow metaphor" to represent a "plethora of attributes people appreciate—or alternatively, detest—in nature." Researchers set boundaries for "convenience" that may be based on a wide variety of attributes from "geomorphological divides" to understanding "a political entity." S. T. A. Pickett and M. L. Cadenasso, "The Ecosystem as a Multidimensional Concept: Meaning, Model, and Metaphor," *Ecosystems* 5 (2002): 1–10.

10. *An Act to Set Apart a Certain Tract of Land Lying Near the Head-waters of the Yellowstone River as a Public Park,* 42nd Cong, 2d sess. (March 1, 1872). 16 U.S.C. 1.

11. *National Park Service Organic Act,* 16 U.S.C. 1–4.

12. 16 U.S.C. 1131–36.

13. The percent of a given park's land base in congressionally designated wilderness varies wildly. Grand Canyon and Yellowstone National Parks have no congressionally established wilderness (although much of those parks is managed as wilderness as a matter of administrative policy). Conversely, Congress has given wilderness status to 95 percent of Yosemite and 97 percent of Sequoia-Kings Canyon.

14. *The [Forest Service] Organic Act of 1897,* 16 U.S.C 473, et seq.

15. *Multiple-Use Sustained-Yield Act of 1960,* Public Law 86-517. 16 U.S.C. 528–31.

16. *Federal Land Policy and Management Act of 1976,* Public Law 94-579. 43 U.S.C. 315 et seq. The BLM was created in 1946 through the marriage of the General Land Office and the U.S. Grazing Service. The BLM had focused on land disposal, grazing, and mineral development. The BLM land base consisted of land not managed by the FS, the FWS, or the NPS.

17. *Omnibus Public Lands Act of 2009,* Public Law 111-11, 16 U.S.C. 1 note. Bureau of Land Management Fact Sheet, "Omnibus Public Lands Management Act of 2009," Washington, D.C., undated, available at www.blm.gov/pgdata/etc/medialib/blm/wo/Law_Enforcement/nlcs.Par.24423.File.dat/Omnibus%20New%20Designations.pdf (accessed September 18, 2010). Bureau of Land Management Fact Sheet, "National Land Conservation Summary Tables," Washington, D.C., April 2010, available at www.blm.gov/wo/st/en/prog/blm_special_areas/NLCS/summary_tables.html (accessed September 18, 2010). The National Landscape Conservation System began as an executive branch initiative in the Clinton administration and was continued under President Bush. The NLCS designation adds a bureaucratic management layer to already-set-aside lands, as the NLCS is made up of national monuments, wilderness areas, national conservation areas, and so forth.

18. As I discuss in the introduction, Congress has shown a strong interest in understanding the cumulative impacts of shifting federal lands out of multiple-use status with regard to oil and gas.

19. Yellowstone National Park contains no congressionally designated wilderness, yet there is little apparent public disenchantment with how the park is managed.

20. *The Wild and Scenic Rivers Act,* Public Law 90-542, 16 USC 1271–87.

21. U.S. Court of Appeals for the Ninth Circuit, *Friends of Yosemite Valley; Mariposans for Environmentally Responsible Growth v. Dirk Kempthorne* et al., no. 07-15791, opinion filed March 28, 2008.

22. Mark Grossi, "Yosemite Seeks Ideas about Crowd Control," *Fresno Bee*, July 8, 2009.

23. *National Environmental Policy Act*, Public Law 91–190, 42 U.S.C. 4332.

24. The Council on Environmental Quality's NEPA regulations appear at 40 CFR parts 1500–1508. Individual agencies have their own regulations implementing those of the CEQ.

25. *Cumulative impact* and *effects* are defined at 40 CFR 1508.7 and 40 CFR 1508.8, respectively.

26. Over a thousand NEPA cases reached the federal courts between 2001 and 2008 alone, according to the CEQ. See their annual litigation summaries, available at http://ceq.hss.doe.gov/legal_corner/litigation.html (accessed September 18, 2010).

27. U.S. Court of Appeals for the Ninth Circuit, *Ecology Law Center v. Austin*, 430 F.3d 1057 (9th Cir. 2005).

28. *Sierra Club v. Bosworth*, 510 F.3d 1016 (9th Cir. 2007).

29. 40 CFR 1508.4.

30. The FS established a categorical exclusion for hazardous fuels treatments when prescribed fire was applied to 4,500 acres or less or when mechanical means were used on tracts of 1,000 acres or less. See Department of Agriculture and Department of the Interior, "National Environmental Policy Act Determination Needed for Fire Management Activities; Categorical Exclusions: Notice," *Federal Register* 68, no. 108 (June 5, 2003): 33814–24.

31. Jerri Zhang, "A New View: Or Just Being Difficult? The Ninth Circuit's View on Categorical Exclusions," *Missouri Environmental Law and Policy Review* 16 (2009): 263–80.

32. Linda Luther, *The National Environmental Policy Act: Streamlining NEPA* (Washington, D.C.: Congressional Research Service, 2007), report to Congress, RL 33267, available at www.nationalaglawcenter.org/assets/crs/RL33267.pdf (accessed September 18, 2010).

33. Dinah Bear, "Some Modest Suggestions for Improving Implementation of the National Environmental Policy Act," *Natural Resources Journal* 43 (2003): 931–60, quotes at 931–32.

34. Bear, "Some Modest Suggestions," 932.

35. Peterson, *Acting for Endangered Species*, x.

36. Peterson, *Acting for Endangered Species*, 31–32.

37. Martin Nie, "Statutory Detail and Administrative Discretion in Public Lands Governance: Arguments and Alternatives," *Journal of Environmental Law and Litigation* 19 (2004): 223–91, quote at 248; internal quote omitted.

38. As quoted in the *Washington Times*, September 1, 2009, 1.

39. *Tennessee Valley Authority v. Hill*, 437 U.S. 153, 180 (1978).

40. Deborah Brosnan, "Science, Law, and the Environment: The Making of a Modern Discipline," *Environmental Law* 37 (2007): 987–1007.

41. A September 23, 2009, query to the scholarly database JSTOR using the term *species problem* and the date range 1995–2009 returned 432 scholarly articles, reviews, and editorials.

42. Dan Tarlock, "The Nonequilibrium Paradigm in Ecology and the Partial Unraveling of Environmental Law," *Loyola of Los Angeles Law Review* 27 (1994): 1121–44, quote at 1112.

43. *National Environmental Policy Act*, Public Law 91–190, 42 U.S.C. 4331.

44. Richard Lazarus, "Courts Continue to Needle on Climate," *The Environmental Forum* 25 (2008): 12.

45. Chief Justice Roberts dissenting (joined by Justices Scalia, Thomas, and Alito) in *Massachusetts et al. v. Environmental Protection Agency et al.*, 549 U.S. 2007, citing *Lujan v. Defenders of Wildlife*.

46. Robert Meltz, *Climate Change Litigation: A Growing Phenomenon, Congressional Research Service* (Washington, D.C.: Congressional Research Service, 2007), report to Congress RL32764, available at http://ncseonline.org/nle/crs/abstract.cfm?NLEid=173 (accessed September 18, 2010).

47. U.S. Court of Appeals for the Ninth Circuit, *Center for Biological Diversity v. National Highway Traffic Safety Administration*, 508 F.3d 508 (9th Cir. 2007).

48. As quoted in Matthew Gerhart, "Climate Change and the Endangered Species Act: The Difficulty of Proving Causation," *Ecology Law Quarterly* 36 (2009): 167–99, quote at 169. This is an excellent piece laying out the difficulties of using the ESA to address climate change. Also see J. B. Ruhl, "Keeping the Endangered Species Act Relevant," *Duke Environmental Law and Policy Forum* 12 (2009): 275–94.

49. Jeanne Nienaber Clarke and Kurt Angerbach, "The Federal Four: Change and Continuity in the Bureau of Land Management, Fish and Wildlife Service, Forest Service, and National Park Service, 1970–2000," pp. 35–51 in *Western Public Lands and Environmental Politics*, 2nd ed., ed. Charles Davis (Boulder, CO: Westview Press, 2001), 49.

50. Perry Backus, "Judge Requires Timber Sale Bond," *Missoulian*, December 23, 2005, available at http://missoulian.com/news/local/article_744b8bab-b149-5bd8-9dd0-6e47e5a8c115.html (accessed September 18, 2010).

51. 25 CFR 2.5.

52. See Department of the Interior Board of Indian Appeals, *Friends of the Wild Swan v. Portland Area Director, Bureau of Indian Affairs*, 27 IBIA 8, Washington, D.C., November 14, 1994, available at www.oha.doi.gov/IBIA/IbiaDecisions/27ibia/27ibia008.pdf (accessed September 18, 2010).

53. For a recent evaluation of moving the Forest Service to the DOI, see Government Accountability Office, *Federal Land Management: Observations on a Possible Move of the Forest Service into the Department of the Interior*, GAO-09-223 (Washington, D.C.: Government Accountability Office, 2009).

54. Roger Sedjo, *The National Forests: For Whom and for What?* PERC Policy Series no. 23 (2001), 4, available at www.perc.org/pdf/ps23.pdf (accessed September 19, 2010).

55. Sally Fairfax, "When an Agency Outlasts Its Time: A Reflection," *Journal of Forestry* 103 (2005): 266.

56. See Allison Berry, *Two Forests Under the Big Sky: Tribal v. Federal Management*, PERC Policy Series no. 45 (2009), comparing timber management on Confederate Salish and Kootenai tribal lands with that on the adjacent Lolo National Forest in northwest Montana, available at www.perc.org/files/ps45.pdf (accessed September 19, 2010). Also see the winter 2005–2006 issue of *Evergreen* magazine devoted to the question "Forestry in Indian Country: Models of Sustainability for Our Nation's Forests?" which, among other things, compares forestry on Colville tribal lands with that on the adjacent Colville National Forest, available at http://evergreenmagazine.com/magazine/issue/Winter_2005_2006.html (accessed September 19, 2010). Tribal forest management in general is not without its shortcomings. For a national assessment, see John Gordon et al., *An Assessment of Indian Forests and Forest Management* (Portland, OR: Intertribal Timber Council, 2003). The report is popularly known as IFMAT II.

57. *The Tribal Forest Protection Act of 2004*, Public Law 108-278.

58. *Herger-Feinstein Quincy Library Group Forest Recovery Act*, Public Law 105-277, 16 U.S.C. 2104.

59. *Valles Caldera Preservation Act of 2000*, Public Law 106-248, 16 U.S.C. 698.

60. President Bush signed Executive Order 13352, *Facilitation of Cooperative Conservation*, on August 26, 2004, available at http://ceq.hss.doe.gov/nepa/regs/Executive_Order_13352.htm (accessed September 19, 2010). Also see "White House Conference on Collaborative Conservation" agenda, available at http://cooperativeconservation.gov/day2resources.html (accessed September 19, 2010).

61. David Sousa and Christopher Klyza, "New Directions in Environmental Policy Making: An Emerging Collaborative Regime or Reinventing Interest Group Liberalism?" *Natural Resources Journal* 47 (2007): 377–444.

62. Sousa and Klyza, "New Directions in Environmental Policy Making," 439.

63. Public Law 104-133, 16 U.S.C. 469bb appendix.

64. Public Law 104-133, 16 U.S.C. 469bb appendix § 104.

65. Interestingly, both the Valles Caldera Trust and the Presidio Trust are to essentially become self supporting, which was Congress's original thought regarding management of the national parks.

66. *Valles Caldera Preservation Act of 2000*, Public Law 106-248, 16 U.S.C. 698.

67. The Santa Fe National Forest has an extensive shared boundary with the preserve, and Bandelier National Monument has a small common boundary with it.

68. For example, in 2008 the bipartisan National Advisory Board of the University of Montana School of Law's Public Land and Resources Law Review published *A Federal Public Lands Agenda for the Twenty-first Century*, calling for a new commission as one of its recommendations for the incoming Obama administration, available at www.umt.edu/publicland/NABreport.pdf (accessed September 19, 2010).

69. *Budget Control Act of 2011*, Public Law 112–25.

70. Since one Congress cannot bind a future Congress, a provision for an up-or-down vote cannot be enforced; however, it would provide an incentive for more statesmanlike voting.

71. *2002 Supplemental Appropriations Act for Further Recovery and Response to Terrorist Attacks on the U.S.*, Public Law 107-206 § 706 (j).

72. Title IV of the Department of the Interior Appropriations Act of 2003 is titled *The Flathead and Kootenai National Forest Rehabilitation Act*, Public Law 108-108 § 403(b).

73. *Healthy Forest Restoration Act*, Public Law 108-148, 16 U.S.C. 6501. The Senate vote was 80–14 and the House vote was 256–170. For a review of fire and the law, see Robert Keiter, "The Law of Fire: Reshaping Public Land Policy in an Era of Ecology and Litigation," *Environmental Law* 36 (2006): 301–84.

74. *Energy Policy Act of 2005*, Public Law 109-58 § 390.

75. Executive Office of the President, Office of Management and Budget, *Fiscal Year 2010 Budget*, OMB-9 (Washington, D.C.: Office of Management and Budget, 2009).

76. I was involved in a two-year negotiation with states (who brought in a variety of interest groups), tribes, local government, the BLM, the BIA, the FWS, and the NPS that resulted in a set of performance measures for the national hazardous fuels program. When it came to determining performance measures for the DOI's hazardous fuels program, OMB staff insisted on including measures this collaborative body specifically rejected.

Conclusion

CUTTING THE GORDIAN KNOT BENEFITS PEOPLE AND THE LAND. Public land management based on cogent, clear, and consistent priorities will yield a landscape offering a widely acceptable balance among the multiple benefits the public expects from its lands and do so based on good stewardship. Getting the courts out of the land-management business, reducing the opportunities for special interests to "monkeywrench" management when they do not get their way in public processes, eliminating the Forest Service, and realigning management boundaries will greatly improve efficiency and effectiveness. Moving decision-making closer to the people directly impacted reflects the simple truth that those with the most at stake should have the greatest voice in decision-making. Society gains on all fronts.

At the outset I noted that we need far-reaching reform, that tugging at the Gordian Knot here or there would not clear away the century of careless *ad hocery* that created the Knot. It will do us no good if Congress moves decision-making closer to affected populations if naysayers can still tie up decisions in the courts. What good will dissolving the Forest Service do if Congress does not also assign a distinct set of management priorities to specific kinds of public lands? I am proposing a package deal.

Our federal lands constitute a national treasure, a part of the fabric of the nation that makes the United States the United States. As such, we should assure we manage them to the best of our ability. Through compromise, collaboration, and political courage we can produce a stewardship regime that is a credit to this and future generations.

Appendix

Federal Acreage (in Thousands) by State, Agency, and Region, 2008

State	BLM	FWS	FS	NPS	Total	As % of State Area
CT	0.0	1.0	0.0	7.8	8.8	0.3
ME	0.0	66.7	53.0	90.3	210.0	1.1
MA	0.0	22.3	0.0	57.9	80.2	1.6
NH	0.0	22.7	734.8	15.9	773.4	13.4
NJ	0.0	74.3	0.0	99.2	173.5	3.6
NY	0.0	29.9	16.2	72.4	118.4	0.4
PA	0.0	10.0	513.4	136.8	660.2	2.3
RI	0.0	2.5	0.0	0.0	2.5	0.4
VT	0.0	33.4	398.2	22.2	453.8	7.6
Northeast	0.0	262.7	1,715.6	502.5	2,480.8	2.4
IL	0.0	155.2	297.1	0.0	452.3	1.3
IN	0.0	65.2	201.5	15.3	282.0	1.2
IA	0.0	117.4	0.0	2.7	120.1	0.3
KS	0.0	58.8	108.2	11.6	178.6	0.3
MI	0.0	120.6	2,872.8	718.2	3,711.6	10.2
MN	1.4	575.0	2,840.7	301.3	3,718.4	7.3
MO	0.0	73.8	1,491.8	83.5	1,649.1	3.7
NE	6.4	179.5	352.3	39.7	577.9	1.2
ND	58.8	1,768.1	1,111.2	72.6	3,010.7	6.8
OH	0.0	9.1	239.0	34.1	282.2	1.1
SD	274.4	1,511.4	2,016.9	297.4	4,100.1	8.4
WI	2.4	239.9	1,530.7	133.8	1,906.8	5.4
Midwest	343.4	4,874.0	13,062.2	1,710.2	19,989.8	4.1

State	BLM	FWS	FS	NPS	Total	As % of State Area
AL	3.5	71.4	668.9	21.1	764.9	2.3
AR	6.1	373.9	2,598.4	105.0	3,083.4	9.2
DE	6.0	2602	0.0	0.0	32.2	2.5
FL	3.1	980.0	1,160.3	2,637.8	4,781.2	13.8
GA	0.0	489.3	866.0	62.9	1,418.2	3.8
KY	0.0	10.8	814.0	95.4	920.2	3.6
LA	16.5	579.1	604.4	21.1	1,221.1	4.2
MD	1.0	46.0	0.0	71.8	118.8	1.9
MS	0.0	228.7	1,174.1	118.9	1,521.7	5.0
NC	0.0	428.6	1,255.2	405.9	2,089.7	6.7
OK	2.0	175.1	400.8	10.2	588.1	1.3
SC	0.0	175.3	629.6	32.6	837.5	4.3
TN	0.0	120.9	707.4	384.4	1,212.7	4.5
TX	11.7	590.4	755.4	1,238.2	2,595.7	1.5
VA	1.0	134.0	1,664.3	363.0	2,162.3	8.5
South	50.9	4,448.8	14,341.8	5,639.9	24,481.4	4.4
AK	81,033.8	76,836.2	21,972.6	54,638.5	234,481.1	64.2
AZ	12,201.9	1,738.1	11,264.4	2,962.9	28,167.3	38.8
CA	15,275.1	479.8	20,802.6	8,107.5	44,665.0	44.6
CO	8,346.2	168.3	14,519.0	673.6	23,707.1	35.7
HI	0.0	299.5	0.0	369.1	668.6	16.3
ID	11,601.9	92.2	20,466.6	517.9	32,678.6	61.7
MT	7,969.3	1,412.0	16,962.7	1,274.4	27,618.4	29.6
NV	47,813.5	2,363.4	5,854.0	778.5	56,809.4	80.9
NM	13,367.9	385.2	9,413.2	391.0	23,557.3	29.6
OR	16,133.1	581.1	15,667.7	199.1	32,581.0	52.9
UT	22,857.7	112.7	8,200.2	2,117.0	33,287.6	63.2
WA	419.7	347.5	9,282.4	1,965.4	12,015.0	28.1
WY	18,367.7	102.8	9,241.2	2,396.4	30,108.1	48.3
West	255,387.8	84,918.8	163,646.6	76,391.3	580,344.5	51.7
Total US	255,782.1	94,504.3	192,766.2	84,243.9	627,296.5	27.7

Sources: Bureau of Land Management, *Public Land Statistics 2008*, 2009, table 1–4. Fish and Wildlife Service, *Annual Lands Report 2008*, 2009, table 2. Forest Service, *Land Areas Report 2008*, 2009, table 4. National Park Service, personal communication with Mike Walsh, NPS Land Division, on April 19, 2010. Data include 5.5 million acres of nonfederal inholdings.

Selected Bibliography

Adams, Jonathan, Bruce Stein, and Lynn Kutner. "Biodiversity: Our Precious Heritage." Pp. 3–18 in *Precious Heritage: The Status of Biodiversity in the United States*, edited by Bruce Stein, Lynn Kutner, and Jonathan Adams. Oxford: Oxford University Press, 2000.

Alexander, Kristina, and Ross W. Gorte. *Federal Land Ownership: Constitutional Authority and the History of Acquisition, Disposal, and Retention*. Washington, D.C.: Congressional Research Service, 2007.

———. *National Forest System (NFS) Roadless Area Initiatives*. Washington, D.C.: Congressional Research Service, 2011.

An Act to Set Apart a Certain Tract of Land Lying Near the Head-waters of the Yellowstone River as a Public Park. 42nd Cong, 2d sess. 16 U.S.C. 1. March 1, 1872.

Anderson, Terry L., Vernon L. Smith, and Emily Simmons. "How and Why to Privatize Federal Lands." *Policy Analysis*, no. 363 (December 9, 1999).

Associated Press. "Thomas Supports Range Lease Ban." *Billings Gazette*, May 30, 2007.

Backus, Perry. "Judge Requires Timber Sale Bond." *Missoulian*, December 23, 2005.

Baden, John, and Donald Snow, editors. *The Next West: Public Lands, Community, and Economy in the American West*. Washington, D.C.: Island Press, 1997.

Baldwin, Pamela. *The National Forest System Roadless Area Initiative—Update of May 18*. Washington, D.C.: Congressional Research Service, 2001.

Balter, Michael. "DNA from Fossil Feces Breaks Clovis Barrier." *Science* 320 (2008): 37–39.

Bayet, Fabienne. "Overturning the Doctrine: Indigenous People and Wilderness—Being Aboriginal in the Environmental Movement." Pp. 314–324 in *Wilderness Debate*, edited by J. Baird Callicott and Michael Nelson. Athens: University of Georgia Press, 1998.

Berry, Allison. *Two Forests Under the Big Sky: Tribal v. Federal Management.* PERC Policy Series no. 45 (2009).

Booth, Douglas. *Searching for Paradise: Economic Development and Environmental Change in the Mountain West.* Lanham, MD: Rowman & Littlefield, 2002.

Bosworth, Dale. "Managing the National Forest System: Great Issues and Great Diversions." Speech before the Commonwealth Club of San Francisco. April 22, 2003.

Bratton, Susan. *Christianity, Wilderness, and Wildlife: The Original Desert Solitaire.* Scranton, PA: Scranton University Press, 1993.

Briggs, John, Katherine Spielmann, Hoski Schafasma, Keith Kintigh, Melissa Kruse, Kari Morehouse, and Karen Schollmeyer. "Why Ecology Needs Archaeologists and Archaeology Needs Ecologists." *Frontiers in Ecology and the Environment* 4 (2006): 180–88.

Brosnan, Deborah. "Science, Law, and the Environment: The Making of a Modern Discipline." *Environmental Law* 37 (2007): 987–1007.

Brower, David. "Introduction." In *Wilderness: America's Living Heritage*, edited by David Brower. San Francisco: Sierra Club, 1961.

———. *Let the Mountains Talk, Let the Rivers Run.* New York: HarperCollins West, 1995.

Brown, Thomas, Michael T. Robins, and Jorge A. Ramirez. "The Source of Water Supply in the United States." Discussion paper. RMRS-WU-4851. Fort Collins, CO: U.S. Forest Service, Rocky Mountain Research Station.

Bryson, Bill. *A Short History of Nearly Everything.* New York: Broadway Books, 2003.

Budget Control Act of 2011. Public Law 112–25.

Butzer, Karl. "The Americas before and after 1492: An Introduction to Current Geographical Research." *Annals of the Association of American Geographers* 82 (1992): 345–68.

California v. U.S. Dept. of Agriculture. 459 F. Supp. 2d 874. N.D. Cal. 2006.

California v. U.S. Dept. of Agriculture. 575 F.3d 999. 9th Cir. 2009.

Callicott, J. Baird, and Michael P. Nelson, editors. *Wilderness Debate.* Athens: University of Georgia Press, 1998.

Chase, Alston. *In a Dark Wood: The Fight over Forests and the Tyranny of Ecology.* Boston: Houghton Mifflin, 1995.

Christensen, Norman, Ann Bartuska, James Brown, Stephen Carpenter, Carla D'Antonia, Robert Francis, Jerry Franklin, James MacMahon, Reed Noss, David Parsons, Charles Peterson, Monica Turner, and Robert Woodmansee. "The Report of the Ecological Society of America Committee on the Scientific Basis for Ecosystem Management." *Ecological Applications* 6 (1996): 665–91.

Citizens for Better Forestry v. U.S. Department of Agriculture. United States District Court for the Northern District of California. No. C 05-1144 PJH.

Citizens for Better Forestry v. U.S. Department of Agriculture. United States District Court for the Northern District of California. No. C 08-1927 CW.

Colburn, Jamison. "Waters of the United States: Theory, Practice, and Integrity at the Supreme Court." *Florida State University Law Review* 33 (2007).

Committees on Appropriations, U.S. Senate and U.S. House of Representatives. "FY 2010 Conference Summary: Interior Appropriations." Summary. October 27, 2009.

Cordell, H. Ken, John Bergstrom, and J. M. Bowker. *The Multiple Values of Wilderness.* State College, PA: Venture Publishing, 2005.

Cronon, William. *Changes in the Land: Indians, Colonists and the Ecology of New England.* New York: Hill and Wang, 1983.

———. "Resisting Monoliths and Tabulae Rasae." *Ecological Applications* 10 (2000): 673–75.

———. "The Trouble with Wilderness." Pp. 69–90 in *Uncommon Ground: Rethinking the Human Place in Nature,* edited by William Cronon. New York: W. W. Norton, 1995.

Daily, Gretchen. "What Are Ecosystem Services?" Pp. 1–10 in *Nature's Services: Societal Dependence on Natural Ecosystems,* edited by Gretchen Daily. Washington, D.C.: Island Press, 1997.

Darby, H. C. "Clearing the Woodland of Europe." Pp. 183–216 in *Man's Role in Changing the Face of the Earth,* edited by William Thomas Jr. Chicago: University of Chicago Press, 1956.

Davis, Mark A., and Lawrence B. Slobodkin. "The Science and Values of Restoration Ecology." *Restoration Ecology* 12 (2004): 1–3.

Diamond, Jared. *Guns, Germs, and Steel: The Fate of Human Societies.* New York: W. W. Norton, 1999.

DiMento, Joseph, and Helen Ingram. "Science and Environmental Decision Making: The Potential Role of Environmental Impact Assessment in the Pursuit of Appropriate Information." *Natural Resources Journal* 45 (2005): 283–309.

Dods, Roberta Robin. "The Death of Smokey Bear: The Ecodisaster Myth and Forest Management Practices in Prehistoric North America." *World Archeology* 33 (2002): 475–87.

Doolittle, William. "Agriculture in North America on the Eve of Contact." *Annals of the Association of American Geographers* 82 (1992): 386–401.

Ecology Center, Inc. v. Austin. 430 F.3d 1057. 9th Cir. 2005.

Endangered Species Act. Public Law 93-205. 16 U.S.C. 1531.

Energy Policy and Conservation Act. Public Law 106-469. 42 U.S.C. 6201.

Fairfax, Sally K. "When an Agency Outlasts Its Time." *Journal of Forestry* (July/August 2005): 264–67.

Fallows, James. "Saving Salmon or Seattle?" *The Atlantic* 286 (2000): 20–26.

Federal Land Policy and Management Act of 1976. Public Law 94-579. 16 U.S.C. 528–31.

Federal Water Pollution Control Act Amendments of 1972. Public Law 92–500. 33 U.S.C. 1251.

Feynman, Richard P. *The Pleasure of Finding Things Out.* New York: Basic Books, 1999.

Fitzgerald, Timothy, and Myrick Freeman III. "Counting the Wealth of Nature: An Overview of Ecosystem Evaluation." Pp. 211–34 in *Accounting for Mother Nature: Changing Demands for Her Bounty,* edited by Terry Anderson, Laura Huggins, and Thomas Powers. Palo Alto, CA: Stanford University Press, 2008.

Fitzsimmons, Allan. *Defending Illusions: Federal Management of Ecosystems.* Lanham, MD: Rowman & Littlefield, 1999.

———. "Ecosystem Health: A Flawed Basis for Federal Regulation and Land Use Management." Pp. 187–98 in *Managing for Healthy Ecosystems*, edited by David Rapport, Bill Lasley, Dennis Rolston, and Ole Nielsen. Boca Raton, FL: Lewis Publishers, 2002.

[Forest Service] Organic Act of 1897. 16 U.S.C. 473.

Fox, Stephen. *John Muir and His Legacy: The American Conservation Movement*. Boston: Little, Brown, 1981.

Frazer, Jennifer. "Oil and Gas Buyback Proposed." *Wyoming Tribune-Eagle*, May 30, 2007.

Fretwell, Holly. *Who Is Minding the Federal Estate: Political Management of America's Public Land*. Lanham, MD: Lexington Books, 2009.

Freyfogle, Eric T. "Goodbye to the Public-Private Divide." *Environmental Law* 36 (2006): 7–24.

Friends of Yosemite Valley v. Dirk Kempthorne. United States District Court for the Eastern District of California Fresno Division. Case no. CV-F-00-6191 DLB.

Futuyma, Douglas J. "Science's Greatest Challenge." *BioScience* 57 (2007): 3.

Gerhart, Matthew. "Climate Change and the Endangered Species Act: The Difficulty of Proving Causation." *Ecology Law Quarterly* 36 (2009): 167–99.

Gildor, Dan L. "Preserving the Priceless: A Constitutional Amendment to Empower Congress to Preserve, Protect, and Promote the Environment." *Ecology Law Quarterly* 32 (2005): 821–62.

Glacken, Clarence. *Traces on the Rhodian Shore: Nature and Culture in Western Thought from Ancient Times to the End of the Eighteenth Century*. Berkeley: University of California Press, 1967.

Glicksman, Robert. "Traveling in Opposite Directions: Roadless Area Management under the Clinton and Bush Administrations." *Environmental Law* 34 (2004).

Glicksman, Robert, and George Cameron Coggins. *Modern Public Land Law in a Nutshell*. St. Paul, MN: Thomson-West, 2006.

Gomez-Pampa, Arturo, and Andrea Kaus. "Taming the Wilderness Myth." Pp. 293–313 in *Wilderness Debate*, edited by J. Baird Callicott and Michael Nelson. Athens: University of Georgia Press, 1998.

Gorte, Russ, Carol Hardy Vincent, Marc Humphries, and Kristina Alexander. *Federal Lands Managed by the Bureau of Land Management (BLM) and the Forest Service (FS): Issues for the 110th Congress—Update of May 17*. Washington, D.C.: Congressional Research Service, 2008.

Gosnell, Hannah, Julia Haggerty, and William Travis. "Ranchland Ownership Change in the Greater Yellowstone Ecosystem, 1990–2001." *Society and Natural Resources* 19 (2006): 743–58.

Government Accountability Office. *Federal Land Management: Observations on a Possible Move of the Forest Service into the Department of the Interior*. GAO-09-223. Washington, D.C.: Government Accountability Office, 2009.

Graber, Linda. *Wilderness as Sacred Space*. Washington, D.C.: Association of American Geographers, 1976.

Grossi, Mark. "Yosemite Seeks Ideas about Crowd Control." *Fresno Bee*, July 8, 2009.

Groves, Craig, Lynn Kutner, David Stoms, Michael Murray, J. Michael Scott, Michael Schafale, Alan Weakley, and Robert Pressey. "Owning Up to Our Responsibilities: Who Owns Lands Important for Biodiversity?" Pp. 275–300 in *Precious Heritage: The Status of Biodiversity in the United States,* edited by Bruce Stein, Lynn Kutner, and Jonathan Adams. Oxford: Oxford University Press, 2000.

Gutierrez, R. J., and George Barrowclough. "Redefining the Distributional Boundaries of the Northern and California Spotted Owls: Implications for Conservation." *The Condor* 107 (2005): 182–87.

Hammond, Katharine, Liana Reilly, and Heidi Binko, editors. "The Northwest Forest Plan Revisited." *Yale Forest Forum Review* 5 (2002).

Hansen, Andrew, Ray Rasker, Bruce Maxwell, Jay Rotella, Jerry Johnson, Andrea Wright Parmenter, Ute Langner, Warren Cohen, Rick Lawrence, and Matthew Kraska. "Ecological Causes and Consequences of Demographic Change in the New West." *BioScience* 52 (2002): 151–62.

Healthy Forest Restoration Act. Public Law 108-148. 16 U.S.C. 6501.

Herger-Feinstein Quincy Library Group Forest Recovery Act. Public Law 105-277. 16 U.S.C. 2104.

Hibbard, Michael, and Jeremy Madsen. "Environmental Resistance to Place-Based Collaboration in the U.S. West." *Society and Natural Resources* 16 (2003): 703–18.

Hobbs, Frank, and Nicole Stoop. *Demographic Trends in the 20th Century.* Census 2000 Special Reports, CENSR-4. Washington, D.C.: U.S. Census Bureau, 2002.

Hoberg, George. "Science, Politics, and U.S. Forest Law: The Battle over the Forest Service Planning Rule." Discussion Paper 03-19. Washington, D.C.: Resources for the Future, 2003.

Howard, James C. *U.S. Timber Production, Trade, Consumption, and Price Statistics 1965 to 2007.* Research Paper FLP-RP-637. Madison, WI: U.S. Department of Agriculture, Forest Service, Forest Products Laboratory, 2007.

Jackson, Philip, and Robert Kuhlken. *A Rediscovered Frontier: Land Use and Resource Issues in the New West.* Lanham, MD: Rowman & Littlefield, 2006.

Johnson, Norman, Jerry Franklin, and Jack Thomas. *Alternatives for Management of Late-Successional Forests in the Pacific Northwest.* A report to the United States House of Representatives; Committee on Agriculture, Subcommittee on Forests, Family Farms, and Energy, and the Committee on Merchant Marine and Fisheries, Subcommittee on Fisheries and Wildlife, Conservation and the Environment. Corvallis, OR: Department of Forest Resources, Oregon State University, 1991.

Keele, Denise M., Robert W. Malmsheimer, Donald W. Floyd, and Jerome E. Perez. "Forest Service Land Management Litigation 1989–2002." *Journal of Forestry* (June 2006): 196–202.

Keiter, Robert B. *Keeping Faith with Nature.* New Haven, CT: Yale University Press, 2003.

Kemmis, Daniel. *This Sovereign Land.* Washington, D.C.: Island Press, 2001.

Lackey, Robert. "Science, Scientists, and Policy Advocacy." *Conservation Biology* 21 (2007): 12–17.

Lands Council v. McNair (Lands Council II). 537 F.3d 981. 9th Cir. 2008.

Lazarus, Richard. "Courts Continue to Needle on Climate." *The Environmental Forum* 25 (2008): 12.

Leopold, Aldo. "Grass, Brush, Timber, and Fire in Southern Arizona." *Journal of Forestry* 22 (1924): 1–10.

——. "Piute Forestry vs. Forest Fire Prevention." Pp. 68–70 in *The River of the Mother of God and Other Essays by Aldo Leopold*, edited by Susan Flader and Baird Callicott. Madison: University of Wisconsin Press, 1991 [1920].

Levin, Simon. "The Problem of Pattern and Scale in Ecology." *Ecology* 73 (1992): 1943–67.

Lowenthal, David. "Is Wilderness 'Paradise Enow?' Images of Nature in America." *Columbia University Forum* 36 (1964): 34–40.

Mann, Charles C. *1491: New Revelations of the Americas before Columbus*. New York: Vintage Books, 2006.

Mann, Charles, and Mark Plummer. "The High Cost of Biodiversity." *Science* 260 (1993): 1868–71.

Marcot, Bruce G., and Jack Ward Thomas. *Of Spotted Owls, Old Growth and New Policies: A History since the Interagency Scientific Committee Report*. Forest Service, Pacific Northwest Research Station, General Technical Report PNW-GTR-408, 1997.

Meinig, D. W. *The Shaping of America, Volume 2: Continental America 1800–1867*. New Haven, CT: Yale University Press, 1993.

Meltz, Robert. *Climate Change Litigation: A Growing Phenomenon*. Washington, D.C.: Congressional Research Service, 2007.

Morton, W. E. *The Wisconsin Centennial Story of Disasters and Other Unfortunate Events 1848–1948*. Madison: Wisconsin State Centennial Committee, 1948.

Muir, John. *Nature Writings*. New York: Library of America, 1997.

Multiple-Use Sustained-Yield Act of 1960. Public Law 86-517. 16 U.S.C. 528–31.

Nagel, John. "The Spiritual Value of Wilderness." *Environmental Law* 35 (2005): 955–1003.

Nash, Roderick. *Wilderness and the American Mind*. 4th ed. New Haven, CT: Yale University Press, 2001.

National Environmental Policy Act. Public Law 91–190. 42 U.S.C. 4331.

National Park Service Organic Act. 16 U.S.C. 1–4.

National Research Council. *Hardrock Mining on Federal Lands*. Washington, D.C.: National Academy Press, 1999.

National Wildlife Refuge System Administration Act of 1997. Public Law 105-57. 16 U.S.C. 668dd–668ee.

Natural Resources Defense Council v. Callaway. 392 F. Supp 685. D.C. 1975.

Nelson, Robert. *A Burning Issue*. Lanham, MD: Rowman & Littlefield, 2000.

Nie, Martin. *The Governance of Western Public Lands*. Lawrence: University of Kansas Press, 2008.

——. "Statutory Detail and Administrative Discretion in Public Lands Governance: Arguments and Alternatives." *Journal of Environmental Law and Litigation* 19 (2004): 223–91.

Nienable, Jeanne Clarke, and Kurt Angerbach. "The Federal Four: Change and Continuity in the Bureau of Land Management, Fish and Wildlife Service, Forest Service, and National Park Service, 1970–2000." Pp. 35–54 in *Western Public Lands and*

Environmental Politics, 2nd ed., edited by Charles Davis. Boulder, CO: Westview Press, 2001.

Norton, Bryan G. *Sustainability: A Philosophy of Adaptive Ecosystem Management.* Chicago: University of Chicago Press, 2005.

Noss, Reed. "Values Are a Good Thing in Conservation Biology." *Conservation Biology* 21 (2007): 18–20.

O' Toole, Randal. "A Matter of Trust: Why Congress Should Turn Federal Lands into Fiduciary Trusts." Cato Institute *Policy Analysis* no. 630, January 15, 2009.

Omnibus Public Lands Act of 2009. Public Law 111–11. 16 U.S.C. 1 note.

Peterson, Cass. "Sea of Grass' Future Rests on a Reed-Thin Compromise: Public vs. Private Interests at Issue." *Washington Post,* December 25, 1987, section A.

Peterson, Shannon. *Acting for Endangered Species.* Lawrence: University of Kansas Press, 2002.

Pickett, S. T. A., and M. L. Cadenasso. "The Ecosystem as a Multidimensional Concept: Meaning, Model, and Metaphor." *Ecosystems* 5 (2002): 1–10.

Pincetl, Stephanie. "Conservation Planning in the West, Problems, New Strategies and Entrenched Obstacles." *Geoforum* 37 (2006): 246–55.

Power, Thomas, and Richard Barrett. *Post-Cowboy Economics: Pay and Prosperity in the New American West.* Washington, D.C.: Island Press, 2001.

Pyne, Stephen. *Fire in America: A Cultural History of Wildland and Rural Fire.* Seattle: University of Washington Press, 1997.

Ramachandra Guha. "Deep Ecology Revisited." Pp. 271–79 in *Wilderness Debate,* edited by J. Baird Callicott and Michael Nelson. Athens: University of Georgia Press, 1998.

———. "Radical American Environmentalism and Wilderness Preservation: A Third World Critique." *Environmental Ethics* 11 (1989): 71–83.

Rapanos et ux. v. United States. 547 U.S. 715. 2006.

Riebsame, William, editor. *Atlas of the New West.* Boulder, CO: Center for the American West, University of Colorado, 1997.

Righter, Robert. *The Battle over Hetch Hetchy.* Oxford: Oxford University Press, 2005.

Ruhl, J. B. "Keeping the Endangered Species Act Relevant." *Duke Environmental Law and Policy Forum* 12 (2009): 275–94.

Sagoff, Mark. *Price, Principle, and the Environment.* Cambridge: Cambridge University Press, 2004.

Sauer, Carl. "The Agency of Man on Earth." Pp. 49–69 in *Man's Role in Changing the Face of the Earth,* edited by William Thomas Jr. Chicago: University of Chicago Press, 1956.

Schlickeisen, Rodger. "The Argument for a Constitutional Amendment to Protect Living Nature." Pp. 221–42 in *Biodiversity and the Law,* edited by William J. Snape III. Washington, D.C.: Island Press, 1996.

Scott, J. Michael, Janet Rachlow, Robert Lackey, Anna Pidgorna, Jocelyn Aycrigg, Gabrielle Feldman, Leona Svancara, David Rupp, David Stanish, and Kirk Steinhorst. "Policy Advocacy in Science: Prevalence, Perspectives, and Implications for Conservation Biology." *Conservation Biology* 21 (2007): 29–35.

Sedjo, Roger. *The National Forests: For Whom and for What?* PERC Policy Series Number 23. Bozeman, MT: Property and Environment Research Center, 2001.

Siikamali, Juha. "Biodiversity: What It Means, How It Works, and What the Current Issues Are." *Resources* 168 (2008): 13–17.

Simpson, John Warfield. *Dam: Water, Power, Politics, and Preservation in Hetch Hetchy and Yosemite National Park.* New York: Pantheon, 2005.

Smith, W. Brad, Patrick Miles, John Vissage, and Scott Pugh. *Forest Resources of the United States,* Forest Service, North Central Research Station, General Technical Report NC-241, 2004.

"Smoke from Louisiana Leads to Health Warning." *Houston Chronicle,* March 8, 2001, 20.

Society of American Foresters. *State of America's Forests.* Bethesda, MD: Society of American Foresters, 2007.

Solid Waste Agency of Northern Cook County v. United States Army Corps of Engineers. 531 U.S. 159. 2001.

Sousa, David, and Christopher Klyza. "New Directions in Environmental Policy Making: An Emerging Collaborative Regime or Reinventing Interest Group Liberalism?" *Natural Resources Journal* 47 (2007): 377–444.

Squatriglia, Chuck. "Blueprint to Beautify, Restore Yosemite Tangled Up in Court." *San Francisco Chronicle,* January 21, 2007, A-1.

Star-Tribune Editorial Board. "Gov Makes Good Case to Protect Wyoming Range." *Casper Star-Tribune,* May 7, 2007.

Stein, Bruce, Cameron Scott, and Nancy Benton. "Federal Lands and Endangered Species: The Role of Military and Other Federal Lands in Sustaining Biodiversity." *BioScience* 58 (2008): 339–47.

Stewart, Omer C. "Fire as the First Great Force Employed by Man." Pp. 115–33 in *Man's Role in Changing the Face of the Earth,* edited by William Thomas Jr. Chicago: University of Chicago Press, 1956.

Straub, Noelle. "Sportsmen in D.C. Lobby for Wyoming Range." *Casper Star-Tribune,* February 16, 2007.

Styles, Daniel. *National Park Visitor Spending and Payroll Impacts.* Washington, D.C.: National Park Service, 2007.

Swedlow, Brendon. "Scientists, Judges, and Spotted Owls: Policymakers in the Pacific Northwest." *Duke Environmental Law and Policy Forum* 13 (2003): 187–278.

Tallgrass Historians, L. C. *Tallgrass Prairie National Preserve Legislative History, 1920–1996.* Omaha, NE: National Park Service, 1998. Available at www.nps.gov/history/history/online_books/tapr/index.htm. Accessed November 27, 2011.

Tarlock, Dan. "The Nonequilibrium Paradigm in Ecology and the Partial Unraveling of Environmental Law." *Loyola of Los Angeles Law Review* 27 (1994): 1121–44.

Taylor, Joseph, III. "The Many Lives of the New West." *Western Historical Quarterly* 35 (2004): 141–55.

Tennessee Valley Authority v. Hill. 437 U.S. 153, 180. 1978.

Thomas, Jack Ward, and Alex Sienkiewicz. "The Relationship between Science and Democracy: Public Land Policies, Regulation and Management." *Public Land and Resources Law Review* 26 (2005): 39–69.

Thomas, Jack Ward, Jerry Franklin, John Gordon, and Norman Johnson. "The Northwest Forest Plan: Origins, Components, Implementation Experience, and Suggestions for Change." *Conservation Biology* 20 (2006): 277–87.

Thomas, Jack Ward, Eric Forsman, Joseph Lint, E. Charles Meslow, Barry Noon, and Jared Verner. *A Conservation Strategy for the Northern Spotted Owl: A Report of the Interagency Scientific Committee to Address the Conservation of the Northern Spotted Owl.* Portland, OR: U.S. Department of Agriculture Forest Service; U.S. Department of the Interior, Bureau of Land Management, Fish and Wildlife Service, and National Park Service, 1990.

Thomas, Jack Ward, M. G. Raphael, M. G. Anthony, E. D. Forsman, A. G. Gunderson, R. S. Holthusen, B. G Marcot, G. H. Reeves, J. R. Sedell, and D. M Solis. *Viability Assessments and Management Considerations for Species Associated with Late-Successional and Old-Growth Forests of the Pacific Northwest.* Portland, OR: U.S. Forest Service, 1993.

Travis, William. *New Geographies of the American West.* Washington, D.C.: Island Press. 2007.

Tribal Forest Protection Act of 2004. Public Law 108-278. 43 U.S.C. 1702.

United States v. Riverside Bayview Homes, Inc. 474 U.S. 121. 1985.

U.S. Army Corps of Engineers. *Wetlands Delineation Manual.* Wetlands Research Program Technical Report Y-87-1. Vicksburg, MS: Wetlands Regulation Center, 1987.

U.S. Army Corps of Engineers Walla Walla District. *Summary: Improving Salmon Passage, Final Lower Snake River Juvenile Salmon Migration Feasibility Report/Environmental Impact Statement.* Walla Walla, WA: Army Corps of Engineers, 2002.

U.S. Bureau of Reclamation. *Water 2025: Preventing Crises and Conflict in the West.* Washington, D.C.: Bureau of Reclamation, 2005. Available online at http:// biodiversity.ca.gov/Meetings/archive/water03/water2025.pdf. Accessed November 27, 2011.

U.S. Congress Committees on Appropriations, U.S. Senate and U.S. House of Representatives. "FY 2010 Conference Summary: Interior Appropriations." Summary. October 27, 2009.

U.S. Department of Agriculture. *Summary Report: 2007 National Resources Inventory.* Washington, D.C.: Resources Conservation Service; Ames, IA: Center for Survey Statistics and Methodology, Iowa State University, 2009. Available at www.nrcs .usda.gov/Internet/FSE_DOCUMENTS//stelprdb1041379.pdf. Accessed November 27, 2011.

U.S. Department of Agriculture, Forest Service. *Fiscal Year 2009 President's Budget: Budget Justification.* Washington, D.C.: Department of Agriculture, 2008.

U.S. Department of the Interior. *Department of the Interior Budget Justifications and Performance Information, Fiscal Year 2011, Wildland Fire Management.* Washington, D.C.: Department of the Interior, 2010.

———. *Fiscal Year 2009 the Interior Budget in Brief.* Washington, D.C.: Department of the Interior, 2008.

U.S. Departments of the Interior, Agriculture, and Energy. *Inventory of Onshore Federal Lands' Oil and Gas Resources and the Extent and Nature of Restrictions or Impediments to Their Development.* Washington, D.C.: Department of the Interior, 2008.

U.S. Energy Information Administration. *Annual Energy Review 2008*. Washington, D.C.: Energy Information Administration, 2009.

U.S. Fish and Wildlife Service. *Final Recovery Plan for the Northern Spotted Owl*. Portland, OR: U.S. Fish and Wildlife Service, 2008.

U.S. Forest Service. *The Process Predicament: How Statutory, Regulatory, and Administrative Factors Affect National Forest Management*. Washington, D.C.: Forest Service, 2002.

U.S. Geological Survey. *Mineral Commodity Summaries 2007*. Washington, D.C.: U.S. Geological Survey, 2007.

Valles Caldera Preservation Act of 2000. Public Law 106-248. 16 U.S.C. 698.

van Wagtendonk, Jan. "The Evolution of National Park Service Fire Policy." *Fire Management Notes* 42 (1991): 10–15.

———. "The History of and Evolution of Wildland Fire Use." *Fire Ecology Special Issue* 3 (2007): 3–15.

Vincent, Carol Hardy. *Land and Water Conservation Fund: Overview, Funding History, and Current Issues*. Washington, D.C.: Congressional Research Service, 2006.

Voicu, Monica. "At a Dead End: Need for Congressional Direction in the Roadless Area Management Debate." *Ecology Law Quarterly* 37 (2010): 478–524.

Weisshaupt, Brad, Matthew Carroll, and Keith Blatner. "Using Focus Groups to Involve Citizens in Resource Management—Investigating Perceptions of Smoke as a Barrier to Prescribed Forest Burning." Pp. 178–85 in *The Public and Wildland Fire Management: Social Science Findings for Managers*, edited by S. M. McCaffrey. General Technical Report NRS-1. Newtown Square, PA: Forest Service, Northern Research Station, 2006.

Wilcove, David, and Lawrence Master. "How Many Endangered Species Are There in the United States?" *Frontiers in Ecology and the Environment* 3 (2005): 414–20.

The Wilderness Act. Public Law 88-577. 16 U.S.C. 1131–38.

Wilkins, Thurman. *John Muir: An Apostle for Nature*. Norman: University of Oklahoma Press, 1995.

Wilkinson, Charles. *The Eagle Bird: Mapping the New West*. Boulder, CO: Johnson Books, 1999.

Williams, Michael. *Americans and Their Forests: A Historical* Geography. New York: Oxford University Press, 1989.

Wilson, E. O. *The Creation: An Appeal to Save Life on Earth*. New York: W. W. Norton, 2006.

Winter v. Natural Res. Def. Council, Inc. 518 F.3d 658, 703. 9th Cir. 129 S. Ct. 365. 2008.

Winterhalder, Keith, Andre Clewell, and James Aronson. "The Science and Values of Restoration Ecology—A Response to Davis and Slobodkin." *Restoration Ecology* 12 (2004): 4–7.

Wood, Robert S. "The Dynamics of Incrementalism: Subsystems, Politics, and Public Lands." *The Policy Studies Journal* 34 (2006): 1–16.

Worster, Donald. *A Passion for Nature: The Life of John Muir*. New York: Oxford University Press, 2008.

———. "Epilogue: Nature, Liberty, and Equality." Pp. 263–72 in *American Wilderness: A New History,* edited by Michael Lewis. Oxford: Oxford University Press, 2007.

Wyoming v. U.S. Department of Agriculture. 570 F. Supp. 2d at 1352.

Yoder, Jonathan, David Engle, and Sam Fuhlendorf. "Liability, Incentives, and Prescribed Fire for Ecosystem Management." *Frontiers in Ecology and the Environment* 2 (2004): 361–66.

Index

About the Author

Allan K. Fitzsimmons retired in 2007 from the Department of the Interior, where he had been a special assistant in the immediate office of the secretary and the department's hazardous fuels coordinator. In earlier stints at DOI he served as a special assistant to the deputy director of NPS and the assistant secretary of fish, wildlife, and parks. He was also special assistant to the deputy undersecretary of energy for policy, planning, and development at the Department of Energy. In those capacities he was involved with a wide variety of public land and natural resource matters ranging from removal of fuels from lands managed by the BLM, the FWS, and the NPS; regulating overflights of Grand Canyon National Park; developing a national plan for protecting wetlands; and preparation of a national energy strategy.

In addition to his government service, Fitzsimmons chaired the Environmental Studies Program at George Washington University and taught courses in conservation, natural resources, and energy there and at other universities. His writing has appeared in *Science, BioScience, Proceedings of the National Academy of Sciences, Natural Resources Journal, Geographical Review,* and *Landscape and Urban Planning.* His first book was *Defending Illusions: Federal Protection of Ecosystems.* He holds a PhD in geography from UCLA, an MA in geography from California State University–Northridge, and a BA in mathematics from the same school.